State Looteries by Henricks and Embrick is a must read for anyone interested in financial justice for all. While implicit bias is often thought of when we discuss the criminal justice system and mass incarceration, rarely is it even considered when we discuss tax policy. That is why this book is so important. It provides a behind the scene look at how a seemingly neutral thing, like state lotteries, can impact taxpayers differently because of their race. Read it and weep.

- Dorothy A. Brown, Vice Provost and Professor
of Law, Emory University

If we really want to comprehend where today's economic justice stands so far as race is concerned, perhaps we should look no further than tax law. Henricks and Embrick do just that in *State Looteries*. With both plain English and piercing analysis, they capture the subtleties of how race and racism shaped the emergence of state lotteries over the past 50 years—a truly fundamental shift in the tax code. This is among the best cases yet for racially-conscious public policy that says enough is enough.

- Kimberlé W. Crenshaw, Director of the Center for Intersectionality
and Social Policy Studies, Columbia University and Distinguished
Professor of Law, University of California at Los Angeles

State Looteries provides a devastating and comprehensive examination of the sustained use of public policies to destroy and expropriate black wealth in America. This is a critical study that helps us understand the origins and persistence of today's enormous racial wealth gap.

- William A. Darity, Samuel DuBois Cook Professor of Public Policy,
African and African American Studies, and Economics, and Director
of the Samuel Cook Center on Social Equity, Duke University

Capitalism pays workers the lowest wages the market will sustain, and then devises ingenious ways to bilk the lower classes of their sparse dollars. *State Looteries* shows how the state is implicated, under the false pretense of sending "deserving" students to college, not only in looting the poor but also of stealing their dreams for deliverance."

- Stephen Steinberg, Distinguished Professor of Urban Studies,
City University of New York—Queens College and
Graduate Center

State Looteries

Fifty years ago, familiar images of the lottery would have been strange, as no state lottery existed then. Few researchers have uncovered the obscure role lotteries play in the changing composition of American taxation. Even less is known about what role race plays in this process. More than simply taxing those on the social margins, the emergence of state lotteries in contemporary American history represents something much more fundamental about state fiscal policy. This book not only uncovers the underlying racial factors that contextualize lottery proliferation in the U.S., but also reveals the racial consequences that lotteries have in terms of redistributing tax liability.

Kasey Henricks is a Postdoctoral Fellow at the Institute for Research on Race and Public Policy at the University of Illinois at Chicago.

David G. Embrick is an Associate Professor in the Department of Sociology and Africana Studies Institute at the University of Connecticut.

Routledge Advances in Sociology

For a full list of titles in this series, please visit www.routledge.com

State Looteries

Historical Continuity, Rearticulations of Racism, and American Taxation

Kasey Henricks and
David G. Embrick

Routledge
Taylor & Francis Group

LONDON AND NEW YORK

First published 2017 by Routledge

2 Park Square, Milton Park, Abingdon, Oxfordshire OX14 4RN

52 Vanderbilt Avenue, New York, NY 10017

Routledge is an imprint of the Taylor & Francis Group, an informa business

First issued in paperback 2020

Library of Congress Cataloging-in-Publication Data
Names: Henricks, Kasey, author. | Embrick, David G., author.
Title: State looteries : historical continuity, rearticulations of
    racism, and American taxation / by Kasey Henricks and
    David G. Embrick.
Description: New York : Routledge, 2016. | Series: Routledge
    advances in sociology ; 180 | Includes bibliographical references
    and index.
Identifiers: LCCN 2016017509 (print) | LCCN 2016028731 (ebook) |
    ISBN 9780415717649 (alk. paper) | ISBN 9781315869803
Subjects: LCSH: Lotteries—United States—History. | Racism—
    United States—History. | Taxation—United States—History.
Classification: LCC HG6126 .H46 2016 (print) | LCC HG6126
    (ebook) | DDC 975.3/80973—dc23
LC record available at https://lccn.loc.gov/2016017509

ISBN: 978-0-415-71764-9 (hbk)
ISBN: 978-0-367-59617-0 (pbk)

Typeset in Sabon
by Apex CoVantage, LLC

Contents

Figures

Tables

Preface
Bound for Glory, A Word of Thanks

Few events can better show how precious life is than the threat to have it taken away. More than 10 years ago, close friends and I stood in a courtroom where our fates would be determined. We were youths not fully comprehending the ramifications of our actions, knowing the law but too stubborn to obey it. I remember the disappointment in my mother's eyes when she picked us up from the juvenile holding facility, her tears running down her face, drowning any words to be said. My fate was no longer in her hands, but in those of the prosecuting attorney.

Though he would determine our futures, at the time it seemed like they had already been chosen. As kids growing up on the wrong side of the tracks in a poverty-stricken Southern city, there was no money for college and few job options aside from fast food. When many in our graduating class were applying for college, I was checking help wanted ads and wondering how my family would make rent. Seeing my mom work 80 hours a week at the local Pizza Hut, I became keenly aware that character, hard work, and dedication did not make our "American Dream" come true. I knew what class oppression was about because this was my experience.

I knew little about racial oppression, though. Because *some of my best friends were black*, I fashioned myself as one of those hip white progressive types. I was "down with brothas," I thought, because my cause and "the black cause" were virtually the same. My friends and I grew up in the same neighborhood, attended the same schools, were raised by single moms, and even worked similar jobs. Our lives were inseparable: bricks of one wall. It was not me who could ever be racist, I thought, but my fellow white Southerners, seemingly uninformed that the Civil War had ended a long, long time ago. My friends never gave me a pass, though, and my self-proclaimed innocence was naïve at best.

Our final day in court came, and I expected the worst. Knowing my friends and I would go through it together calmed me, whatever "it" was going to be. After all, the charges we faced were similar. It was this day, however, that would forever mark our divergent paths. Decisions were made, our punishments set. The court placed my friends' wrists in shackles, and they went to prison. The court gave me a slap on the wrist, and I went to community college.

It was on this day that I began to truly understand the penalties and rewards of race. While my academic interests cannot be reduced to a single event, I share this experience because it represents one reason I became interested in the intersecting areas of racial inequality and law. It is my own biography, which has been shaped by the complex, and at times paradoxical, interaction of vulnerability, privilege, and agency, that grounds my dedication to the subject. For me, the subject is not merely an academic one. It is personal as well as political. This is what motivates me in what I foresee as a career-long devotion to uncovering the broad social impacts of racial inequality on law and legal practices.

Were it not for sociology, I would not have a language to describe, let alone comprehend, these experiences. Learning to see the world through this lens has helped me put into words the dynamic processes of how personal biographies meet history, institutions, and social structure. It has helped me identify some of the causes and consequences of inequality that I have witnessed and reinforced in my own life, but also in the lives of countless others. The promise of sociology, to paraphrase C. Wright Mills (1959), is to uncover blueprints of the broader social fabric that constrains and enables relations of our everyday lives. As a student of racial inequality specifically, and social inequalities generally, the promotion of understanding the world in this way is what informs who I am, and what I hope to accomplish as an activist-scholar.

How This Book Came to Be, and a Word of Thanks

State Looteries began in a voting booth. November 2, 2002, it was my first election. On the ballot was a statewide referendum for a lottery in Tennessee. It passed with a 58 percent approval rate, in part, because proponents claimed it would send "deserving" kids to college.

That was all I needed to hear. Even though I had no intention of playing, the teenage version of me believed the lottery was my winning ticket.

My home state followed a precedent set by Georgia and devised a strategy to set aside lottery proceeds for higher education. Perhaps with bitter irony, depending on your social location, lawmakers created "HOPE" Scholarships, for Helping Outstanding Pupils Educationally. I met most of the eligibility requirements. I was a Tennessee resident, the GPA checked out, my goal was to attend an in-state institution, and so on. Upon closer reading of the fine print, I missed one criterion: graduating from high school or its equivalent in 2003 or after.

The exclusion was not lost on me when I attended Chattanooga State Technical Community College and later Austin Peay State University. Like many other working-class kids, I worked full-time between fast food and construction to keep on the lights while attending classes. Meanwhile, it seemed like most (white) middle class kids I spoke to, and their cousins, were riding waves of lottery money through college—a lottery that my vote helped create. A lack of money, and the daily worry that comes with it, was a problem they didn't recognize. At least that's how I felt; I was bitter at the time.

The bitterness was a privileged kind, to be sure. As much as I stressed about money—or lack thereof—my father and sweet mother, the aunt who raised me, my sister, and other family members sacrificed to provide support along the way, helping to purchase books and cover leftover tuition costs. And my bosses and professors extended me many opportunities and breaks along the way to make a college experience possible. Still, the lottery seemed like a slap in the face to me and similarly situated others, not to mention those who were worse off. At least two things would always temper this feeling, though. One, I couldn't blame those who received HOPE scholarships. I'd cash in on the opportunity if our positions were switched. And, two, college still felt like a privilege to me. Few folks I grew up with got the opportunity to attend, and prison seemed a worse yet more realistic possibility.

Writing was (and continues to be) my outlet, but I didn't know what to do with it until sociology. Original analyses of *State Looteries* began in a sociology classroom nearly 10 years ago, as it was in my courses at Austin Peay, where I first learned to distinguish "public issues" from "private troubles" (Mills [1959] 2000). Mentors like Shirley Rainey-Brown, Tucker Brown, Robert Butler, Yvonne Prather, Roxanne Gerbrandt, and David Steele planted seeds of my sociological imagination. For most term papers, they encouraged me to use the lottery as a vehicle for tracing interrelationships between personal biography and history. In turn, these assignments culminated into a general blueprint for what would later come.

I remained committed to the development of *State Looteries* during my early years of graduate school at Loyola University Chicago. There I met professors like Ayana Karanja, Jerry Steenken, Marilyn Krogh, J. Talmadge Wright, Judson Everitt, Lauren Langman, and Philip Nyden. They made time to engage my work, ask me pointed questions about what's so racial about lotteries, and offer practical advice for improving the project. Colleagues like Reuben Miller, Saher Selod, Bhoomi K. Thakore, Bill Byrnes, Laurie Cooper Stoll, Courtney Irby, Cameron Williams, and Quintin Williams provided an intellectual community to flesh out these ideas. Other department members, including Rosa Negussie, Christine Wolff, and Stephanie Decaluwe, shared their navigational support over the years, and guidance through mazes of university bureaucracy. With the support of everyone at Loyola, I pursued the lottery project for my master's thesis.

Later iterations of *State Looteries* were finalized during my time as a Law and Social Science Fellow at the American Bar Foundation. This opportunity provided the space and resources to pursue my research agenda, and allowed me to deepen what empirical richness and theoretical clarity I could offer. I am especially grateful for the relationships and encouragement from Robert L. Nelson, Laura Beth Nielson, Christopher Schmidt, Elizabeth Mertz, Vicky Woeste, Jothie Rajah, Philip Ashton, Justin Richland, Camilo

Leslie, Terence Halliday, and the Chicago Law & Society Writing Collective. Data collection and analysis were also made possible by funding from the National Science Foundation (SES-1424422) and the Graduate School at Loyola.

Elsewhere in the academy, David G. Embrick and I have been spoiled by the support from a community of mentors, colleagues, and confidants. Eduardo Bonilla-Silva, Rogelio Sáenz, Pamela Anne Quiroz, Matthew W. Hughey, David L. Brunsma, Dorothy Brown, Ashley "Woody" Doane, Wendy Leo Moore, Joyce Bell, Stephen Steinberg, Victor Ray, Nicholas Vargas, Leighton Vila, Melissa Weiner, William "Sandy" Darity, Francine Lipman, Kathleen Fitzgerald, and Anthony Ladd all offered constructive criticisms or affirming words on early versions of the project. Many times, their comments were just what we needed to hear during times of research fatigue or moments of burnout. We are grateful for the allyship.

Though any shortcomings of *State Looteries* fall squarely on David and me, the project benefitted from two anonymous reviewers who were as thoughtful as they were careful. Their comments were a welcome specter that haunted our writing. We have attempted to account for most of their insights, and are grateful for their depth of engagement. In addition, Daina Cheyenne Harvey, Victoria Brockett, and Louise Seamster had a direct hand in the evolution of some of the arguments contained within. Parts of *State Looteries* represent developments of collaborations with them, and their investment has made for a better project.

Special thanks to our editor, Max Novick, for shepherding us through the publishing process and believing in the project from the onset. His investment, enthusiasm, and support mean a lot, and we look forward to working together again. Of course, David and I must also thank our family and friends. The Henricks and Embricks. The Morenos, Millers, and Maldonados. Devon Robinson. For their seemingly bottomless love, we owe them a debt of gratitude that we will never be able to repay.

Let me extend thanks to my co-author, adviser, and friend. David is why I applied, and stayed, in graduate school. During my first year in Chicago, I struggled to find a balance between a full-time job and part-time studies. Two semesters and a family emergency later, I found myself driving around in what was my only shelter. Too prideful and embarrassed to ask for help, David sensed I had problems bigger than graduate school. He offered unwavering support with mentorship unconfined by classroom walls. His helping hand gave me nourishment, both in a literal and intellectual sense. He filled my belly with food, but it was his words on becoming a scholar, future mentor, and a better all-around person that kept me intellectually committed. *State Looteries* would not be possible without his contribution.

Last but never least, I thank my partner Ana Moreno. Bless her soul. She's heard so much about the project that she could have written it herself (and probably said it better too). I can think of no better way to spend my days, in a universe of seemingly infinite time and space, than to share them with her. Ana has brought to my life so much that was not there before we met. Less pride, more humility. Fewer expectations, higher hopes. Less pain, more love. Her love has been greater than what I could have asked, more than I can put into words. "[T]he best gesture of my brain is less than your eyelids' flutter." And I am grateful.

As my fingers stroke these keys, Ana is carrying our first child. With fear and excitement, we wonder how parenthood will look and feel. We wonder what kind of person Gustavo will become. And we wonder about the world he will inherit. Dreams of democracy fill our head, one where freedom is not a mockery and liberty not a lie. *State Looteries* is written in the spirit of public sociology for him, my old friends, and so many others. Perhaps one day we will create a world together where America can become "the dream the dreamers dreamed," where people get opportunities to become the beautiful people they already are, and where all are treated with dignity and respect.

~ kase
Chicago, June 2015

This book is a product of Kasey's many years of hard work, dedication, and endurance. If I added anything as a second author, it was entrance to the world of publishing and perhaps a bit of rugged harshness on those occasions when I told Kasey what I truly thought of his sometimes lofty ideas and fantastical dreams. There were many times when we just talked about the disenchantments of our business—what it means to be a working class, female, minority, or non-heterosexual academic; I suppose I will be forever scarred (or enlightened) by Joanna Kadi's book *Thinking Class: Sketches from a Cultural Worker*. Mostly, though, what I did was pass down the golden nuggets of advice given to me by my own advisor, Eduardo Bonilla-Silva: learn to write clear, simple, and clean; learn to take rejection, lots and lots of rejections; remember where you came from and always, always, always pay it forward. Unlike myself (I recall being an often angry graduate student), Kasey has been the perfect student: always taking notes, always listening, and always taking seriously any advice given to him. Oddly enough, those are also some of the telltale signs of someone with a working-class upbringing (smile). Kasey, I am very proud of you man. You have a critical eye, a kind heart, and a generous soul. I have learned as much from you as you from I (perhaps more). And I predict you will go far in our business. Academia, like the world in which we live, is rife with hypocrites; structural barriers (racism, sexism, homophobia, etc.) mean that we often must tread lightly when we want to scream out loud about the injustices that we not only study, but also face as members of a certain race or gender, or as other scholars of inequality. So keep fighting the good fight, as you always have.

~ DGE
Chicago, June 2015

Foreword
Racialized Taxation: Furthering Racialized Social Systems Theory

All theories are incomplete and partial. This is always the case because no phenomenon—social, physical, or biological—can be isolated to the extent that one can produce a total, holistic explanation for its occurrence. In the realm of race and race theorization, this is undoubtedly the case as well. I, for example, advanced a structural theory of racism almost 20 years ago (Bonilla-Silva 1997), which I labeled the "racialized social system" approach (RSS henceforth). My basic claim was that racial phenomena had a material foundation: that is, I argued that if race existed in societies, it was not because people had "negative ideas" about others, but because a socially defined group (a race) received benefits by labeling others (racializing) as their inferiors. It was upon this fundamental idea that I built a whole theoretical apparatus to explain race matters in social formations.

Even though I stand by the basic arguments in my original article, my general theory had some limitations (I have acknowledged many of them in a recently published paper, see Bonilla-Silva 2015). One limitation was that my theory was at the macro-level analysis and said precious little about the meso- and micro-levels of racially based social action. Albeit my work on the "new racism" (Bonilla-Silva and Lewis 1999) was in part an attempt of getting at these levels of analyses, I have not done a complete and satisfactory job of answering my own call for unearthing "the specific mechanisms, practices, and social relations that produce and reproduce racial inequality at all levels" (Bonilla-Silva 2001: 48; see also Hughey et al. 2015). This is a monumental job, both theoretically and empirically, and truly requires, as I have alluded in many forums, collective theoretical and empirical efforts. I believe, and hope, that like-minded race analysts who regard racism as structural or institutional should work to develop theories, arguments, and social facts to explain and document how racism works as a structure and forms a racial regime.

Enter "State Looteries"

State Looteries by Henricks and Embrick (and one has to love the title of their book) is a serious effort at both theorizing *and* empirically detailing how a very important component of the racial structure operates at the *meso*-level. Their argument in this ingenious book is that taxation is a racialized mechanism that transfers capital to whites (they call this "white wealthfare") by literally looting the impoverished black and brown masses. They contend that "*State Looteries* represents our attempt to learn more of the general (i.e., RSS) through attention paid to the specific (i.e., the lottery tax), and in the process situate the empirical within the theoretical" and add that, by doing this, their "work places data and theory on equal footing, so that any gaps between the two can be bridged" (Henricks and Embrick 2016: 186). I welcome their critical engagement with my work enthusiastically as this is the only way we will advance racial theory. Their book, hence, is a solid contribution to both racial theory and the empirical documentation of how race matters in "post-racial" America, and it is much more. I place their work in the broad field of economic sociology, particularly in the relatively new field of fiscal sociology, but their specific contribution to this field is to examine the racial component of taxation through an analysis of state lotteries. This is key, as economic sociology has grown tremendously in recent years, but has been mostly blind (or shall I say, colorblind?) to the way that race is embedded in all economic relations and transactions.

This brings me to the final contribution of their book. Although many have written on the regressive taxation character of lotteries, few have highlighted its racial aspects as well as its colorblind appeal. Presumably lotteries are not racially targeted, but Henricks and Embrick show their historical connection to "tax rebellions," all of which, since the 19th century, have had a racial angle (see Chapter 3). All the states that lowered taxes still had a need for revenue; hence, state lotteries became a favorite fiscal solution. This solution has been presented time and again across states in the nation as a neutrally structured means to increase much needed revenues for education, pensions, and the like. State lotteries have also been presented as something good for the "common man" (see Chapter 5). Yet, as is the case with many seemingly neutral practices, policies, and institutions in our "post-racial" times (e.g., college admissions tests, many voter registration regulations and voting procedures, etc.) nothing is what it seems. Lotteries allow states to lower taxes for all, but since blacks and Latinos are poorer than whites, they do not benefit equally from tax cuts. Blacks and Latinos, however, play more lottery than whites (about 36% more), which is not a surprise because lottery agencies racially target players through advertisement (see their example of the Illinois Lottery) and even through some of the games they promote (e.g., the "numbers" games).

The revenue state lotteries generate on the backs of folks of color is then seemingly redistributed for all state residents via expenditures in services such as education; however, in many states, the revenue goes to the General Revenue Fund, which allows legislatures to use the money as they see fit. And even in states when the revenue is used for things such as education, the distribution does not favor those who contribute the most and need the most. For instance, the authors show how, although Chicago contributes 70 percent of the funds generated by the state lottery (and particularly from the areas where black and brown people are hyper-concentrated), it receives a fraction of the revenue. Thus, states "loot" and do not "reboot" areas in desperate need for state investment.

This book is rich in details, deep in history, solid in analysis, and is definitely a book that will help advance racial theory. Therefore, my hope is that many people will read Henricks and Embrick's book, as it is a well-executed effort in trying to ascertain one of the central mechanisms used to reproduce racial inequality in so-called post-racial America.

~ Eduardo Bonilla-Silva, Duke University

Acknowledgments

The following images are reproduced with permission:

"Anti-busing Rally at Thomas Park, South Boston." Spencer Grant Collection, State of Massachusetts, Boston Public Library.
"Photo: PA83–42–1975–9–6–11." Collections of the Texas/Dallas History and Archives Division, Dallas Public Library.
"Untitled Photograph." Carmen A. Roberts Papers, Box 1, photographs, Bentley Historical Library, University of Michigan.

We would like to express our appreciation to the copyright holders for sharing the rights.

Introduction
Black Dollars, White Pockets
Looting by Another Name[1]

How far has America come on the issue of race? November 4, 2008. The first black man is elected president of the United States, and journalists like Richard Cohen (2008) of *The Washington Post* conclude that the country has transcended race. Yet in many ways, racism continues to color the Obama years as much now as in the past. One might say his election has been a cover to proceed with an established system of state-sponsored looting and pillorying in black communities (Bonilla-Silva [2003] 2014). Whereas some consider America's racist institutions like those during Jim Crow as temporary aberrations to an otherwise well-functioning, morally compliant system, a counterview sees them as enduring features of democratic capitalism (Feagin 2006). Though Jim Crow no longer exists (at least formally), its ghost lies on, unwilling to die.

"Black codes"[2] that compelled emancipated slaves into involuntary, underpaid, or sometimes unpaid labor have been replaced by a criminal justice system that oversees more black people than were enslaved in 1850 (Alexander 2010). Poll taxes, literacy tests, and residency requirements that denied people of color suffrage have evolved into Voter ID laws that thwart participation in electoral politics (Bell [1973] 2008). Racial violence of yesterday has become the "shoot first, ask questions later" practices of today in places like Ferguson, Missouri. Courtroom silence on ugly displays of racial violence parallels how lynch mobs would leave bodies to hang for days, like Ida B. Wells (1892) describes, as a message to keep minorities "in their place."

The body of an unarmed, "hands held high" teenager lay lifeless from being shot at least six times and twice in the head. His killer, Police Officer Darren Wilson, did not see a human being, only a "thing." According to Wilson's grand jury testimony,

> "he looked up at me and had the most aggressive face. That's the only way I can describe it, it looks like a demon, that's how angry he looked. He comes back toward me again with his hands up"
>
> *(State of Missouri v. Darren Wilson, Grand Jury Volume V* 2014: 224–225).

Several shots later, Michael Brown goes down for the last time. Officer Wilson had stripped from him his humanity as well as his life.

There on Canfield Drive, Michael Brown's corpse would rest in open view, for nearly four hours, under the unrelenting summer sun. A white sheet was draped over most his body, but neither his feet nor the blood were covered. Much as in the extreme forms of Jim Crow, Michael Brown was transformed into a racial spectacle—into a warning (Embrick 2015). Blood is on the hands of police officer Darren Wilson, but he is not the only one. White people are responsible for this tragedy. We are implicated in a social fabric that has long made communities like Ferguson possible and has reduced black people to a slush fund for our own racial interests. For this reason, and many more, blood is on everyone's hands.

Jim Crow marked an era of two nations—one white and the other black—state-sanctioned as "separate but equal." Why would anyone suspect taxation to fall outside this purview? People of color were subjected to a different tax code whereby they generated revenues for their own *de jure* segregated institutions as well as white mainstream ones (Anderson 1988; Du Bois [1935] 1992). Legal gains brought by the blood, sweat, and tears of the Black Freedom Struggles ended black codes, at least by name if not practice, but these codes did not fully fade into America's past. Echoes of the past can be heard if one listens closely enough. Ferguson represents one rearticulation of Jim Crow, unwilling to die.

Jim Crow, Then and Now

Fast forward to today. Government no longer imposes "blacks-only" taxes, nor does it afford exclusive opportunities to whites. That is, no longer are these things *explicit*. During the 1950s, '60s, and '70s, the Black Freedom Struggles pushed for minority inclusion into "mainstream" institutions, seeking integration in schools and housing as well as access to social safety net policies. All these gains would signify acceptance into larger society. When preliminary steps toward these ends occurred, whites retreated from superficial commitments to racial justice initiatives and they collectively organized to redesign the very institutions that represented racial inclusion (Seamster and Henricks 2015; Steinberg [1995] 2001).

As we discuss in more detail later, white racial resentment became (and continues to be) expressed through tax revolts, anti-welfare and "social entitlements" discourse, and the decimation of state revenues. Seemingly neutral tax policies at various levels of government have taken shape, ones that privilege whites at racial minorities' expense (in addition to the poor in general). These include the lottery tax but many others too. In effect, whites have reappropriated black gains for their own material interests.

Examples abound. Some might point to "urban renewal" developments, or what James Baldwin labels "negro removal" initiatives (see Clark and Baldwin 1963: 27), through tax increment financing and "entrepreneurial" government (Farmer and Poulos 2015; Quiroz and Lindsay 2015). Others might point to incentives that subsidize "segregation academies," or what some of us may simply call high school (Black and Black 1987; Bonastia 2012), as well as the persistence of "white-only communities," what some call home (Loewen 2005). Then there lies the twisted case of Ferguson, Missouri. This is a black-majority city in which a white-led city government, municipal court system, and police force colluded to prioritize raising revenue above all else.

Ferguson's Fiscal Context: New Song, Same Old Tune

Ferguson is a case study whereby the meaning of "serve and protect" transformed into "plunder and profit." Not unlike other cities, the money-deprived city resorted to taxation by other means, relying upon its cops and courts to extract millions in fines and fees. These revenues do not constitute efficient state finance. Rather, they are among the few options available to local politicians often facing budgetary shortfall. This situation was set in motion by actions in the 20th century. Over two-thirds of states followed California's lead with Proposition 13, otherwise known as the People's Initiative to Limit Property Taxation, to pass reforms restricting how local governments raise revenue (Martin 2008).[3]

Many state coffers are, in other words, trapped in a procedural straight-jacket, unable to alleviate the fiscal crises they often confront. Missouri is no exception to the trend. Following the lead of Mel Tucker, founder of "The Taxpayer Survival Association" and eventual U.S. Congressional Representative, the state's voters passed a referendum he authored in 1980: "The Hancock Amendment." Provisions of this law (see Article 10, Sections 16–24 of the Missouri Constitution) set forth procedural barriers for how politicians can generate money. Most new local taxes, licenses, or fees must be voter-approved through a ballot referendum.

Reforms like these accomplish at least two things. First, they limit what taxes can be levied on an institution to which people of color have been denied access: housing. Between 1930 and 1970, for example, census records report that the percentage of Americans owning a home increased from 47.8 to 62.9 percent. This increase was an exclusive one built upon racially discriminatory lending initiatives backed by the Federal Housing Authority and Veteran's Administration (Jackson 1985). As this form of "white wealthfare" ended with civil rights reforms, whites rebelled against property taxes seen as paying for unpopular initiatives like "busing" (Sears and Citrin 1982). They limited their tax liability through ballot referendums, and in the process, created subsidies to preserve wealth generated under a formal apartheid state.

And second, "Unable to raise tax rates, many municipal governments have only one tool at their disposal: lowering them. They cannot raise money, but they can give it away" (Johnson 2015: 9). Through "development-driven" initiatives, politicians presume that luring new business with improved infrastructure and property tax abatements will ease their fiscal woes. Throw money at the corporations, the narrative goes, and they will bring jobs, raise property values, increase sales tax revenue, attract other business, and so on. Often the costs exceed the benefits, though, and local residents, especially those already marginalized, have their political voice silenced and are collateralized to foot the bill (Seamster 2015). This is among the reasons that Ferguson received only $68,000 in property taxes for 2013 from Emerson Electric, a Fortune 500 company with a 152-acre headquarters of prime real estate, which is barely enough to pay a municipal judge for all those infamous petty fees and fines that were distributed (Johnson 2015).

When Black Dollars Become a White Slush Fund

Petty fines and fees offer politicians one of the few options permissible for generating revenue under the Hancock Amendment. They can be levied on a range of "deviant" activities like jaywalking, not cutting grass or maintaining one's property, wrongfully removing trash, wearing "saggy" pants, and disturbing the peace, among many other broadly defined but selectively imposed infractions (Balko 2014). The city budget reports that petty fines and fees comprise Ferguson's second-highest revenue source, just behind sales taxes but ahead of franchise taxes (usage fees on telecommunications, natural gas, and electricity) and property taxes (City of Ferguson 2012, 2013). "Ferguson's law enforcement practices," concluded the U.S. Department of Justice (2015), "are shaped by the City's focus on revenue rather than by public safety needs" (p. 2).

Why prioritize revenue over public safety? Because Ferguson, the St. Louis area, and Missouri in general have a century-long record of policy choices that prioritize white and corporate interests above most everything else (Gotham 2002). Whiteness yields, to borrow George Lipsitz's (1998) words, a certain cash value:

> [I]t accounts for advantages that come to individuals through profits made from housing secured in discriminatory markets, through the unequal educations allocated to children of different races, through insider networks that channel employment opportunities to the relatives and friends of those who have profited most from present and past racial discrimination, and especially through intergenerational transfers of inherited wealth that pass on the spoils of discrimination to succeeding generations
> (p. vii; see also Hamilton et al. 2015; Kirp et al. 1995; Massey and Denton 1993; Oliver and Shapiro [1995] 2006; Ross and Yinger 2002).

The value of whiteness accrues through outright exploitation or opportunity hoarding, so that disadvantages confronting people of color are systematically interconnected with advantages afforded to whites.

Unequal racial arrangements do not require individually initiated actions that assert or defend racial interests in a direct manner (Feagin and Eckberg 1980; Haney-López 2000; Wellman [1977] 1993). These relations are buffered by institutions that routinize how benefits are monopolized by whites or extracted from others who supply them. The fiscal state is one interwoven institution that buffers racist relations. In Ferguson, the distinct functions of city government, local courts, and the police department broke down, and in their place emerged a convergence of money generation. About a quarter of Ferguson's collected revenue, for example, came from petty fines and fees in the 2010s ("U.S. Department of Justice" 2015). These have seen steady growth, with $1.38 million in 2010, $1.41 in 2011, $2.11 million in 2012, and $2.46 million in 2013, which indicates that an expansion in the number of filed charges and cases on the court's docket.

Ferguson's municipal courts confused its role as an arbitrator of justice and used "its judicial authority as the means to compel the payment of fines and fees that advance the city's financial interests" ("U.S. Justice Department" 2015: 3). In 2013, 96 percent of all those arrested due to an outstanding warrant were black ("U.S. Department of Justice" 2015). Compared to their counterparts, black folks were 68 percent less likely to have their court cases dismissed, 50 percent more likely to have their cases lead to an arrest warrant, and accounted for 92 percent of arrest warrants issued. Over 9,000 warrants were issued in 2013, the highest number in the state, for minor violations regarding parking, traffic, and housing code infractions. They did not always require jail time, though, so long as fines were paid. Should a person be unable to pay, the courts sometimes denied people eligibility for public assistance ("ArchCity Defenders" 2014). Other times, they imposed something akin to an 18th-century-style "debtors' prison." They were locked up for weeks at a time.

According to data compiled by the Ferguson Police Department, many offenses seem to be exclusively reserved for black folks. They comprised 85 percent of all traffic stops, 90 percent of all citations, and 93 percent of all arrests between 2012 and 2014 ("U.S. Department of Justice" 2015). Census records show that blacks comprise only 67 percent of the city's population ("U.S. Census Bureau" 2013). When stopped for traffic violations, they were more than twice as likely as their white counterparts to be searched; all despite the fact they were 26 percent less likely to possess contraband ("U.S. Department of Justice" 2015). While four or more citations were issued during a single incident only twice to nonblacks, black folks received four or more citations on 73 occasions. Between 2011 and 2013, 95 percent of "Manner of Walking in Roadway" and 94 percent of "Failure to Comply" charges were levied against black people. Of the documented force used by Ferguson Police Department officers, 90 percent and every canine bite was against a black person. These events were not Bull Connor's Birmingham, Alabama, of the 1960s; they are present-day occurrences in Ferguson, Missouri.

Neither the Ferguson Police Department nor the municipal courts were acting out of their own volition; they had plenty of encouragement and, at times, extortion from city government. After 2011, the City Manager and City Council upped the money available to the courts and added new positions to handle an expanding caseload ("U.S. Department of Justice" 2015). This helped ensure that the arbitrators of justice could continue "setting new all-time records in fines and forfeitures" on a monthly basis, as well as maintain capacity to "increase the revenues" (Ferguson's City Manager qtd. in "U.S. Department of Justice" 2015: 9). Municipal judge Ronald Brockmeyer willfully complied. Further transforming his courtroom into a cash cow, he added a host of fees for clearing warrants, "failure to appear," and stepped-up fines for repeat offenders or subsequent charges.

Meanwhile, local politicians pressured the FPD with emails like: "unless ticket writing ramps up significantly before the end of the year, it will be hard to significantly raise collections next year. What are your thoughts? Given that we are looking at a substantial sales tax shortfall, it's not an insignificant issue" (Ferguson's Finance Director qtd. in "U.S. Department of Justice" 2015: 10). The Police Chief, Thomas Jackson, replied with assurance. Once the FPD hired more officers, placed more of them on the streets, and extended shift durations, he claimed, the city would generate the revenue it needs. To further ensure that collections increased, officers were evaluated by their level of ticket-pushing "productivity," operationalized as distributing a minimum level of fines and fees—an average of 28 per month. Were these quotas left unmet, officers could be punished with reassignment or some other discipline.

There Is No Ferguson, There Are Fergusons

An insidious truth of Ferguson is that black dollars financed the court-approved death of Michael Brown. When "the Great Recession" hit in the mid-2000s, Ferguson responded not by downsizing but expanding government (Johnson 2015). The city issued bonds to finance renovation to the police station worth $3.5 million, issued an 8 percent raise to police officers (and all municipal employees), and purchased three Chevy Tahoes and 60 police handguns. When returns on the bonds could not be satisfied by revenues generated from typical tax sources, the city, courts, and cops turned to the black community and imposed taxation by another name. Presumably, Darren Wilson was driving one of these Tahoes and carrying one of these firearms the day he killed Michael Brown. Petty fines and fees are a part of a broader fiscal picture that made "Ferguson" possible.

Ferguson is no anomaly. Similar underhanded financial schemes occur in other urban cities across America, including Chicago (Wildeboer 2012). In fact, the U.S. Supreme Court has ruled practices like these as constitutional (*Schilb v. Kuebel* 404 U.S. 357 [1971]). The money we are talking about here is the same money that pays for local infrastructure. It helps pay for police departments like those in Ferguson, as well as other local services that most residents partake in. These kinds of revenues are the lifeblood of our public schools, roads and highways, community hospitals, and so on. The revenues do not come from just anyone, though.

We live in a system that did not just let a racialized finance system happen. It was built this way by design, a point that escapes white logic (Mills 1997). As many of our white sisters and brothers preoccupy themselves with judging looters and protesters or commenting on black etiquette, they miss the point that we intentionally created this mess. Ferguson is a community marked by white racism that is so fundamental to an American way of life that body cameras for police will not nudge the nation toward a racial democracy. As much is evident from events that took place in Staten Island, New York. A police officer was caught on video strangling an unarmed black man, yet another grand jury silently consents to the racist status quo. Staten Island is Ferguson. It is not singular; we have Fergusons. This is Oakland. This is Cleveland. This is Baltimore. This is . . .

. . . This Is the Lottery

The lottery is like the petty finance scheme of Ferguson. Both represent rearticulations of Jim Crow practices, only the lottery is dressed in more socially acceptable clothing. Few other state products, perhaps except higher education, are promoted and advertised on the same scale by the state. Even the enterprise of education is open to competition, so that students can attend both private and public schools. Lotteries are not set up in this way. State legislatures have designed them in such a way that states are guaranteed to be sole providers of lottery products. This monopolizes the industry, preemptively flattens competition, and fattens profit rates. "In terms of state products that citizens can purchase directly," Charles Clotfelter and Philip Cook (1989) observe, "the lottery ranks second, right after higher education" (p. 30). That said, lotteries surpass higher education—and other state-sanctioned services like hospitals, parks and recreation, and utility service providers—when it comes to profitability. No other public enterprise offered by the state compares to lotteries in this respect.

Modern state lotteries lie at a strange crossroads of government operations. On the one hand, they seem like another regulatory agency, but on the other hand, they act more like private industry. Bureaucratically speaking, "[lotteries] are held out to be just another square on the organizational charts of government, and allegedly are designed to be vaguely 'regulatory' in nature" (Karcher 1989: 47). As David Nibert (2000) argues, they live up to this description in some ways by establishing guidelines to preserve the integrity and accountability of their daily operations, and perhaps most importantly, to prevent corruption. The regulatory nature of lotteries helps preserve their own legitimacy in the public's eye, but at the end of the day, these institutions exist to maximize tax revenues and increase the bottom line.

The Bottom Line Is a Color Line: Looting by Another Name

The lottery is a tool of government designed with seemingly noble intentions. As the advertisements tell us, "everyone's a winner." Most state lotteries also follow legal frameworks so that proceeds are 1) returned to lottery players through prize winnings, 2) used to pay for operating costs, and 3) redirected to state finance. Of course some variance exists across states, but most lotteries are more alike than they are unalike. Newer lottery states have followed the legal models of what worked for their predecessors, and often duplicate the formula to initiate their own (Cook and Clotfelter 1989; Karcher 1989; Nibert 2000).

Our central goal in *State Looteries* is to uncover hidden biases of the lottery tax and expose some of the racial consequences for financing public services in this way. Some of the central questions we take up in this book are: What does race have to do with the proliferation of state lotteries during the late 20th century? From whom does lottery money come, and on whom is it spent? How might these tax practices constitute a form of institutional discrimination? In what ways does taxation create and recreate racial inequalities? Drawing from multiple data sources, which consist of public datasets, historical archives, and information collected through government audits, we utilize a mixed-methods approach to illuminate the racial underpinnings of how lotteries have reconfigured America's tax composition in ways that end up reproducing, or perhaps exacerbating, existing racial inequalities.

Proponents claim that lotteries help alleviate fiscal crises, and in some cases, extend opportunities to "deserving," well-to-do people. Like petty fines and fees in Ferguson, however, the emergence of state lotteries during the past 50 years is a reconfiguration of the tax code—one that racializes "new" ways that capital is hoarded by some groups and redistributed from others. Legally, no one racial group is required to pay the lottery tax, but this does not negate the fact that it carries implicit biases. This is particularly true when state-sponsored advertising targets black folks, as well as engages in other tactics of racial profiling, and then substitutes other sources of revenue with lottery money. These state-sanctioned exchanges end up routinizing inequitable transfers of material resources, so that white coffers remain untouched and people of color pay more for public services that continue to fail them. So, just how far has America come when it comes to race? Perhaps a better question we might ask ourselves is how far America has yet to go. We would suggest much, much further than November 4, 2008. #BlackLivesMatter

Notes

1   An earlier iteration of this chapter appeared as editorial commentary in *Humanity and Society* (see Henricks and Harvey 2015).
2   "Black codes" refer to laws established in postbellum Southern states (and some in other regions too) that restricted black emancipation, and effectively reduced

their condition back to "slavery by another name" (Blackmon 2008). One common example included vagrancy laws that targeted unemployed black folks and equated not working with criminal behavior.

3 Though California sparked tax revolts that would ignite the nation during the 1970s, these types of constitutional limitation movements have a deep history that dates to at least the 1870s. In Alabama, for example, white "Redeemers" created a new reactionary constitution that effectively defunded the common schools established under Reconstruction and set up legislative barriers that prevented policymakers from doing anything about it (McMillan [1955] 1978).

1 "No Taxation Without Discrimination"

"The Lottery Tax," State Finance, and Racism

"Racism is like a Cadillac, they bring out a new model every year."

~Malcolm X[1]

The above quote is one Malcolm X would often tell his followers. Although newer models look much different than older ones, the fact of the matter is that a Cadillac is still a Cadillac. Likewise, racism is still racism, regardless of how it has changed throughout the years. Time and time again, when minority groups gain access to public services, white backlash follows suit. One instance in which this occurred includes the post-bellum era when newly freed black slaves entered into developing public schools. White communities banded together to oppose black education and engage in political tactics that hoarded white resources from funding black education. Another includes the civil rights era, when de jure segregation was outlawed and federal orders mandated schools to integrate. Ruby Nell Bridges Hall in Louisiana, the courageous Little Rock Nine in Arkansas,[2] Rita Buchanan and Linda McKinley in Nashville, Tennessee, and countless others across the U.S. witnessed white outrage that ranged from derogatory racial remarks to racial terrorism to tax revolts.

Taxes are often seen as the resources making public schools possible, and thus, they are consistently singled out as a symbol of angst by white reactionary movements. Perhaps we should expect as much when considering the words of Eduardo Bonilla-Silva (2001), "fundamental changes in racialized social systems are accompanied by struggles that reach the point of overt protest" (p. 43). Though this point has been long stressed by those looking at overt protests spearheaded by people of color (e.g., Franklin and Moss 1947), we want to emphasize new ways in which dominant group members reassert their interests to alter tax practices during eras of changing racial dynamics.

Taxes say something about the ever-changing structures of social life. They offer a blueprint, in both symbolic and concrete terms, for uncovering the primary arrangements in society—racial hierarchy included. *State Looteries* revisits some formative episodes of tax rebellion throughout American history, as well as other moments that many may have forgotten or never known. In this book, we devote most our attention to dissecting the consequences these rebellions have caused; consequences like the proliferation of lotteries and the fundamental reconfiguration of America's tax code. The intent is to uncover how racialized tax practices change in patterned yet resilient ways. Soon after the Civil War ended, as Eric Foner (1988) points out, for example, a wave of tax revolts proliferated in the South. Self-proclaimed white "Redeemers" were angered to see their own tax dollars spent on a welfare state they perceived to be as extravagant as it was coercive (Du Bois 1910).

Before His Time, Early Observations on Racialized Taxation

A young W.E.B. Du Bois and his colleagues (1901) were the first, and still among the only, to identify racialized processes of hoarding and redistribution via taxation:

> "We congratulate the South on resisting . . . the many millions it has spent on Negro education. But it is only fair to point out that Negro taxes and the Negroes' share of the income from indirect taxes and endowments have fully repaid this expenditure, *so that the Negro public school system has not in all probability cost the white taxpayers a single cent since the war"*
>
> (p. ii, emphasis original).

Despite this observation, Du Bois never undertook a systematic study of these revolts. However, some historians, like John Hope Franklin ([1961] 1994), J. Mills Thornton (1982), and others, have offered insights on the matter. They detail various ways that whites collectively organized and retaliated against a scallywag, carpetbagger, and a black Republican Party.

Fed up with the idealism of emancipation, as well as an "imposter," bayonet rule government that vastly expanded the state's size and scope, white Redeemers rebelled with legal reforms to roll back Reconstruction's accomplishments (Franklin [1961] 1994). These included instituting new taxes, establishing universal education, extending social services, and investing in infrastructure (Du Bois 1910, [1935] 1992; Kousser 1980; McMillan [1955] 1978; Woodward 1971). Among the new taxes levied were those on property, which, for the most part, only whites possessed (Woodward 1971). In some states, property taxes increased four- to eightfold during Reconstruction (Thornton 1982; see also Du Bois 1910), and debt more than quadrupled (McMillan [1955] 1978). White Southerners confronted not only losing the war, but living in a devastated economy of evaporated wealth (i.e., former slaves) and worthless currency.

Meanwhile the Reconstruction government expected them to pay taxes that financed services such as education for emancipated slaves, as well as to sit idly by while their perceived unequals gained legal protections (e.g., Civil Rights Act of 1866, Congressional Reconstruction Acts of 1867), such as the right to create and enforce contracts, purchase and sell property, and participate in court proceedings (Foner 1988). From a Redemption standpoint, Reconstruction had surpassed its point of excess and many whites aspired to reclaim their "rightful" social standing (Franklin [1961] 1994). Some wore sheets and practiced physical and mental violence. Others wore suits and preferred peaceful exploitation. It was exploitation, nonetheless. As the federal government was turning its back on Reconstruction, and eventually withdrawing federal troops from the South, Redemption campaigns began retrenchment strategies state-by-state to recapture political control and bring about an idealized racial state. They accomplished this feat by many measures, through black voter suppression with poll taxes, voter identification laws, gerrymandering, and replacing elections with appointments, among a host of other tactics (Rogers 1970). Once political control was in hand, reforming the tax code was a logical starting point for change.

Racial Retrenchment in the Tax Code under Redemption

During the U.S. Supreme Court's landmark case *Oliver Brown et al. v. Board of Education of Topeka, et al.* (1954), numerous whites spoke in favor of preserving segregated schools. They presumed that black folks did not pay enough taxes to get a say in government spending, and therefore fell outside the burdens and benefits of citizenship (Walsh Forthcoming). These types of narratives are old hat and echo sentiments present in the late 19th century. "[R]edemption governments, often describing themselves as the 'rule of the taxpayer,'" writes C. Vann Woodward (1971), "frankly constituted themselves champions of the property owner against the property less and allegedly untaxed masses" (p. 59). Making these claims, white Redeemers pursued retrenchment strategies of tax reform that hoarded what resources they possessed, redistributed capital others had accumulated, or sometimes a hybrid of both.

In Alabama, for example, a reclaimed Democratic gubernatorial office moved to replace the 1868 Constitution (McMillan [1955] 1978). Leaders of the movement, like Leroy Pope Walker, denounced the document as:

> a piece of unseemly mosaic, composed of shreds and patches gathered here and there, incongruous in design, inharmonious in action, discriminating and oppressive to the burthens it imposes, reckless in the license it confers on unjust and wicked legislation, and utterly lacking in every element to inspire popular confidence and the relevance and affection of the people
>
> ("Journal of the Convention" 1875: 5).

Claiming the mantra of "reverse discrimination," Walker and others called for a constitution that acknowledges "the perfect political and civil equality of all men, of whatever race, color, or previous condition" as well as limit government's fiscal capacity because the "power to tax is power to destroy" ("Journal of the Convention" 1875: 5–6). Another leader, Francis Strother Lyon, claimed,

> The highest aim of the late convention was to insure the safety of the people against the possibilities of extravagance and corruption
> ("Journal of the Convention" 1875: 169).

Redeemers aimed to return the out-of-touch, extravagant, and crooked fiscal state to "the people" of Alabama and protect their interests from overreaching BIG government (Du Bois 1910).

Paralleling events that transpired in California nearly a century later (Martin 2008), Alabama's property tax rates were reduced across the board and constitutional obstacles to tax increases were put in place. These feats were accomplished by replacing the Reconstruction Alabama Constitution of 1868 with a Redeemer Alabama Constitution of 1875, which was backed by the white supremacist Democratic Party and a reclaimed gubernatorial office (McMillan [1955] 1978). The newly enacted constitution segregated schools (Article XIII), abolished the state's board of education (Article XVII), placed a debt ceiling on spending (Article XI), required a two-thirds majority for appropriations (Article III), and limited the tax powers of state, county, and municipal governments (Article XI). The changes had a direct effect on education finance, with funds reducing from $484,000 to $348,891, or 27.9 percent, during the 1875 Constitution's first year in effect (McMillan [1955] 1978). Inadvertently, these reforms rolled back government's size and scope, and entrenched a tax structure for decades to come through procedural barriers yet to be fully overcome (Newman and O'Brien 2011).

Contrary to Alabama, other states moved to expand rather than contract their tax structure. In Kentucky (1874), legislators enacted a "uniform"[3] system of school finance. What came with it was a number of tax laws that promoted white interests at the expense of blacks. "The sources of the revenue for the schools" writes Gilbert Thomas Stephenson ([1910] 1969), "were (1) a tax of twenty cents on the hundred dollars upon the property of Negroes, (2) their poll taxes, (3) their dog taxes, (4) taxes on deeds, suits, and licenses collected from colored persons, (5) fines, penalties, and forfeitures collected from them, (6) sums received from Congress, provided the apportionment to each colored child did not exceed that to each white child, and (7) gifts, donations, and grants" (p. 197). These laws were later ruled unconstitutional in 1885 (see *Dawson v. Lee, 83 Ky. 49)*, but they nonetheless represent a pattern that proliferated across the South, and later in other regions, whereby people of color were held liable to pay for their own "public" benefits (Du Bois [1935] 1992).

Historical Echoes: The Continuities of Race-Driven Tax Revolts

Were W.E.B. Du Bois alive to witness the emergence of lotteries as part of modern state finance, we doubt he would be surprised. Many of the same trends he identified in the 1870s and 1880s would repeat themselves throughout the nation a century later. Soon after the formal end of Jim Crow, white-led tax revolts emerged in California and then most states. These reactionary movements were largely responding to growing militancy among the Black Freedom Struggles. As Kenneth Neubeck and Noel Cazenave (2001) point out:

> By the mid-1960s, it was increasingly clear to most African Americans that gaining fundamental legal civil rights in the South was not enough. The primary goal of the civil rights movement began changing to economic equality with whites for African Americans everywhere, North and South. This goal threatened the race-based economic privileges enjoyed by all whites
>
> (p. 120).

This is among the reasons why, argue Thomas Byrne Edsall and Mary Edsall (1991), whites responded during the 1970s with racial discourse that came to embody all that was wrong with unbalanced budgets, bureaucratic incompetence, programs in the war on the racialized poor, school desegregation efforts, and a coercively redistributive tax state.

Growing white animosity drove them to rebel against the state for what they saw, once again, as policies that pandered to minorities. Clarence Lo (1990) points out that many whites organized to cut government "waste" by slashing taxes seen as undermining and destroying their quality of life. Government initiatives, like integration mandates in public schools, became viewed as costly programs that undercut white interests paid out of pocket by their own "hard-earned tax dollars." An expanding population, comprised by mostly Latina/o and Asian immigrants, further stroked white anxiety. Words like "tax revolt" had become, pointed out Senator George McGovern (1978), codespeak for race. These "mad as hell" white folks retaliated by taking to the ballot box, and in the process, they fundamentally reformed state tax codes. Through the passage of state-level amendments that set up institutional barriers to progressive taxation (e.g., tax limitations, supermajority requirements), ones that emulate Redeemer constitutions, they all but forced politicians to entertain alternative ways to keep state finances in order.

Enter the lottery tax.

Taxation, a Neglected Subject of Study

Despite the practical and substantive importance of taxation in people's everyday lives, few contemporary scholars, including social scientists and even those in sociolegal studies, have examined this presumably dreary and lifeless topic as a central subject of study. Charles Tilly (2009) offers three reasons why scholars need to pay attention to taxation:

> First, over the long run it constitutes the largest intervention of governments in their subjects' private life, so much so that the history of state expansion becomes a history of violent struggles over taxes, and the history of state consolidation becomes a history of tax evasion by those who have guile and power to frustrate the fisc. Second, follow the money: the circulation of resources from subjects to government-initiated activities provides a sort of CT scan for a regime's entire operation. Third, it dramatizes the problem of consent [regarding the "Social Contract"]
>
> (p. xiii)

As a whole, we as scholars have ignored the broad implications of taxation and how it cuts across a seemingly endless list of institutional domains. All these oversights occur, argue Isaac William Martin, Ajay Mehrotra, and Monica Prasad (2009), despite the fact that it is through taxes that group relations are formalized (see also Martin and Prasad 2014).

Matters of the individual and society, bureaucratic administration, distributions of public and private capital, and, what is most important to this study, the reproduction of racial inequality all run through taxation. For these reasons, Joseph Schumpeter ([1918] 1991) wrote:

> The spirit of a people, its cultural level, its social structure, the deeds its policy may prepare—all this and more is written in its fiscal history, stripped of all phrases. He who knows how to listen to its message here discerns the thunder of world history more clearly than anywhere else
> (p. 101).

Only until recently, this call for "fiscal sociology" has mostly fallen on deaf ears. The study of taxation has been left to those mostly in the realm of applied research. Centers like the Center on Budget and Policy Priorities, Citizens for Tax Justice, Council On State Taxation, Institute on Taxation and Economic Policy, National Taxpayers Conference, Tax Foundation, and Tax Policy Center have been the ones to address a subject matter that affects most everyone.

Under what has been labeled "the new fiscal sociology," some notable scholars have taken up Schumpeter's call to unmask "the thunder of world history" through the study of taxation. This nascent movement has yielded numerous insights. James O'Connor ([1973] 2002), for example, identifies how budgetary shortfalls in government are inevitable under capitalism, since the state must simultaneously perform contradictory functions of maintaining business profit and preserving social harmony. Kimberly Morgan and

Prasad (2009) offer a comparative historical analysis of France and the United States to show what role taxation has played in shaping these countries' different trajectories of state development. Lo (1990) and Martin (2008) trace the nexus between taxation, social movements, and constitutional change by illuminating the bottoms-up reactionary origins of the 1970s property tax revolts in California. Katherine Newman and Rourke O'Brien (2011) offer a historically comparative focus that contrasts how tax regimes of the South (and later the West) have diverged from all other regions, since this region not only has the highest regressive tax system but the highest concentration of poverty in the nation. One notable omission from much research within "the new fiscal sociology," with some exception, regards matters of race, racism, and racial conflict.

Towards a New Fiscal Sociology of Race, Racism, and Racial Conflict

Whereas most of the aforementioned scholars argue, to varying extents, that taxation represents the Social Contract of modernity, our understanding flows from the work of philosopher Charles Mills (1997) in viewing this contract as inherently a racial one. The United States was founded under the premise of racially inspired, Anglo-Saxton notions of "manifest destiny" (Horsman 1981), and would become what others have labeled a "*herrenvolk* democracy" (van den Berghe 1967) or a "white republic" (Saxton 1990). From the 1787 Philadelphia Convention, whereby people of color, especially black slaves, were stripped their humanity, declared three-fifths a person, reduced to chattel property, and rendered incapable of self-rule (Marable [1983] 2000), to the Naturalization Act of 1790 that pronounced whiteness as a precondition for citizenship and formal political participation (Haney-López 1996; Harris 1993), formation of the U.S. commenced with the codification of a rigid racial hierarchy. Whites were declared both the de jure and de facto "ruling race."

"No taxation without representation!" These iconic words of tax rebels like Samuel Adams and the "Sons of Liberty" marked the birth of a new nation. Yet when these words became formally codified under law, they cannot be fully understood without reference to race. Consider, for example, the text of Article I, Section 2 in the United States Constitution:

> Representatives and Direct Taxes shall be apportioned among the several States which may be included within this Union, according to their respective Numbers, which shall be determined by adding the whole Number of free Persons, including those bound to Service for a Term of Years, and excluding Indians not taxed, three fifths of all other Persons.

This passage represents a compromise, as Robin Einhorn (2006) shows, between elite white men of Northern and Southern states that grew out debates beginning shortly after the adoption of the Declaration of Independence and initial meetings of the Continental Congress. On both sides of the sectional debate, racial oppression was rationalized for their own benefit. When it came to congressional representation, Northern representatives like John Adams and James Wilson wanted to regard black slaves as much less than three-fifths a person to ensure their own political control, but when it came to taxation, these same delegates argued that black slaves be counted much higher than 60 percent for a tax system based not on absolute property but population size (Wills 2003).

Southern delegates like Samuel Chase, James Madison, and Thomas Lynch objected to higher tax burdens and lower representation, and they assumed positions in direct opposition to their Northern brethren. According to Jefferson's notes on this debate, Samuel Chase of Maryland countered with the following argument:

> [T]axation should always be in proportion to property; that this was, in theory, the true rule; but that, from a variety of difficulties, it was a rule which could never be adopted in practice . . . He considered the number of inhabitants as a tolerably good [alternative] criterion of property, and . . . thought it the best mode which we could adopt, with one exception only: he observed that negroes are property, and, as such, cannot be distinguished from the lands or personalities held in those states where there are few slaves. . . . There is no more reason, therefore, for taxing the Southern States on the farmer's head, and on his slave's head, than the Northern ones on their farmers' heads and the heads of their cattle; that the method proposed would, therefore, tax the Southern States according to their numbers and their wealth conjunctly, while the Northern would be taxed on numbers only
>
> ("The Debates in the Several State Conventions on the Adoption of the Federal Constitution, Vol. I" [1777] 1888: 70–71).

Other Southerners argued that their constituents, themselves, were victims of slavery, and therefore deserved an exclusive tax break that would be undeserving for Northerners. According to John Adams' notes on an earlier debate, William Hooper of North Carolina argued:

> A gentleman of three or four hundred negroes don't raise more corn than feeds them. A laborer can't be hired for less than twenty four pounds a year in Massachusetts Bay. The net profit of a negro is not more than five or six pounds per annum. I wish to see the day that slaves are not necessary
>
> ("Journals of the Continental Congress, in June 5 —October, 8 1776, Volume V" [1776] 1906: 1080).

In Orwellian style ([1949] 1961), these words defended Southern tax relief on the basis that "freedom is slavery." Owning other human beings, according to this rationale, caused slaveholders to incur economic losses not gains.

Einhorn (2006) points out that it was James Madison who suggested the three-fifths ratio. In a good faith pledge of the South's allegiance to the Union, Madison offered "that in order to give proof of the sincerity of his professions of liberality, he would propose that slaves be rated as five to three" ("The Debates in the Several State Conventions on the Adoption of the Federal Constitution in 1787, Vol. V" [1787] 1845: 79). This proposal mediated unsettled ground between New Englanders, who wanted a 3:4 ratio of slaves to free persons and Southerners who preferred a 3:1 or 4:1 ratio (Einhorn 2006). Later Madison and others like Hugh Williamson of North Carolina built upon earlier sentiments expressed by Chase and Hooper nearly 10 years earlier, but did so in ways where they simultaneously condemned slavery and justified favorable tax treatment for slave states in the same breath. According to Williamson, "he was principled agst. Slavery, but that he thought slaves an incumbrance to Society instead of increasing its ability to pay taxes" ("Letters of Delegates to Congress: Volume 20 March 12, 1783 —September 30 1783" [1783] 1976: 120). On the very day Madison pledged the ratio, it became adopted by Congress (Einhorn 2006).

It did not hurt that Madison's position was affirmed by prominent Northern leaders, like the known abolitionist Alexander Hamilton. Consider Hamilton's accommodation in his own words:

> Much has been said of the impropriety of representing men, who have no will of their own . . . It is an unfortunate situation of the Southern States, to have a great part of their population, as well as property in blacks. . . . But representation and taxation go together—and one uniform rule ought to apply to both. Would it be just to compute these slaves in the assessment of taxes; and discard them from the estimate in the apportionment of representatives? Would it be just to impose a singular burthen, without conferring some adequate advantage?
>
> ("The Debates in the Several State Conventions on
> the Adoption of the Federal Constitution in 1787,
> Vol. II" [1788] 1836: 237).

Hamilton's concession to slavery lies in his complicity. Perhaps this was political maneuvering. After all, the main federal source of revenue at this time, the tariff, benefitted the economic interests of industry in general and Northern state in particular far more than it did the agrarian-based Southern economy. Whichever is the case, Hamilton did not question the fundamental master/slave relationship in debates over taxation. Instead he went to great lengths, as the passage shows, to defend it.

A long story short, the "three-fifths clause" was not merely a compromise regarding how to enumerate the population. It emerged out of nearly two decades of debate over the apportionment of taxation and representation, two contentious items that nearly thwarted the formation of a young nation (Einhorn 2006). Though the first laws were written in the language of liberalism with words like common deference, liberty, and promoting the general welfare, debates leading up the enactment of the Constitution were entrenched within colonial discourse whereby people of color were framed as objects of power to be owned and taxed as property and counted as apportionment without representation, and as potential threats to the social order. This racial ideology manifests itself, as the "three-fifths clause" attests, in the word of law. And herein lay the very beginning of how racial politics shaped, and was shaped by, conflicts over taxation. It marks the beginning of, to extend Mills' (1997) theory, "The Racial Contract of Taxation."

Of All the Matters of Taxation, Why the Lottery Tax?

Looking beyond the boundaries of social science, a subgroup of sociolegal scholars who label themselves "critical tax theorists" has gone to great lengths during the past two decades to dissect racial implications of various tax codes. Their analyses have spanned a broad range of statutes such as charitable institution exemptions (Brennen 2004), the Earned Income Tax Credit (Abreu 2001; Brown 2012; Moran 2010), homeownership subsidies (Brown 2010; Moran and Whitford 1996), federal income taxes (Moran 2010), "the marriage penalty" (Brown 2007), and payroll taxes of Social Security and Medicare (Lipman 2011), among others. The insights of this scholarship greatly influence our own approach to the subject, but a glaring omission within this body of work lies in its bias toward federal tax law (Martin and Beck Forthcoming; Newman and O'Brien 2011).

State and local taxes, which include the lottery tax, represent a growing staple of smaller government and yield steady streams of revenue that make public services possible (Martin and Beck Forthcoming). In fact, these taxes comprise a significant portion of the Gross Domestic Product, an indicator conventionally used to gauge a nation's standard of living. Local and state tax revenues, for example, grew about three points from 13.5 to 16.3 percent of the GDP between 1972 and 2005 (Rueben and Rosenberg 2008). As these figures indicate, much important tax action is occurring at lower levels of government that have yet to be studied by critical tax theorists. Even scanter attention has been paid to the lottery tax. We argue, however, that this area of research provides a potent opportunity for understanding the relationship between race and taxation, and how it helps negotiate order and preserve racial hierarchy.

In contrast to what economist Edwin R. A. Seligman (1895) once labeled "the worst tax in the civilized world" (p. 61), otherwise known as the property tax (Lo 1990; Martin 2008), the lottery might be considered the most loved tax. Can we point to other state activities that are now sanctioned and even celebrated by popular culture, media, and the state, but were once rendered illegal? Do any other industries exist in which the state declares an exclusive right to sell a consumer product of implicit taxation? What other government agencies not only accommodate demand but stimulate it for its own tax revenues? Which other government enterprises encourage one consumer behavior through advertisements, on the one hand, and implicitly condemn this same behavior with gambling treatment programs, on the other? To state the obvious, all these questions are rhetorical. The lottery is a "peculiar institution" if you will, and an aspect of state finance that has few comparisons.

Like most taxes, the lottery tax formalizes what obligations individuals have to the state and society, and vice versa, while at the same time it signifies the legitimate expansion of bureaucratic administration in distributing public and private resources. Because lotteries are relied upon to finance an elaborate set of social services and resources, they are deeply embedded within various social institutions that impact people's daily lives and a host of social outcomes. For these reasons, lottery studies have much to reveal about social life, change, and, perhaps above all, inequality. Few other taxes are more implicit as modern state lotteries in the United States, but these new forms of taxation did not emerge quietly in the night. Their emergence coincides and directly follows some of the most visible and intense tax revolts in the nation's history (Lo 1990; Martin 2008; Sears and Citrin 1982).

Jean-Baptiste Colbert, the finance minister of Louis XIV before the French Revolution, once declared,

> The art of taxation consists in so plucking the goose as to obtain the largest amount of feathers with the least possible amount of hissing
> (qtd. in Evans [1665] 1968: 680).

His point was that effective, sustainable state finance could be achieved when revenue is maximized while protest is simultaneously minimized. Despite the fact that this truism is not only several centuries old but is often quoted by those who study taxation, these same scholars generally have few answers as to what provokes tax rebellions, why people demand specific tax policy changes to certain unpopular taxes, and how come some taxes inflame more animosity than others (Martin 2008). Yet the structure of taxation is defined by critical junctures like property tax revolts, diverging and converging historically contingent paths, and legally codified continuities. Schumpeter ([1918] 1991) noted, the history of conflicts over taxation, and taxation in general, reveals "the driving forces of the fate of nations, as well as into the manner in which *concrete* conditions, and in particular organizational forms, grow and pass away" (p. 101, emphasis in the original).

The Contemporary World of Taxes Seen Through Racial Conflict

Does race have a place in contemporary tax law? Some sociolegal scholars say no (e.g., Bryce 1998; Galvin 1998). In his own words, Charles Galvin (1998) writes:

> A tax system should be neutral in its effect on each citizen's decision-making. Therefore, *assuming a democratic ideal of a free society with equal opportunity for all*, the framers of tax policy should strive for a system that is blind as to gender and color
>
> (p. 1749, emphasis added).

The premise of colorblindness becomes an ideological starting point by which sociolegal scholars like Galvin and others interpret the world of taxation. Our view contrasts this position. In virtually all areas of life, race remains an organizing principle of how social, cultural, economic, and symbolic rewards or penalties are distributed (Bonilla-Silva 1997, 2001). The area of taxation is no exception. Though notions of neutrality, freedom, and equality opportunity may embody democratic ideals worth striving toward, one would be in serious error to presume them as self-evident. Doing so constitutes a normative judgment that ignores how race continues to structure what circumstances, opportunities, and resources are available to people.

On the contrary, we understand taxation as a site of racial conflict between differently positioned groups who have opposing interests. This is because race is irreducible to any other basis of social relations (e.g., class, ethnicity, and so on), and as Michael Omi and Howard Winant ([1986] 1994) argue, it remains "a *fundamental* axis of social organization" (p. 13, emphasis original). This means that it takes on a life of its own, and operates in independent and autonomous ways to shape the individual psyche and collective social forces. To fully appreciate the immediacy race has for social conflict, Omi and Winant ([1986] 1994) develop an alternative framework they label "racial formation." This concept is defined "as the sociohistorical process by which racial categories are created, inhabited, transformed, and destroyed" (p. 55). It links representation and structure with racial meanings that organize consciousness and political economy. In the authors' estimation, the state is a preeminent site for understanding racial formation processes because this is where highly contested racial conflict occurs—taxation included.

Practices of the state, taxation included, are embedded within the broader set of relations that define how society is organized. Because these relations are characterized by racial conflict that is subject to ongoing change, as C. Wilson (1996) argues, the role of the racial state is not constant but shifting. The state can possess a seemingly contradictory nature because it represents multiple interests. This is why, for instance, racially oppressive tax practices can fluidly mold themselves over time from explicit "black codes" in the 1870s to colorblind taxation like the lottery in the present day. While it is undeniable that racial change transpired as a result of social movements during the 1950s, 1960s, and 1970s, these concessions, which outlaw explicit discrimination and prohibit the imposition of race-specific taxes, did not alter the structure that arranges a rigid racial hierarchy (Bonilla-Silva 1997, 2001; Feagin 2006; Steinberg [1995] 2001; Wellman [1977] 1993). In fact, these concessions to minorities intensified white backlash (Rubin 1972; Warren 1976). We argue that this is especially true in regards to the implicit and explicit racial politics of property taxes, conflicts regarding whom this money is expended upon, and struggles over who carries their fair share of tax burden.

Taxation within a Racialized Social System

The overarching theoretical framework guiding our argument is what Bonilla-Silva (1997) labels a "racialized social system" (henceforth RSS). Beginning from the premise that race is a central, but not exclusive, organizing principle for how rewards and penalties are distributed along domains of the economic, political, cultural, social, and symbolic. This is not to say that racial groups, in and of themselves, are real in any natural sense. On the contrary, race is a biological fiction but a social fact (Bonilla-Silva 1999). It results from political struggles rooted in practical matters of the everyday, matters that include taxation. Once a previously racially unclassified social relation, practice, or group takes on racial meaning, or becomes racialized (Omi and Winant [1986] 1994), a set of racial relations that consist of practices and ideas that influence, and become influenced by, all levels of society. Though these processes of racialization were first initiated by power interests (e.g, the converging interests of capitalists, planters, and colonizers captured in the codification of the three-fifths tax clause), once racial categories came to organize a set of social relations, they assumed an independent, though not exclusive, role in shaping social structure (Bonilla-Silva 1997, 1999).

What constitutes this racial structure, to be more specific, is the systemic culmination of racialized practices, and the ideas that rationalize them, across multiple interlocking domains (Bonilla-Silva 1997). Beginning from the premise that race is about power and conflict, ideas and practices of taxation work together as a means for sustaining racial inequality. They do so, however, in ways that are subject to revision over time. This makes racial ideas and practices a highly dynamic phenomenon. What remains constant, however, is that life circumstances, opportunities, and resources continue to be organized along racial lines, which cements dissimilar, opposing interests between groups. Whites have vested interest to preserve the status quo because they stand atop the racial hierarchy, whereas people of color are positioned to transform it. Because race operates systemically, all individuals are implicated in racial affairs (Bonilla-Silva 1997, 2001, [2003] 2014).

Not everyone is implicated to the same extent, though. White nationalists, for instance, tend to overtly promote their racial interests; meanwhile, well-meaning, racially tolerant white individuals often advance their interests in more discreet and seemingly nonracial terms (Hughey 2012). As much is often true when whites choose to live in racially homogeneous suburban communities (Shapiro 2004), send their children to racially exclusive private schools (Lewis 2003), or oppose racial justice initiatives (e.g., affirmative action) on the logics of liberalism (Berry and Bonilla-Silva 2008; Gallagher 2003). Nonetheless, this broad-sweeping implication does not mean that whites (or minority group members for that matter) act upon their racial interests in an intentional or conscious manner. "[W]e all constantly make use of a whole set of frameworks of interpretation and understanding," argues Stuart Hall (1984), "often in a very practical unconscious way, and [those] things alone enable us to make sense of what is going on around us, what our position is, and what we are likely to do" (p. 7).

Though the RSS framework has broad reaching implications, so far it has predominantly been tested in narrow empirical terms. A number of scholars (e.g., Bell and Hartmann 2007; Doane 2006; Embrick and Henricks 2013; Gallagher 2003; Hughey 2012; Lewis 2003; Mayorga-Gallo 2014; Moore and Bell 2011; Quiroz 2007) have anchored the RSS framework in communicative interaction, and in the process, revealed the vast everyday penetrability of colorblind ideology. This work maps the contours of modern racial discourse and its slippery, often subtle "now you see it, now you don't" style. The cornerstone of colorblind ideology (i.e., abstract liberalism) even provides whites (and some people of color) the moral upper hand by infusing ideals of rugged individualism (e.g., personal choice) with market fundamentalism (e.g., equal opportunity) to explain away racial inequality or justify not doing anything about it.

Racial ideology matters because it is essential in rationalizing (and resisting) various racial practices. In the realm of taxation, for instance, paying taxes, or at least the perception of who pays them, says something about a group's position of social belonging and civic engagement. Perhaps in many people's minds, it settles the question of: "Do you pay into the system, or simply take from it?" The enduring, pejorative racial stereotypes of "welfare queens," "anchor babies," and "social parasites," among others, reinforce the ill-contrived perception that minority groups do not contribute to the system, ensuring their continued marginalization and alienation (Haney-López 1996). On the other hand, emphasis on ideology without reference to political economy runs the risk of overlooking the practical implications of racial oppression. It may not showcase how racial oppression operates in a material sense. Herein lays an area of the RSS framework yet to be tested. According to Bonilla-Silva (1997, 2001, [2003] 2014), the preservation of a rigid racial hierarchy is not dependent upon ideology alone, but the interacting nature of ideology *and* practice. Consider his notion of "new racism" to make our point.[4]

New racism refers to the process by which the overt, formal, and humiliating ideas and practices commonly affiliated with Jim Crow have been displaced, to some extent, by new ideas and practices that are institutional, covert, and seemingly nonracial in character.[5] Even though these new practices and ideas eschew direct racial reference, they are perhaps all the more effective as instruments of racial domination. This is because most of the systemic mechanisms that reproduce racial exclusion, which persists on virtually every socioeconomic indicator available to social scientists, are rendered hidden from plain view.[6] The aforementioned authors have brought to light how these processes work on an ideological level, but they do not show how these ideas connect to a variety of practices that unevenly (re)distribute circumstances, opportunities, and resources along racial lines. They cannot explain, for instance, how change in not only racial ideology, but racial practices is a "normal" historical outcome of conflict between races (Bonilla-Silva 1997: 475). To fill this missing link between ideas and praxis under an RSS framework, our intent is to: 1) trace the genealogy of race-driven antitax crusades that culminated in broad-reaching legislative change, 2) understand various racial underpinnings regarding the recent proliferation of state lotteries, and 3) demonstrate how these events have reconfigured America's tax code to redistribute tax liability along racial lines. *State Looteries* sheds light on specifics of what scholars still do not know enough about: the mechanisms, practices, and social relations that reproduce racial domination and subordination.

No Taxation Without Discrimination

Taxation, and the formalized relationships it represents between people, the state, and social order, is under constant flux since changing actors among dominant groups perpetually seek to renegotiate tax obligations to their own advantage (Tilly 2007). Extending this thought to account for how the state becomes racialized, Kevin Gotham (2000) argues that this tension can only be reformed, not resolved, so long as race remains an organizing principle for how the state mediates asymmetrical distributions of power. An analysis of how lotteries emerged out of tax protests sharply draws attention to these reforms, the political mobilizations that prompted them, and the historical contingencies in which they occurred, meanwhile a focus on tax practices of the lottery illuminates how individuals, action, and change are implicated, in interconnected ways, to preserve a variable yet persisting racial structure. These tax revolts matter because once the dust settles, the resulting lottery proliferation is codified into tax law and will continually affect future generations; particularly through the distribution of capital to maintain general infrastructure. Taxes have long been designed and revised, after all, to accommodate the ever-changing structures of social life, and they have a way of uncovering what is most important in society (Schumpeter [1918] 1991).

Given that racial oppression is an endemic feature of the U.S. political arena (Bonilla-Silva 1997), the often obscured and overlooked area of study likely holds many stories of an untold racialized history of taxation. Few scholars have shown how racial structure operates through concrete everyday practices like taxation that are state-sanctioned.[7] As Neubeck and Cazenave (2001) argue,

> Social scientists really do not have a systematic theory that addresses the state's racial character, racist practices by the state, or the role of the state in maintaining racial inequalities
>
> (p. 22).

This omission is problematic because the state has long assumed an active role (e.g, slavery, formal Jim Crow) in preserving white dominance through racial discrimination.[8] In what many have labeled "the Post-Civil Rights Era,"[9] this discrimination does not necessarily operate like early mainstream social scientists (e.g., Allport 1958; van den Berghe 1967) conceptualized it, though. Discriminatory acts can occur among individuals acting out some prejudiced dispositions, but the form of discrimination that preoccupies our focus concerns broader social actions of the state.

Drawing inspiration from Stokely Carmichael[10] and Charles Hamilton (1967), we see discrimination "as vastly greater than the beliefs and acts of misguided individuals, but rather as something that was embedded in institutions, so much so that it [can] be perpetuated through routine institutional practices without racist intent" (Steinberg 2007: 90).[11] Instead of stressing explicit ideas of bigotry endorsed by individuals, the perspective we endorse emphasizes racial practices that are reiterated over time to protect a group's social, political, economic, cultural, and symbolic position (Feagin and Eckberg 1980; Haney-López 2000; Wellman [1977] 1993). This means that even well-meaning, good-intentioned white folks can nonetheless participate in discriminatory acts through collective action (Downs 1970; Knowles and Prewitt 1969). Various judges, including those of the U.S. Supreme Court, have echoed these sentiments in their written legal opinions. In *Griggs et al. v. Duke Power Co.* (401 U.S. 424 [1971]), for example, the majority opinion defined institutional discrimination as interactions, exchanges, and practices that are negative in effect even though they may be fair in form.

In other words, the state plays a prominent role in sustaining racial antagonism. Its complicit or endorsed participation in explicit legal discrimination has been constitutionally abolished, at least on paper, if not in practice, but modern tax codes serve as an illustrative example that represents a disguised, yet robust system of racial domination. Though seemingly nonracial, the lottery tax represents a state-sanctioned apparatus of racial domination that occurs through legal codification of taxation. The colorblind language of these codes has potential to render these practices as overlooked, and perhaps even invisible. But, as we show throughout the book, they none-theless serve as an effective social control mechanism that maintains asymmetrical power relations between racial groups. The state allocates material rewards to whites at the expense of people of color. In this way, Jim Crow has merely been redesigned with colorblind language, not ended.

Notes

1 Quote taken from: Lipsitz, George. 1998. *The Possessive Investment in Whiteness: How White People Profit from Identity Politics.* Philadelphia: Temple University Press.
2 The Little Rock Nine included: Minnijean Brown, Terrance Roberts, Elizabeth Eckford, Ernest Green, Thelma Mothershed, Melba Patillo, Gloria Ray, Jefferson Thomas, and Carlotta Walls.
3 According to Einhorn (2001), uniformity clauses became commonplace in Southern constitutions after the Civil War. They represent another procedural barrier that protects elite white interests through tax limitation. Under abstract notions of "fairness," and not taxing one form of capital more than another, these clauses impeded the formation of progressive tax structures and gave rise to more regressive sources of revenue like the sales tax (Newman and O'Brien 2011).
4 Elements of this argument were developed earlier in a book chapter written by Bonilla-Silva and Amanda Lewis (1999).
5 "New racism" is a conceptual building block that falls under the umbrella of Bonilla-Silva's broader RSS framework. See also Bonilla-Silva and Lewis (1999).
6 By systemic mechanisms, we mean the complex, interconnected, and interdependent processes that consist of practices that (re)create uneven distributions of capital between racial groups.
7 The state has not been fully omitted from Bonilla-Silva's work. In his analysis of new racism, for example, he addresses how people of color continue to be politically repressed by a white-controlled state through barriers in the electoral process, underrepresentation of elected and appointed officials, and state brutality through racial profiling, mass incarceration, and capital punishment (see Bonilla-Silva 2001: 100–111). Nonetheless, such a focus emphasizes racially explicit state practices that are hardly colorblind in practice. In our study, we aim to show how the state preserves racial inequality in seemingly nonracial ways through the lottery tax.
8 This claim is less true today than when it was made nearly two decades ago. Works by Bracey (2015), Darity (2008), Jung (2015), Jung et al. (2011), Moore (2014), Moore and Bell (2010), and Saito (2009), among others, have taken up "the racial state" as a central subject. What we hope to add to these studies is a discussion at the intersects of race, the state, and taxation. The emphasis on taxation is of particular importance, since it determines state capacity altogether (Martin et al. 2009; Martin and Prasad 2014).
9 We use the term "Post-Civil Rights Era" with caution. This is because the term implies a rupture from a preceding time period, affirming the notion that the current era is beyond "civil rights." This does a disservice to the plurality of racial resistance articulated during the Black Freedom Struggles of the 1950s, 1960s, and 1970s. These consisted of multiple movements with multiple goals, many of which that have never been conceded. Some of the more modest, reformist goals were accomplished by various Civil Rights Acts, but parts of the struggle articulated much more radical demands for racial (and economic) justice; ones

that challenged fundamental arrangements of society (Neubeck and Cazenave 2001). In fact, many scholars who endorse the "Post-Civil Rights era" language nonetheless invoke some of the same political solutions advocated years ago by these radicals. For these reasons, among others, we argue that a war of position over civil rights wages on and the "Post-Civil Rights era" has not occurred yet. An alternative label we suggest posits the current era as *the Late Jim Crow.* Such language more aptly captures how Jim Crow practices of old persist in modern times and often coexist alongside colorblind practices of racial aggression, all under one unified historical epoch. As we show throughout this book, for example, many contemporary tax codes are extensions of often overlooked Jim Crow practices, ones that are racial in every way but name.

10 Stokely Carmichael became later known as Kwame Ture.
11 It should be noted, however, that Carmichael and Hamilton locate racial prejudice as the fundamental motivational factor of institutional racism (Feagin and Eckberg 1980).

2 Lottery Studies and Their Discontents

A Critical Review

"This mania, so generally condemned, has never been properly studied."

~ Honré de Balzac[1]

These words ring as true today as they did when written more than 150 years ago. Throughout history, scholars have dismissed or overlooked lotteries rather than attempted to understand them. Few have connected their role in state finance to matters of social inequality generally, let alone racial inequality specifically. This blind spot is part of a broader trend across the academic literature. Though classical theorists from Adam Smith and Vilfredo Pareto onward devoted much of their careers to analyses of public finance, recent scholars who label themselves the new fiscal sociologists have rightfully argued that rarely has much attention been paid to taxes as a central subject (see Martin, Mehrotra, and Prasad 2009). Even seminal thinkers like Karl Marx ([1852] 1963) who understood taxes as the "lifeblood" of the capitalist state failed to anticipate how lotteries would become a vital revenue-raising instrument for government.

The lottery is an anomalous form of taxation. Because of its unimposing nature and reliance on voluntary participation, some lottery scholars like Charles Clotfelter and Philip Cook (1989) have labeled it a "painless tax" (p. 215). Contrary to conventional definitions of the new fiscal sociologists who conceptualize a tax as an "obligation to contribute money or goods to the state" (Martin et al. 2009: 3), people purchase lottery tickets as consumer products out of their own volition. The state then implicitly retains a fraction of the proceeds, while simultaneously avoiding political backlash often associated by sheer mention of the "t-word." In fact, this lottery tax is so implicit that those who purchase lottery tickets are not referred to as taxpayers. They go by another name. As former New Jersey State Senator Alan J. Karcher (1989) argues, "Lottery advocates have devised other euphemisms to shield the playing public from realizing they are being taxed. Ticket buyers are always referred to as 'players,' never as taxpayers" (p. 38).[2] Regardless of how these lottery revenues are collected, though, they carry the same value as do any other taxes. For these reasons, among others, the lottery can be defined as a form of taxation (Beckert and Lutter 2009; Clotfelter and Cook 1989; Nibert 2000).

Critics like John Mikesell and Kurt Zorn (1986, 1988) recognize that lotteries generate tax dollars, but suggest that mechanisms behind them are more representative of a "fickle form of finance." Because leftover lottery proceeds are subsumed by administrative costs, sales fluctuate drastically from year to year, and earmarked proceeds pale in comparison to other tax revenues, they claim that lotteries add little to nothing to state treasuries. However, some researchers at the National Opinion Research Center (NORC 1999) argue that the social costs associated with lotteries outweigh their benefits. They estimate, for example, that pathological gambling costs the U.S. "$5 billion per year and an addition $40 billion in lifetime costs for productivity reductions, social services, and creditor losses" (NORC 1999: ix).

There is evidence to support some of these contestations but not all of them. Despite these criticisms, we and others argue that it is premature to dismiss lottery contributions as inconsequential. Clotfelter and Cook (1989) have shown, for instance, that lotteries generate more money than all other forms of gambling combined, are more profitable than any other public enterprise operated by state governments, and trump most excise taxes in their ability to generate state income. In 2011 alone, for example, lottery proceeds generated more than $18 billion for state governments, who then spent this money to finance nearly every public service imaginable ("U.S. Census Bureau" 2011a).

The lottery tax is commonly lumped into the "sin tax" category, but this presumption can be misleading. Unlike tobacco and alcohol taxes, for example, the state owns a monopoly on who creates and sells lottery tickets. What is sold to most buyers, with the exceptions of a few lucky winners, are rectangle-shaped pieces of paper. This enables overhead costs for state lotteries to be considerably lower than those associated with alcohol and tobacco products. Lottery tickets, for example, are not harvested by farmers or brewed by brew masters, which helps to lower production costs and increase profit margins. Whereas excise taxes on alcohol and tobacco may yield the state about 10 percent of every transaction, lottery tickets typically offer between 20 to 40 percent of every dollar transaction.[3] The money is then earmarked by states for public services or placed in general budgets.

According to census data ("U.S. Census Bureau" 2011a), about half the gross sales of lottery tickets are returned to players through prize winnings, slightly more than 10 percent cover operating costs, and proceeds directed to states' public services represent about one-third of all lottery sales in any given year.[4] These proceeds are not in the same class as income and property taxes, but politicians would be hard-pressed to replace this money or reject their contribution as negligible. Lottery proceeds generally comprise between 0.5–3.5 percent of the total annual revenue available in most state treasuries ("U.S. Census Bureau" 2011a). This number often doubles, however, when lottery proceeds are strictly compared as a percentage of total state tax revenues. In comparison, state taxes comprise only slightly more than half of all state revenue. Therefore, contributions from the lottery tax are significantly understated when solely compared to total state treasuries rather than revenues from state taxes.

Not all academics reduce lotteries to "a fickle form of finance" or dismiss them altogether. Those who engage the lottery as a serious topic of rigorous analysis have tended to narrow their focus to three general questions: 1) How did modern lotteries emerge, 2) why (and how) do people play the lottery, and 3) who plays the lottery? These topical areas demarcate the major focal points and lines of debate across the interdisciplinary field of lottery studies. What follows is a survey and critique of the various answers that have been provided to these questions. In rendering a fairly robust survey of lottery studies, our ultimate goal is to prompt an overdue discussion of the ways lotteries can, and often do, reproduce racial inequality.

How Did Modern Lotteries Emerge?

Prior to the 1960s, familiar lottery images would have been strange. No lottery drawings would have bombarded your local nightly newscast, no advertisements would have decorated the local convenience store, and no losing scratch-off tickets would litter local community streets. This is because no state lotteries existed then. Their (re-)emergence represents a recent phenomenon in the United States.[5] New Hampshire was the first to adopt one in 1964, after which lotteries proliferated across the nation. Today, only seven states do not have one. How did this happen? Explanations vary widely.

Lottery scholars have tended to attribute the rise of lotteries to one or more of the following reasons: 1) interstate competition and regional diffusion, 2) conducive political environments, or 3) fiscal stresses on the state. These explanations, however, limit our understanding of the rapid rise of lotteries in America because they do not reach beyond the point of description.[6] What the literary field of lottery studies is missing is a robust synthesis of not only how but why lotteries emerged at a particular historical juncture rife with social, economic, and political conflict. Moreover, virtually all lottery scholars fail to adequately discern the role race has played in shaping, and becoming shaped by, this conflict.

Keeping Up with the Joneses

The common idiom, "keeping up with the Joneses," succinctly captures the argument many scholars offer to explain the proliferation of state lotteries (Alm et al. 1993; Berry and Berry 1990; Calcagno et al. 2010; Caudill et al. 1995; Coughlin et al. 2006). Keeping up with the Joneses is about living up to certain social standards of some outside influence. If these standards cannot be met, then this represents some sort of shortcoming or downright failure. In terms of taxation and the lottery, keeping up with the Joneses is about interstate competition. For example, politicians of "State B" see how much revenue the lottery generates for "State A." They become envious, so State B then mimics State A, initiates its own lottery, and deepens the pockets of its state treasury. Meanwhile, politicians of "State C" observe this whole process, and they, too, realize they are missing out on easy money. So State C gets its own lottery. Like a domino effect, this process spreads on and on to other nearby states.

Interstate competition over lottery tax dollars, in other words, leads to regional diffusion of state-sponsored lotteries (Alm et al. 1993; Berry and Berry 1990; Calcagno et al. 2010; Caudill et al. 1995; Coughlin et al. 2006). This process, however, is more than just peer-pressure coming from neighboring states. The "everybody's doing it" explanation only goes so far and misses some of the tangible economic benefits that come with lottery adoption. This is why some of those who support the "keeping up with the Joneses" thesis have supplemented their position with additional reasons. They argue that it is in states' best interests to start a lottery because this keeps gambling revenues within their borders, attracts tourists from outside states, and even exports taxation onto nonstate citizens (Calcagno et al. 2010; Garrett and Marsh 2002; Ghent and Grant 2007).

The "keeping up with the Joneses" argument can be quite convincing and much evidence is available to support it, but those who support this explanation nonetheless sidestep several questions. These include but are not limited to:

1)   What sociohistorical circumstances prompted the initial rise of lotteries?
2)   How is it that many states (e.g., Arizona, Georgia, Michigan, New Hampshire, Washington) have adopted their own lottery even though no one surrounding them had one?
3)   Why have some states (e.g., Alabama, Mississippi, Utah, and Wyoming) continued to resist lottery adoption despite all those surrounding lottery states?
4)   If regional diffusion of lotteries promotes interstate tax competition, then why do a majority of states cooperate in interstate lotteries like the Powerball?
5)   Whose interests—in terms of social, economic, political, and perhaps most importantly, racial—are served by implementing lotteries for public finance?
6)   And what consequences might lotteries have on racial inequality specifically, and social inequality generally?

While it is true that interstate tax competition exists and lotteries can yield much revenue for state treasures, these reasons do not fully explain the recent rise of lotteries in the United States.

Fertile Ground and a Conducive Environment

For those of us who remember *Schoolhouse Rock!*'s "I'm Just a Bill" song, we already know that policymaking does not occur in a vacuum. It is contextual and has much to do with timing and political climate. Basically, a second group of scholars drive home this point in their research (Alm et al. 1993; Berry and Berry 1990; Caudill et al. 1995; Clotfelter and Cook 1989; Erekson et al. 1999; Wetzel 2012). Lotteries, they argue, emerge in conditions where partisan bickering is set aside, lawmakers are sympathetic, and constituents hold favorable attitudes (or are at least indifferent) towards gambling. Without these conditions present, states are likely to remain without a lottery.

Just like that bill sitting on Capitol Hill, it waits and remains an idea that key policymakers and political influences debate. As of 2013, only seven states in the union are without a lottery. Cletus Coughlin, Thomas Garret, and Rubén Hernández-Murillo (2006) argue that this is because lingering political influences present too large an obstacle to overcome. In states like Alabama, Mississippi, Utah, and Wyoming, where conservative religious groups are dominant, politicians and their constituencies have uncompromisingly opposed lottery adoption. Taking the moral high road, members from these groups draw from the Protestant ethic to "charge that gambling is based on selfishness, that it undermines the stewardship of resources, and that, by relying on chance, it denies providential control over human life" (Clotfelter and Cook 1989: 47). Religious influences are not the only deterrent, though. In Nevada, no state lottery exists because influential members of the casino industry see it as a threat to their own profits. Couching their opposition in antistatist, free market rhetoric, segments of this group have gone to great lengths to flex their political muscle to make sure that all gambling money stays in their pockets (Wetzel 2012).

That said, money is what makes the world go round. When states need it but do not have it, opposition to the lottery can be tempered. This is especially true when their implementation means tax relief for a public that sees itself as taxed too much already. Various studies have shown that moral arguments fall to the wayside when lotteries are framed as an alternative to new taxes or tax hikes (Davis et al. 1992; Filer et al. 1988; Glickman and Painter 2004). Lotteries tend to receive bipartisan support during periods of budgetary shortfalls, as they provide both Democrats and Republicans a way to generate huge sums of money with little to no resistance. Their reliance on voluntary participation eschews unwanted, mandatory taxation in a political environment characterized by a permanent tax revolt (Martin 2008). Not only does this make lotteries more politically feasible than other tax alternatives, but the dire need for revenue-raising attests to the looming elephant in the room: fiscal crisis.

An Economic System in Need of Stitches,
How about a Band-Aid?

Money may smooth over moral and political differences, but why is this money needed to begin with? Some say to relieve fiscal stress. In this view, the lottery is like a pressure release valve on a strained fiscal machine. It offsets budgetary shortfalls caused by external tensions outside the machine itself. Scholars of this persuasion contend that state lotteries emerged from the zenith of economic problems like the 1970s oil shocks, taxing and spending reforms from the 1960s to 1980s, and the recession of the early 1980s (Alm et al. 1993; Coughlin et al. 2006; Erekson et al. 1999). Lottery proliferation across American did not occur simply because states wanted to keep up with the Joneses or because the political environment was conducive. They were adopted out of economic circumstance at a particularly historical moment of the latter part of the 20th century. This era marked the end to unprecedented growth in the United States, and the beginnings of globalizing markets, deindustrialization in manufacturing cities, and the deregulation of corporate businesses (Fischer and Hout 2006). All these factors culminated together to erode the tax base available to government.

Though much insight is to be gleaned from this perspective, in many ways it does not go far enough. Simply identifying various consequences of fiscal crisis does not resolve the question of how these consequences originated, nor does it illuminate the processes that created them. The release valve analogy does not hold up because it presumes the fiscal machine was properly designed from the forefront. It implicitly romanticizes capitalism as a functionally efficient economic system, and never questions its contradictions, how it sows the seeds of its destruction, and ultimately becomes its own gravedigger (Marx and Engels [1848] 2002). It misses what James O'Connor ([1973] 2002) identified as the legitimation crisis of the state. Government has this problem because it must simultaneously satisfy two incompatible tasks: making business profits possible while preserving social harmony.

In attempting to do both, budgetary shortfalls are the inevitable result. Profit is made possible by paying workers less than the fruits of their labor are worth, a point even Adam Smith ([1776] 2010) acknowledged, but to keep these profits coming, the state must maintain aggregate demand. It does this through actions that ensure social harmony. For instance, it casts a safety net that maintains a basic standard of living and invests in institutions like education that support the ideological creed of social mobility and success through merit. Under capitalism, though, the demand for these services is outpaced by the ability to pay for these services. Although lotteries offer some money to reduce budgetary shortfalls, as David Nibert (2000) and Donald Peppard (1987) rightfully point out, they never resolve this underlying tension. This is why lotteries represent a false solution to a deeper crisis they cannot solve. It is a band-aid approach to something that needs stitches.

While we sympathize with Nibert and Peppard, our perspective offers a compatible but unique take on the lottery. We see the proliferation of state lotteries as a result of broad transformations in the capitalist political economy, but our position stresses the centrality of race throughout this process. In fact, we argue that the emergence of state lotteries and the recent reconfiguration of American taxation, in general, cannot be understood fully without the consideration of racial antagonism. This argument is developed further in the following chapter, but a short comment is warranted here.

Modern lotteries emerged during a period when many whites blamed people of color, especially blacks and Latinas/os, for their own economic insecurities caused by real income stagnation and looming tax debts (Feagin 2012; Omi and Winant [1986] 1994). It was this white racial backlash that fueled the fire of tax revolts starting in California and spreading throughout the nation (Lo 1990; Sears and Citrin 1982). For many vulnerable, angry whites, taxes had transformed "big government" into a coercive and redistributive state, especially when spent on programs (e.g., welfare, affirmative action) seen as pandering to minority interests (Edsall and Edsall 1991).

Race-driven tax revolts had devastating consequences on government's ability to raise revenues. All the while, people still expected, or even demanded, public services made possible only by taxes (Sears and Citrin 1982). Despite racialized anti-tax rhetoric, infrastructure investment like public education, roads and highways, parks and recreation, and hospitals, among many other examples, remain wildly popular. Yet without tax revenues, none of these are possible. Since government still needed money to make these services possible, many policymakers turned to piecemeal tax alternatives to help make up the difference. That said, the emergence of lotteries is part of a broader trend in America's changing tax composition. And since few politically feasible alternatives are available for state governments to collect money, they show little sign of being abandoned any time soon.

Why (and How) Do People Play the Lottery?

> The Lottery, with its weekly pay-out of enormous prizes, was the one public event to which the proles paid serious attention. It was probable that there were some millions of proles for whom the Lottery was the principle if not only reason for remaining alive. It was their delight, their folly, their anodyne, their intellectual stimulant. Where the Lottery was concerned, even people who could barely read and write seemed capable of intricate calculations and staggering feats of memory. . . . Winston had nothing to do with the running of the Lottery, which was managed by the Ministry of Plenty, but he was aware (indeed everyone in the Party was aware) that the prizes were largely imaginary
>
> (Orwell [1949] 1961: 73).

Though the question of why people play the lottery is not the focus of our study, we would be remiss to avoid the topic altogether. This question, perhaps above all others, has preoccupied the minds of scholars for the past few decades. Answers to this question have been multiple, contradictory, and, in our estimation, shortsighted. Much of what has been offered derives from what classical theorists like Karl Marx, Georg Simmel, Adam Smith, and Vilfredo Pareto said on the topic, but it is perhaps most succinctly captured in the passage above from the dystopian novel *1984*. Just like the story of the proles, lottery scholars have argued that people play the lottery for a variety of reasons, from maximizing self-interest (Clotfelter and Cook 1989; Guryan and Kearney 2008) to escaping economic deprivation (Blalock et al. 2007; Bloch 1951; Devereux [1949] 1980; Nibert 2000; Stranahan and Borg 1998) to personal gratification (Conlisk 1993; Hartley and Farrell 2002; Forrest et al. 2002; NORC 1999; Walker 1998) to lasting beliefs in mysticism (Clotfelter and Cook 1989; Reith 1999).

While each of these contentions is substantively important, the preoccupation with what motivates lottery play has closed off, rather than opened up, other important lines of inquiry. In doing so, this narrow focus has limited the field as a whole and what can be learned from lotteries. Other questions that are equally, if not more important, to ask include:

1) How have lottery revenues altered state finance?
2) From whom does lottery money come and on whom is it spent?
3) Do lottery transactions circulate capital from some groups to others?
4) And how might lotteries create and recreate inequalities?

Unfortunately, most lottery scholars have not addressed these questions or answered them fully. Their focus on why people play the lottery has diverted too much of their attention.

Maximizing Self-Interest: It's All About the Benjamins

People play the lottery because money is not everything—but having it is. With a simple handful of lucky numbers, a person's life could be forever changed. Though most will lose, someone is guaranteed to eventually win. For those who do win, dreams of wealth and riches come true. Perhaps these people finally have enough money to pay all the bills without worry or buy that dream house they always wanted. The inevitable outcome that someone will win the lottery can be deceptive, though. For a number of lottery scholars, it is this "someone has to win" mentality that has induced many to play in the first place (Clotfelter and Cook 1989; Guryan and Kearney 2008). It transforms lottery players into rational strategists seeking to maximize their self-interest through risk-taking behavior.

It is as though lottery players perform a cost-benefit analysis each time they make a purchase, all the while keeping their eyes on the prize of those handsome dividends. Even though lottery payouts are proportionally less frequent than any other form of commercial gambling, many believe that the jackpot will be theirs if only they develop the right skill set or master the game's craft (Clotfelter and Cook 1989; Guryan and Kearney 2008). This is the self-proclaimed wisdom of Richard Lustig (2010), author of the popular-selling book *Learn How to Increase Your Chances of Winning the Lottery*. Drawing from his 25 years of experience, and many years of losing, Lustig (2010) describes himself as a veteran lottery player with a method that will increase everyone's chance of winning. For skeptics who insist that he basically does not know his apple butter from bullshit, his response is always along the lines: "Well, I have won the lottery seven times."

Lustig's method of winning the lottery echoes exactly what Clotfelter and Cook (1989) observed many years ago. Lottery players develop "skill sets" to manage risk and beat the odds. Some of these include:

1) playing numbers they think are unpopular,
2) studying winning numbers over time to observe some overarching pattern,
3) and selecting the same set of numbers every day.

Once these are perfected, the logic is that these "skill sets" will eventually pay off. Unfortunately, this type of thinking commits the quintessential "gambler's fallacy." That is, it assumes that lottery winnings follow some discernible pattern over time, and once a person understands this pattern, she or he can predict future outcomes. This presumption ignores the fact that the proverbial house will always win. Lottery winnings are not patterned but randomized, and most states pay out a predetermined fraction (usually around 33 percent) of all generated revenues.

Because some grossly overestimate their odds of winning, Adam Smith ([1776] 2010) said long ago that lottery play is for those who cannot calculate probability. "Adventure upon all the tickets in the lottery, and you lose for certain," he wrote, "and the greater the number of your tickets the nearer you approach to this certainty" (p. 103). Of those that could do math but still played lottery, Smith ([1776] 2010) stated that they suffered from impulsive folly and self-delusion:

> The vain hope of gaining some of the great prizes is the sole cause of this demand. The soberest people scarce look upon it as a folly to pay a small sum for the chance of gaining ten or twenty thousand pounds; though they know that even that small sum is perhaps twenty or thirty per cent more than the chance is worth
>
> (p. 103).

The bottom line of this perspective is that players have serious errors in judgment.

While Smith's words are more than 200 years old, these ideas remain alive and well. Many see lottery play, especially the kind motivated by reason and maximizing self-interest, as pathological behavior that is destructive to the players themselves and those around them (Lesieur 1998; Lesieur and Blume 1987). It causes a host of costly social consequences, such as higher rates of illness and poorer health outcomes, increasing divorce rates, expanding levels of criminal activity, arrests, and incarceration, swelling debts and declared bankruptcies, escalating reliance on welfare aid and unemployment insurance, and growing measures of worker absenteeism and lost productivity (NORC 1999). From this perspective, lottery play is comparable to a cancer that afflicts an otherwise healthy body of society. Those who see it as pathological understand gambling as a disease that reflects shortcomings in the cultural values of those who purchase lottery tickets in the first place. Therefore, they recommend policy suggestions like enhanced "gambling education" and expanded psychological support programs (NORC 1999).

With codified words like "crime" and "welfare," among others, cloaked within the language of cultural values, the pathological emphasis is one that implicitly perpetuates commonsense understandings of the poor generally and people of color specifically as deficient (Bonilla-Silva [2003] 2014; Essed 1991; Omi and Winant [1986] 1994). As William Ryan (1971) pointed several decades ago, research of this persuasion asserts that " 'these people' think in different forms, act in different patterns, cling to different values, seek different goals, and learn different truths" (p. 10). It is as though these people are culturally inadequate, caught up in a social mindset that creates their own cycles of poverty. They buy lottery tickets, in other words, out of their own impulsiveness, short-sighted rationale, or outright ignorance.[7] When lottery play is thought of as a pathological problem located within the individual, the people who purchase lottery tickets are seen to lack self-respect and ambition to better themselves. "Which is to say that they are strangers, barbarians, savages" (Ryan 1971: 10). Lottery scholars like Henry Lesieur and Shelia Blume, among many others, "blame the victim."[8]

Not all lottery players are victims, though, or even blamed as such. As Tim Wise ([2003] 2008) points out, this is because people are not consistent about the standards they impose on social groups:

> Short-term orientation is supposedly why the poor squander money on lottery tickets, preferring the long shot of get-rich-quick over the daily grind of steady employment. But when William Bennett blows several million dollars in casinos it's just a hobby, passing the time, or entertainment, not viewed as evidence of a flawed value system
>
> (p. 320).

Bennett is a former cabinet member of the Ronald Reagan and George H. W. Bush Presidential Administrations, author of *The Book of Virtues*, and a self-professed national spokesman on morality. He has professed a message of "personal responsibility" throughout his career, claiming that the poor could lift themselves out of poverty if only they practiced this virtue (Bennett 1993). That said, Bennett does not always follow his own advice.

Reports estimate Bennett's known gambling losses to surpass more than $8 million just in the past decade ("The Associated Press" 2009). By this criterion alone, he might be considered a pathological gambler. Yet Bennett insists he is different from those who need a little personal responsibility in their lives. He does not gamble the family's "milk money" ("The Associated Press" 2009). Herein lays the double standard: When Bennett squanders millions, it is considered his own business, but when the poor or people of color lose a couple dollars on lottery tickets it is labeled a "cycle of poverty" or "tangle of pathology." The point is that the same "morally imprudent" behavior practiced by members of high-status groups often remains ignored, scrutinized less harshly, and free from stigmatizing their entire group.

In and of itself, lottery play is not a social problem. Yet some lottery scholars who argue that gambling is motivated by self-interest and risk-taking behavior imply just that (e.g., Guryan and Kearney 2008; Lesieur 1998; Lesieur and Blume 1987; NORC 1999). The question of why people play the lottery is transformed into one that primarily reflects moral character. What defines a social problem, though, as Harold Blumer (1971) shows, is not some objective, intrinsic condition or arrangement within individuals. It is processes of collective definition amongst people situated within power relationships. Lottery play becomes a social problem when people of power react and label it as such. To ignore processes like these is to divorce lottery play from its embedded social context.

Escaping Economic Deprivation: Lotteries as the "Opium of the Masses"

When writing of religion, Marx ([1844] 1972) said the following:

> *Religious* suffering is, at one and the same time, the *expression* of real suffering and a *protest* against real suffering. Religion is the sigh of the oppressed creature, the heart of a heartless world, and the soul of soulless conditions. It is the *opium* of the people
>
> (p. 12, emphasis original).

The last phrase of this passage, "opium of the people," is perhaps one of Marx's best-known quotes. Though it is often decontextualized and reduced to some kind of slogan, even those who have not read Marx's ideas are familiar with this phrase. What perhaps most do not know, including many premier Marxist scholars, is that Marx derived these words from someone else who used them first to describe the lottery.[9] A few years prior to Marx's deployment of this phrase, as Antonio Gramsci ([1949] 1974) points out, these words were written by one of Marx and Engels' most profound contemporary influences: French novelist and playwright Honoré de Balzac ([1842] 1897) in *La Rabouilleuse* (translated as *The Black Sheep*).

Balzac ([1842] 1897) described "the lottery, the most powerful fairy in the world," as "the opium of poverty" (p. 98). Like a drug, it works up people's magical hopes of escaping their own problems. Not only does it numb them from their desperate conditions of reality, but it offers a small glimmer of hope for the hopeless. What is especially cruel about this opiate is that it taunts the poor's dreams of wealth with their own everyday lived nightmares. The riches of the lottery, to adapt Haile Selassie's ([1963] 1972) words, "will remain but a fleeting illusion to be pursued, but never attained" (p. 467). It inverts fantasy as farce, with the joke falling on the poor. How Marx ([1844] 1972) describes religion echoes Balzac's take on the lottery. In many ways, both religion and the lottery "[are] the sigh of the oppressed creature, the heart of a heartless world, and the soul of soulless conditions. [They are] the opium of the people" (Marx [1844] 1972: 12).

The spirit of these words lives on today. Many contemporary lottery scholars agree that the lottery opiate remains a person of color or poor person's drug (Blalock et al. 2007; Bloch 1951; Devereux [1949] 1980; Heberling 2002; Nibert 2000; Stranahan and Borg 1998). As Devereux ([1949] 1980) explains, it represents "a tiny hole in the 'closed system' of toil and budgeting, a 'safety valve' through which the repressed wishes crowd for escape" (p. 781). In doing so, the lottery offers release to those on the margins, a release for whatever feelings of despair and depravation they may have. Among those who have trouble satisfying basic levels of sustenance, the depravation thesis sees lottery play as the equalizer of chance. It is the closest many in these groups get to the American ethos of "equal opportunity."

Seen this way, lotteries level the playing field. Especially during times of economic instability and growing inequality, more and more people recognize that prudence, hard work, and investment in the future take someone only so far (Nibert 2000). The lottery, however, offers equal opportunity to all individuals. Just listen to the lottery advertisements over the years. One television commercial promoting the Illinois Lottery displayed images of a mansion with the following voiceover:

> In America we do not have kings nor queens or even dukes. What we have is far more democratic. It is called the Superlotto and it gives each individual a chance for untold wealth. So play Superlotto because, even though you can't be born a king, no one said you can't live like one
> (qtd. in Nibert 2000: 93).

Other campaign slogans, as Michael Heberling (2002) shows, have included the following:

- "This could be your ticket out." (Illinois)
- "Work is nothing but heart-attack-inducing drudgery." (Massachusetts)

- "All you need is a *Franklin ($100)* and a *fantasy.*" (New York)
- "How to Get from Washington Boulevard to Easy Street." (Illinois)

According to Nibert (2000), messages like these "entice people to dream of wealth by dangling extravagant homes and cars before their eyes." He further notes that "In some instances advertisers even use fantasy to induce fantasy" (p. 14). All the while, ads like these implicitly communicate that work is for suckers. When a campaign equates labor with heart-attack-inducing drudgery, it validates employee dissatisfaction and denigrates work altogether by offering a narrow-mined alternative (Nibert 2000). It says do not be a fool, get yours. After all, "all you need is a Franklin and a fantasy." Buy a ticket, win the lottery, and quit work . . .

. . . unless you happen to already be living the proverbial dream. According to the deprivation thesis, though, these are not the ones playing the lottery. It is the poor in general, and people of color in particular, who tend to play the lottery. When ads of the Illinois Lottery read "How to Get from Washington Boulevard to Easy Street" or "This could be your ticker out," this begs the question: out of where? The common-sense answer, of course, is: the ghetto. Robert Goodman (1995) reveals that these Illinois ads were selectively placed in blighted, run-down neighborhoods where minorities are concentrated. Just in case desperate conditions are not enough of a nightmare, lottery advertisements taunt these residents with messages of wealth beyond their dreams. Perhaps they even conjure allusions to Dr. Martin Luther King Jr.'s vision from the mountaintop.

Consider these lottery ads and their not-so-racially implicit message (Heberling 2002):

- "All you need is a dollar and a dream." (New York)
- "His vision lives on . . . honor the dream." (Washington D.C.)

If audiences miss implications of the infamous "March on Washington," background pictures of the civil rights leader are surely to be inescapable. Perhaps what messages like these communicate is some twisted vision of Dr. King's dream. It is as though when his eyes saw the glory of the coming of the Lord, these ads say that glory could be purchased with some lucky lottery dollars.[10] Honor his vision. Avoid those difficult days that lie ahead. Buy a ticket to the promised land.

Lottery advertisements that twist Dr. King's words are more than watered-down versions of his message. They are co-optations of his message. When Dr. King's words are stripped of context and meaning, they are transformed into deceptively insincere ploys to make a sale. Dr. King could not have been an avid lottery player because most states did not have one during his lifetime. The first modern state lottery did not emerge onto the American scene until 1963, when New Hampshire initiated its own. Last time we checked, Dr. King did not spend much of his time there. Yet ads like the ones above suggest that Dr. King was an avid lottery player, so you should be too. And by "you," these advertisements mean people of color—especially given that most are concentrated in their neighborhoods.

It is predatory advertisements like these, a number of lottery scholars argue, that induce those with limited means to gamble away what they do not have (e.g., Heberling 2002; Nibert 2000; NORC 1999; Stranahan and Borg 1998). Perhaps this is true. It might explain, as Harriet Stranahan and Mary Borg (1998) argue, why states that pursue advertising slogans like the ones we have sampled have much higher lottery sales. Then again, correlation is not causation. A major limitation in many studies where this argument is presented is a sin of omission. Silenced is the voice of lottery players because most were never consulted in these studies. For lottery advertisements to be as predatory as some claim, analysts must understand that lottery players are not quiescent, passive dupes who mindlessly do whatever ads tell them to do. They are active agents who interpret advertisements on their own terms, decide what to do with this information, and play the lottery out of their own volition. Therefore, studies need to treat them as such.

Seen differently, predatory lottery ads say less about lottery players and more about who produced these messages in the first place. Not only do advertisements allude to the target audiences of lotteries, but they reveal what messages the ad creators think will resonate with this audience. Solely from the slogans above, the targeted audiences seem to be the poor and people of color who prefer to escape their circumstances and get rich quick without merit or hard work. These representations reinforce defamations of character for those who play the lottery, all the while ignoring the needy masses that opt to spend their earned dollars on food, shelter, and general bills. The lottery is the opiate of the poor, if not in reality, then by representation.

Alternative Explanations: "I Do It for the Rush" or "My Fortune Cookie Said I'd Win"

Not convinced by the self-interest or deprivation explanations, others have offered alternative theories for why people play the lottery. Vilfredo Pareto ([1920] 1980), for example, was among the first classical theorists to argue that people gambled for the rush of it. In fact, he utilized the lottery to illustrate what he meant by the notion of "residues." For him, this concept represents an intermediary between people's natural inclinations and their belief systems. Whereas the former cannot be known, let alone studied, the latter can. Pareto ([1920] 1980) contends that, blindsided by fantasies of wealth, especially big lottery jackpots, people catch lottery fever and inevitably invert fiction as fact. They deny reality by transforming an extremely low-probability event into one that is within the realm of possibility. Lottery players uphold the few lucky winners as exceptions that disprove the rule. Once seen this way, people justify their lottery purchases and become caught up in the sheer thrill of playing.

Many other contemporary lottery scholars echo these sentiments (Conlisk 1993; Forrest et al. 2002; Hartley and Farrell 2002; NORC 1999; Reith 1999; Walker 1998). The lottery gives people an excuse to get caught up in the moment. As Gerda Reith (1999) writes,

> Time freezes, and gamblers become absorbed in a total orientation to the immediate Here and Now. In this state they become creatures of sensation; seeing, but not really aware of their surroundings; perceiving, but not truly cognizant of what is going on
>
> (p. 132).

Imagining what life would be like with millions to spend offers a great source of gratification, and this activity alone is often enough to keep people playing. Unlike those who subscribe to the self-interest or deprivation theories, the gratification thesis posits that it is not the final outcome that motivates lottery play. Rather, it is the process of playing itself, and all the excitement this entails, that motivates lottery purchases. While some find this argument convincing, critics point out that it begins with the premise it seeks to explain (Beckert and Lutter 2013; Garvía 2007; Guillén et al. 2012; Hartley and Farrell 2002). This logic makes the theory circular and non-falsifiable: People gamble for the thrill, and the thrill causes them to gamble.

An alternative explanation of lottery play turns to people's lasting belief in superstition, mysticism, and magic (Clotfelter and Cook 1989; Reith 1999; Wohl and Enzle 2002). Why do people play certain lottery numbers? For the same reason others might cross their fingers, spill the salt, or blow on dice. It makes them lucky, or so they believe. This luck can then be transferred to someone's wheel of fortune and increase their odds of obtaining some desirable outcome. In contrast to all the other theories discussed so far, this one rejects rationalism as a driving force behind lottery play. Rather, people are motivated to play the lottery for symbolic reasons captured in "the ancient arts of astrology, numerology, and dream interpretation" (Clotfelter and Cook 1989: 79).

It is as though the ghosts of dead beliefs still haunt the modern world because feudalistic ideas, or what Max Weber ([1919] 1946) described as an ethos of "romantic irrationalism," are still among us (p. 143). According to this view, people long for supernatural explanations. They believe some things in this world are beyond science and reason, and cannot be understood let alone tamed. In a culture of superstition, players assign symbolic significance to certain numbers they play. Where these numbers can come from varies drastically. Perhaps they represent a wedding anniversary or birthday, maybe they came from the burgeoning cottage industry of dream books, or possibly they are just the numbers from a recent fortune cookie. The point is, as Clotfelter and Cook (1989) argue, that this culture of belief must be taken seriously because it has created much demand for lottery products.

Not Why but How People Play the Lottery:
"Everybody's Doing It"

Unsatisfied by explanations of lottery play that are often atomized and individualistic, a group of lottery scholars primarily comprised of sociologists has begun to shift the conversation (Adams 2001; Beckert and Lutter 2013; Clotfelter and Cook 1989; Garvía 2007; Guillén et al. 2012). These scholars ask not why but how people play the lottery. This focus shifts attention away from the players, themselves, and emphasizes the act of playing. An underlying assumption of this approach is that people do not act as isolated, (ir)rational actors who use lotteries as a means to some ends. Instead, lotteries represent a foundation for ritualized social interaction. A lottery ticket comes to represent an "object infused with symbols meaningful to [the player], and often to members of his or her primary network of social relations" (Adams 2001: 456).

Perhaps the most visible manifestation of the social network explanation is syndicate play. Garvía (2009) defines this as "a social practice by which friends, relatives, or co-workers share lottery tickets" (p. 609). The practice redefines a lottery ticket altogether. No longer is it simply a claim to some potential jackpot, but a social symbol that evokes collective membership. The lottery ticket helps create shared experiences and reasons for communication between members of a group (Adams 2001; Beckert and Lutter 2013; Garvía 2009; Guillén et al. 2012). For these reasons, syndicate play buffers the liability of repeatedly losing because lottery play becomes less about winning a jackpot and more about fostering group solidarity.

Despite the breath of theoretical fresh air these scholars offer lottery studies, some have the tendency to overstate the implications of their research. In suggesting new avenues of inquiry, for instance, one of the leading scholars of this perspective contends:

> research on lottery syndicates could look at other important issues within economic sociology, including the perpetuation of inequality. Research has unequivocally established that lotteries are fiscally regressive. . . . Qualitative data suggest that the attracting power of syndicating can either reverse or reinforce this scenario
> (Garvía 2007: 644).

It is one thing to claim that syndicate play can alter how regressive or progressive lottery play can be, but it is altogether another thing to state that lotteries perpetuate inequality. Garvía (2007) gets ahead of himself, logically and empirically, when he does not consider the spending side of taxation. After all, it is possible for lottery expenditures on marginalized groups to exceed their contributions. Regressive taxation may translate into the perpetuation of inequality, but this causal relationship should be empirically supported, not theoretically presumed.

Who Plays? Who Pays? The Lottery Money Trail

Long has it been presumed that the lottery is played by those who can least afford it. Consider, for example, the words of classical theorist Georg Simmel ([1907] 2004). He writes:

> The tragedy in all this is that people whose income provides only the minimum level of existence, and who therefore should not risk anything at all, are most strongly subjected to such temptations. Not only is the profit that is based on probability denied to those whose situation places them in most need of it and who are prevented from obtaining it by the logic of their situation, but their security against losses based on probability is also denied them—and it is precisely these people who can least bear such losses
>
> (p. 262).

Though many contemporary lottery scholars corroborate Simmel's position, not all studies share this consensus. A number of studies reveal that low-income individuals spend higher proportions of their income on lottery tickets compared to high-income individuals (Beckert and Lutter 2009, 2013; Borg et al. 1991; Hansen et al. 2005; Miyazaki et al. 1998; Pirog-Good and Mikesell 1995). Other studies show how education affects lottery play, with those of lower attainment levels playing more than individuals with higher levels (Brown et al. 1992; Price and Novak 1999). Though these trends tend to confirm a consistent pattern, not all analysts agree that the lottery is a regressive source of revenue.

It is quite the opposite, in fact. In Illinois, John Mikesell (1989) finds that income has a proportional relationship to lottery play at all levels. Emily Oster (2004) confirms similar findings for Powerball lotteries that offer larger jackpots in Connecticut. Ann Hansen (1995) shows that in Colorado people with higher education attainment purchase lottery tickets more so than their counterparts. Surveying lottery play in three states (Colorado, Florida, and Virginia), Harriet Stranahan and Mary Borg (1998) find that middle income groups play the lottery more frequently than their peers (though they may not spend more). These trends have been further confirmed at the national level. Drawing from a Gallup poll, Ludwig (1999) offers evidence that the lottery is a progressive tax structure in which groups with higher income and education levels play at higher rates compared to other groups. Taken altogether, all these studies complicate, and in some instances directly challenge, common knowledge about who plays the lottery. It is not always a socioeconomically regressive source of revenue.

When race and ethnicity are considered as a factor in lottery play, the picture of who plays becomes even murkier. Studies report inconsistencies. Some identify little to no differences among groups in the frequency of lottery play (McCrary and Palvak 2002; Stranahan and Borg 1998).[11] When it specifically comes to Latinas/os, some suggest they spend more money on lottery tickets that cost less and yield smaller rewards (Hansen 1995; Price and Novak 1999).[12] That said, considerably little is known about Latina/o lottery habits compared to whites and blacks. Even less is known about any other nonwhite racial groups (e.g., Asians, Native Americans, multiracials), as they are virtually absent from the literature or are methodologically subsumed under umbrella categories of nonblack or nonwhite (Henricks 2014). Dichotomizing race in these ways not only dilutes precise measurement, but it oversimplifies how racial dynamics work. Because the presence of multiple racial groups complicates how symbolic and material resources are distributed (Bonilla-Silva et al. 2003), scientific inquiries need revision so that findings cannot be as readily dismissed as artifacts of the method. In light of these discrepant findings, more research needs to be completed to reveal exactly from whom lottery revenues are generated.

Only then will analysts be able to determine if, or to what extent, the lottery is a regressive source of revenue in terms of income, education, and race and ethnicity. This question, however, is not the only one that needs to be asked. In addition to uncovering from whom lottery money comes, an equally important question is what this money is spent on. Unfortunately, most lottery scholars have failed to take up this question. Such an omission, as Mary Borg, Paul Mason, and Stephen Shapiro (1991) note, considers "only half the issue–the tax side of incidence" (p. 15). How about the spending side of the lottery tax? Without addressing this question, some scholars' (e.g., Beckert and Lutter 2009; Garvía 2007; Nibert 2000; Peppard 1987) appraisal of the lottery as exploitative, inequitable, or perhaps even unjust, remains premature. Though this judgment may resonate with moral reservations about the lottery, these claims are empirically unproven. It is possible that regressively generated revenue can be progressively distributed when marginalized groups receive more lottery expenditures than they contributed in the first place.[13] For analysts to claim that lotteries perpetuate inequality, they need to borrow one of the oldest rules of journalism and "follow the money."

Are Lotteries the Anti-Robin Hood Tax?

Politicians frequently argue that states need lotteries for the money, and once finally adopted, designated public services like K-12 education will finally get all the funds they have long gone without. In reality, though, lotteries tend to displace other sources of revenue, such as corporate, property, and income taxes (Borg and Mason 1988, 1990). The sequence of this infrastructural redesign raises questions that remain largely unanswered, if asked at all. Namely, how do lotteries help redistribute tax liability? If lotteries disproportionately generate money from marginal groups, then this process is comparable to a classic bait-and-switch scheme, one that is anti-Robin Hood in nature. Fiscal policy reform like this not only frees elite interests, defined in terms of race and class, from obligatory taxes, but it causes marginal groups to increasingly pay for public services that all groups enjoy.

If one turns to the literature to learn how lottery revenues are spent across the country, one will find inconclusive answers. Unfortunately, this is because the question has long been ignored by lottery scholars (Borg et al. 1991). Some recent scholarship diverts from this trend, but most is limited to case studies of particular states or large metropolitan areas (e.g. Borg et al. 1991; Henricks 2014; McCrary and Palvak 2002; Stranahan and Borg 2004). In the states of Georgia and Florida, for example, McCrary and Palvak (2002) and Stranahan and Borg (2004) find state lotteries to redistribute capital upwards through college scholarships from low income, nonwhite, less educated households to high income, white, educated households. In Chicago, Illinois, Henricks (2014) shows how lottery money supplanted other taxes once earmarked for education, and consequently, shifts the tax responsibility of paying for public education onto those who play the lottery most: communities of color and working-class communities.

While findings from these studies are quite suggestive, their conclusions are hardly comprehensive. No study, to our knowledge, attempts to show how lottery revenues are spent on a national scale.[14] This gap in the literature needs to be filled, especially since lottery revenues have injected new cash flows into America's reconfiguring tax code. Over the past half-century, we argue, lotteries have assumed larger roles in finance and altered how states pay for public services. In addition, these case studies are inhibited by certain methodological and substantive choices that bring their findings into question. When Borg et al. (1991) sampled their population via mail surveys, for example, their results yielded a dismal 17.8 response rate. Though McCrary and Palvak (2002) obtained better results when they opted for the telephone interview, they too had problems tapping their purported population of interest. They report a response rate of 51.3 percent, but only 26.2 percent of all participants identified as active lottery players. In both these studies, the samples were oversaturated by whites, females, and homeowners. It was this group that the authors confirmed as least likely to play the lottery. Bearing these shortcomings in mind, new research designs should avoid problems of the past and advance what knowledge lottery studies have to offer. More evidence is needed to comprehensively conclude whether the lottery is exploitative, inequitable, and unjust.

Concluding Thoughts: The Lottery Tax and Institutional Racism

Nearly 150 years after Balzac ([1842] 1897) first wrote that lotteries are misunderstood and improperly studied, we conclude our review by parroting those same thoughts. Our critique is an attempt to elaborate this point by identifying some of the key limitations in what recent lottery scholars have said on the subject. Our goal is to prompt new ways sociologists and other scholars can think about the role of lotteries in the reproduction of inequalities, especially in terms of race. In their short modern existence, lotteries have emerged onto the American scene to provide relief for eroded tax bases of state governments under fiscal crisis (Nibert 2000; Peppard 1987). The fact that lotteries are paid only by the willing adds to their insidious nature (Clotfelter and Cook 1989). Though often initiated on the promise to provide additional funds, they tend to replace alternative forms of taxation that are relatively progressive (Borg and Mason 1988, 1990). And in the process, we argue, the initiation of lotteries entails hidden biases that redistribute tax responsibilities and hoard resources along lines of race (and class).

The lottery removes exploitive relationships by at least one degree. Those who routinely benefit from it—vis-à-vis tax relief or expenditure receipts—are not required to directly perform acts of expropriation. Rather, lotteries become an institution by which a state entity—one designated for "good causes" like the education of children, environmental protection, senior care, and so on—diverts private resources from the poor generally and people of color specifically, all in the name of financing services deemed as "public." Structuring tax finance this way shifts control from individuals who belong to dominant groups to institutions erected to serve their interests. No longer are people who profit from processes of resource distribution (or hoarding) required to actively assert their interests. The state does it for them. Through everyday transactions, each lottery purchase enacts and affirms unequal racial arrangements. Rarely are lotteries seen from this vantage point, though.

Those who benefit from these larger social forces often too eagerly adopt self-flattering views and remove themselves from the equation of inequality. Consider the words of Mary Jackman (1994) when she writes:

> The institutionalization of inequality releases the individual members of the dominant group from any sense of personal complicity. As they seek to interpret the happy situation in which they find themselves, they have no reason to feel personally defensive—after all, they have personally taken no steps to extract from others the benefits that regularly come their way
>
> (p. 65).

When it comes to taxation, dominant group members can make "sincere" arguments in the name of local self-determination and taxpayers' rights to shape how revenues are (not) distributed and who receives them—even if it means shutting down public schools to oppose desegregation (Bonastia 2009, 2012). When people are assumed as makers of their own destiny, larger social forces at hand, such as the increasing dependence of government finance on lottery money, are often diminished as contributors to inequality. The voluntary nature of lotteries further obscures these exploitive tax arrangements, and lets dominant group members "off the hook."

An expanding reliance on lotteries to finance public services comes with a host of social consequences that we intend to bring to light. When boiled down in simplest form, the lottery tax represents monetary exchanges that circulate money from some groups to others with the state acting as an intermediary. Though lottery expenditures vary from state to state, this money pays for the schools children attend, roads and highways people drive on, parks and recreation areas everyone visits, corrections systems that police the social order, and healthcare available to senior citizens, among many other services. This process raises a number of questions that beg to be comprehensively answered: from whom does this money come, and on whom is it spent? How might these tax practices constitute institutional discrimination? In what ways does taxation create and recreate inequalities?

Notes

1 Quote taken from Balzac, Honoré de. [1842] 1897. *La Rabouilleuse*. Philadelphia: George Barrie & Son.
2 Perhaps a parallel in today's context would be how some corporations have long called their employees "associates" rather than workers or something else. The idea behind the strategy is the same, even if the context is different.
3 Because taxes for alcohol, tobacco, and lottery products vary from state to state (and sometimes even more at the local level of government), this comparison is subject to vary. Even by conservative estimate, though, it is safe to conclude that the rate of tax proceeds for each lottery unit sold will be considerably more compared to tax proceeds from alcohol and tobacco.
4 Given that lottery winnings (but not losses) are considered "income," governments at the federal, state, and even local level subject them to income taxes—especially the larger jackpots. Any winnings that are $600 or more are subject to federal tax liability. This frequently reduces net income from lottery winnings to about half the gross amount (Nibert 2000). In light of these indirect taxes, the estimates of lottery proceeds to state treasuries that I have provided thus far are highly conservative.
5 In truth, lotteries in America have much deeper historical roots. During colonial times, for example, many lotteries were in existence, but they existed in a variety of forms. Governments did operate them in this era, but they did not own a monopoly on them like they do today. In fact, it was quite common to see private businesses and even churches run their own lotteries. And they were wildly popular then, just as they are today. This all began to change, however, in the late 19th century. Various social movements (e.g., women's rights, abolitionists, antiwar groups, education reformers, and prison reformers, among others) converged in their opposition to lotteries for their own reasons, and they mobilized for federal reform that culminated in the prohibition of all lotteries by the end of the 1800s. It was only after a half-century of dormancy that lotteries reemerged in their modern state-sponsored form. For a much more in-depth overview of this history, see Chapter 3 of Clotfelter and Cook's (1989) *Selling Hope*.
6 Some notable exceptions (e.g., Nibert 2000; Peppard 1987) diverge from this trend.
7 A number of studies that emphasize cultural theories of lottery play, but nonetheless directly challenge, the pathological gambling perspective are worth noting here. Various scholars (e.g., Kaplan 1987; Eckblad and von der Lippe 1994; Larsson 2011) have found lottery players to exhibit values of modesty, caution,

and restraint through behavior they describe as self-restrained realism. Even after their respondents won large jackpots, most did not go on lavish spending sprees but instead paid off their debts, donated to charities, invested in their futures, and continued working their regular jobs.

8 "Blaming the victim" explanations of lottery play, poverty, or inequality in general represents the tendency to deny group-based privileges and/or penalties, locate social problems within cultural deficiencies, and scapegoat marginalized peoples for their own exploitation (Darity 2002; Steinberg 1995). It places the responsibility of exploitation within the exploited themselves, often through narratives like "black people are lazy" or "they just don't have their act together," and in the process obscures the actual relations of domination and who does the dominating (Bonilla-Silva [2003] 2014).

9 It is worth noting that elsewhere in his writings, Marx ([1852] 1963) expresses other sentiments about the lottery. In *The Eighteenth Brumaire*, he bemoans the French state of Louis-Napoleon Bonaparte for its use of lottery revenues to purge the poor from France to the *golden* state of California. Perhaps more importantly, though, Marx ([1852] 1963) worried about the effects the lottery might have on revolutionary uprisings. "[G]olden dreams," Marx ([1852] 1963) wrote, "were to supplant the socialist dreams of the Paris proletariat" (p. 84). If people became complacent with fantasies of wealth and instant gratification, he thought, the lottery could thwart collective social action. It meant his communist utopia might be sold out to a game of chance in which most everyone is a loser.

10 Here, we are alluding to Dr. King's last public speech given in Memphis, Tennessee, on April 3, 1968: "I Have Been to the Mountaintop."

11 These same studies do reveal, however, that blacks disproportionately spend more money on lottery products than other racial groups.

12 Much of the literature privileges the term "Hispanic" over "Latina/o" or treats the terms as interchangeable. Throughout the article, we employ the term "Latina/o" as an alternative to "Hispanic" for political reasons. The latter pan-ethnic label is intricately intertwined with historical European oppression because it refers to those who are of Spanish origin but is broadly imposed on anyone of Latin American ancestry (Sáenz and Murga 2011). Thus, the term is a symbolic imposition directly rooted in conquest and colonization.

13 Borg et al. (1991) found in Florida that a vast majority of households enjoyed a net gain from lottery expenditures on education. In other words, most households received more from the lottery than they contributed in the first place.

14 One exception to this rule includes Clotfelter and Cook's (1989) *Selling Hope*, which is perhaps the gold standard of lottery studies. It was the first of its kind, and at the time of publication, it was a fairly exhaustive analysis of American state lotteries. That said, its analysis is dated. Most data analyzed were collected between the mid-1970s and -1980s, the number of state lotteries has since nearly doubled, and the historical, social, economic, and political contexts have changed considerably.

3 "Mad as Hell" Tax Rebels and a Changing Tax Composition
A Historical Corrective for How State Lotteries Emerged[1]

Today, lotteries are everywhere (see Figure 3.1), but their emergence is a recent historical development. If we time-travelled to a year as recent as 1963, the pervasively familiar imagery of lotteries would be non-existent. This is because they were outlawed for over 70 years in the United States (Clotfelter and Cook 1989). That is, until New Hampshire broke the streak. Confronted with one of the country's least-funded public education systems, largely as a result of no state income or sales tax in addition to resistance of property tax hikes, its state legislators had few options other than to establish a lottery for much-needed funds (Nibert 2000). On March 13, 1964, Governor John W. King became the first player of the modern state lottery. Soon thereafter, New York adopted its own lottery in 1967. Then during the 1970s and 1980s, state lotteries spread like wildfire across the nation. In just these two decades, the number of state lotteries, including the District of Columbia, increased thirteen-fold—from two to 26. As we write this book, all but seven states operate their own lottery. Though much ink has been spilled on how this trend came to be, few lottery scholars connect it to broader trends in government finance. More specifically, what remains less understood is the obscure role lotteries play in the changing composition of American taxation. Even less is known about *the role of race and racial antagonism* in this great transformation. In this chapter, we provide a historical corrective that sees the emergence of lotteries through the lens of race.

What Does White Backlash Have to Do With Tax Revolts?

The history of racism must be written as "a series of experiences or incidents which are resented by a dominant group and construed as affronts, unwarranted aggressions and attacks—usually as signs of a possibly more abiding and threatening attack" (Blumer [1939] 2000: 191). These words foreshadowed the racial antagonism that transpired during the 1970s and 1980s. Many whites met the entrance of people of color in once excluded areas of education, employment, housing, and immigration with apprehension and hostility. Unaccustomed to physical contact with people of color in their schools and workplaces, let alone intimate spheres of neighborhoods they called home, many whites perceived these changing trends as threats

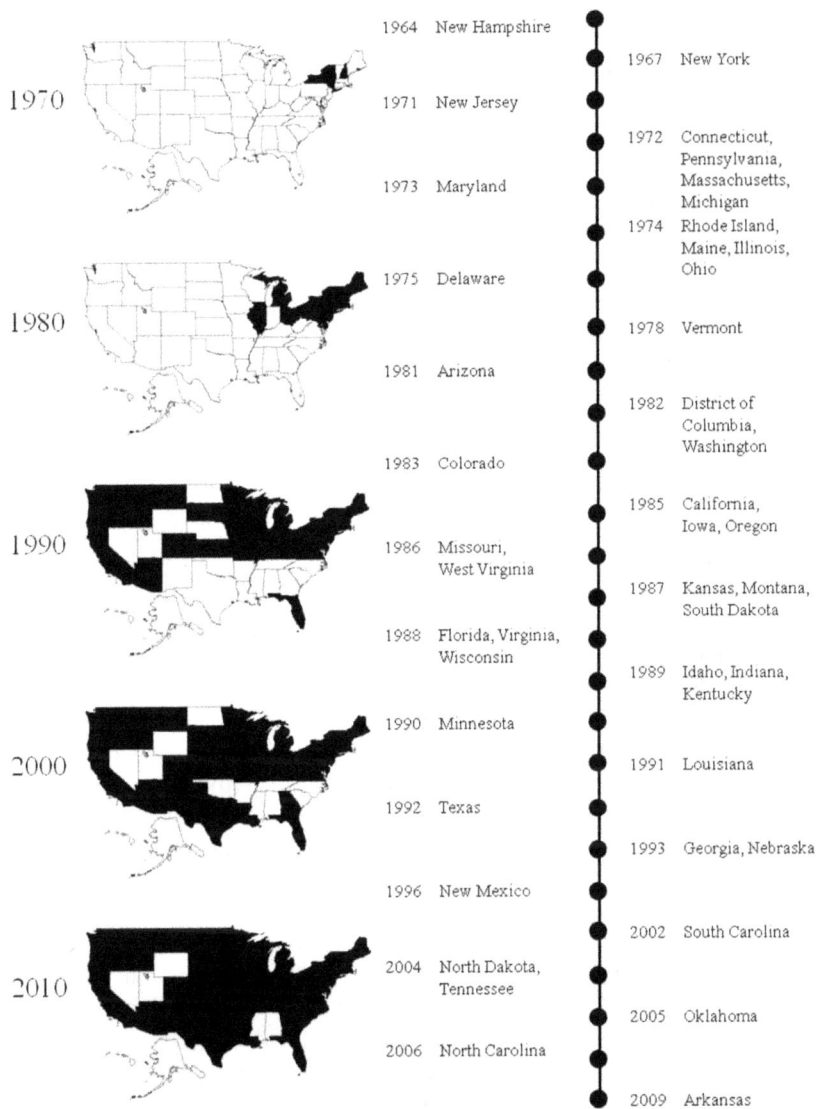

	1964	New Hampshire	
			1967 New York
1970	1971	New Jersey	
			1972 Connecticut, Pennsylvania, Massachusetts, Michigan
	1973	Maryland	1974 Rhode Island, Maine, Illinois, Ohio
	1975	Delaware	
1980			1978 Vermont
	1981	Arizona	
			1982 District of Columbia, Washington
	1983	Colorado	
			1985 California, Iowa, Oregon
1990	1986	Missouri, West Virginia	
			1987 Kansas, Montana, South Dakota
	1988	Florida, Virginia, Wisconsin	
			1989 Idaho, Indiana, Kentucky
	1990	Minnesota	
2000			1991 Louisiana
	1992	Texas	
			1993 Georgia, Nebraska
	1996	New Mexico	
			2002 South Carolina
	2004	North Dakota, Tennessee	
2010			2005 Oklahoma
	2006	North Carolina	
			2009 Arkansas

Figure 3.1 Timeline of Modern State Lottery Proliferation (through 2010)

to their own social position (Bobo 1983, 1988).[2] Out of this insecurity, as Harold Blumer ([1939] 2000, 1958) predicted, they came to view people of color and racialized symbols like interventionist government as a frontal challenge to their status, security, and general welfare.

Whites blamed people of color for their own economic uncertainties (Feagin 2012; Omi and Winant [1986] 1994). The golden era of unprecedented American growth that entailed racially exclusive opportunities of massive homeownership expansion, property development, and community creation (see Oliver and Shapiro [1995] 2006) came to an end. Broader shifts in the political economy (e.g., deindustrialization, deregulation, privatization, and globalization) left a majority of all Americans confronted with real income stagnation, growing inflation, and rising unemployment (Fischer and Hout 2006). For the first time ever, many experienced declines in their standard of living.

Rather than attribute these problems to "the increasing significance of class" (see Wilson 1978), many whites displaced their anxieties onto people of color and government initiatives that symbolized minority interests.[3] National surveys confirm that state interventionist strategies—i.e., housing and education desegregation, affirmative action, immigration reform, and social welfare programs—became central targets of this white backlash (Feagin 2012; Omi and Winant [1986] 1994).[4] The pushback of this era was unlike racial animosity that had preceded it (Sears and Kinder 1971).

Less frequent was opposition to government initiatives of minority incorporation framed in the racially explicit language of Jim Crow. Political positions became couched within the ideological framing of abstract liberalism (Bonilla-Silva 2001). Many whites deployed rhetorical strategies that infused economic principles of "free choice" and individualism with political principles of "equal opportunity" to reject a broad range of public policies perceived as promoting minority inclusion, and to even deny that racial hierarchy exists altogether (Bonilla-Silva 2001; Crenshaw 1997; Gallagher 2003). In other words, most whites supported ideals of racial equality, but they opposed public policies that might practically achieve it (Schuman et al. [1985] 1997). And even though many advanced racially exclusive interests, they refused to see themselves as racist (Wellman [1977] 1993).

Consider results from the 1972 General Social Survey for example. More than 85 percent of whites supported integrated schools in principle, but when asked if they supported busing efforts to desegregate schools, about 86 percent rejected this measure (Bobo et al. 2012). Such logic was applied to a host of issues in addition to education. In "the city too busy to hate," for example, Kevin Kruse (2005) shows how white Atlantans opposed housing integration policies during the 1970s and 1980s. Avoiding expressions of explicit prejudice and bigotry, they contested racial initiatives in the name of abstract notions of freedom, choice, and fairness by alleging that government had overstepped its role. They opposed alleged state intrusion and defended individual rights to "select their neighbors, their employees, and their children's classmates" (Kruse 2005: 9). These sentiments are not regionally exclusive to the Deep South, though. Lillian Rubin (1972) and Leland Saito (2009) uncover similar patterns in California.

Much of the white pushback was directed at blacks, but they were not the only targeted group. Exemplified in recent work by Samuel Huntington (2004), the "foreign invasion" of Latinas/os (and some Asians) triggered a particular anxiety amongst many whites too.[5] He argues that Latinas/os in general, and Mexicans in particular, are essentially "taking over" the job market, dropping workers' wages, free-riding public services, abusing the welfare system, and refusing assimilation to "American" culture.[6] Many whites react to these exaggerated observations as threats to their social, economic, and cultural status (Doane 1997). Though these claims have been empirically disproven (see Sáenz et al. 2007), they represent a form of domestic colonization that justifies why Latinas/os, especially those of darker skin and stereotypical indigenous features, are positioned near the bottom of America's stratification ladder (Bonilla-Silva 2004; Murguia and Sáenz 2002; Vargas 2015). As long as this group remains subordinated, the material and symbolic interests of whites are preserved.[7]

Ironically, many whites invert empirical realities of racial hierarchy to claim the mantel of racial victimhood (Mills 1997). A clear example of this is found in persisting claims of so-called "reverse discrimination" (Pincus 2003). For many whites, government initiatives of minority incorporation represent unmeritocratic group preferences viewed as a zero-sum gain. Inclusion and expansion of rights to minority groups requires not only the interests of whites to be sacrificed, but it unfairly intensifies competition during uncertain, vulnerable economic times. All the while, such claims dismiss how whites have long profited from excluding people of color and extracting socioeconomic rewards from their devalued, underpaid, and unpaid labor (Feagin 2000). Allegations of reverse discrimination serve a powerful ideological function, and when channeled effectively, can elicit a potent collective force of white backlash.

When accepting his party's nomination at the 1984 Republican National Committee Convention, President Ronald Reagan ([1984] 1989) rhetorically asked a series of questions like "[I]s there really any doubt at all about what will happen if we let them win this November?" and "Is there any doubt that they will raise our taxes?" (p. 210). The cadences separating one moment from another were filled by chants of "no" from the audience, even though answers to these questions were obvious and could have otherwise gone unsaid. At times, Reagan ([1984] 1989) elaborated his message more fully, professing the government's role as limited and promoting *the interests of all*:

> [W]e're here to see that government continues to serve the people and not the other way around. Yes, government should do all that is necessary, but only that which is necessary.
>
> We don't lump people by groups or special interests. And let me add, in the party of Lincoln, there is no room for intolerance and not even a small corner for anti-Semitism or bigotry of any kind. Many people are welcome in our house, but not the bigots
>
> (p. 212).

Couched in colorblind rhetoric, erroneous narratives like these diminish historical and ongoing racial discrimination while simultaneously inverting government initiatives of minority inclusion as discriminatory to the dominant group (Bonilla-Silva 2001; Crenshaw 1997; Gallagher 2003).[8] Reagan delivers this message to predominantly white audiences, who often see the tax state as coercively redistributive (Edsall and Edsall 1991). If one asks "redistributive to whom?" Reagan's next sentence offers an implicit answer. He singles out minorities in the codified language of "groups" and "special interests," but does so in a way that preemptively flattens accusations of racism. Reagan condemns bigotry while pairing his message with imagery of Lincoln. As if they were two bricks of the same proverbial wall, he symbolically claims the political heritage of the "Great Emancipator"—a point that foreshadows what later comes:

> . . . Down through the welfare state to statism, to more and more government largesse accompanied always by more government authority, less individual liberty and, ultimately, totalitarianism, always advanced as for our own good. The alternative is the dream conceived by our Founding Fathers, up to the ultimate in individual freedom consistent with an orderly society.
>   We don't celebrate dependence day on the Fourth of July. We celebrate Independence Day
>
> (Reagan [1984] 1989: 212–213).

The crowd responds, in hymnal fashion, "USA! USA! USA!" In the name of liberty and damnation of totalitarianism, Reagan promises "emancipation" for a new generation. Unlike Lincoln, though, it was not intended for racial minorities deemed dependent on welfare, statism, and growing government largesse. The proclamation was for his constituency, a message intended, by and large, for white people (Feagin 2012).

The politics of racial inequality came to embody all that was wrong with unbalanced budgets, bureaucratic incompetence, and a coercively redistributive tax state (Quadagno 1994). While "undeserving" minorities were alleged to prefer, to paraphrase President Bill Clinton's ([1996] 1998) words, a welfare check to a paycheck, the growing animosity among whites drove them to rebel against "big government" for what they saw as pandering to minority interests (Gilens 1999; Neubeck and Cazenave 2001). It was, after all, this alleged pandering that caused many whites to sense a downward slippage in their social position (Bobo 1983, 1988). Government initiatives like certain welfare programs (e.g., Aid to Dependent Family and Children), immigration reform, integration mandates in schools, and prohibition of restrictive housing covenants, among others, became viewed as costly programs that undercut white interests paid out of pocket by their own hard-earned tax dollars.

No longer were whites, of both lower and upper class, going to put up with "big government" that permitted minorities to scam and squander their hard-earned tax dollars, all the while remaining in entangled pathologies and parasitic dependency (Neubeck and Cazenave 2001). This is why Reagan's storylines, like the fictitious "welfare queen" from Chicago's south side, were so effective. On the 1976 campaign trail, for example, he said,

> She has 80 names, 30 addresses, 12 Social Security cards and is collecting veterans' benefits on four nonexisting deceased husbands . . . She's collecting Social Security on her cards. She's got Medicaid, getting food stamps and she is collecting welfare under each of her names. Her tax-free cash alone is $150,000
>
> (qtd. in Neubeck and Cazenave 2001: 127).

Narratives like this are not simply lies agreed upon, inverted as gospel truth, they are ideological appeals for support and calls to action (Bonilla-Silva et al. 2004).

Alleged moral shortcomings of imaginary welfare queen types ultimately are seen as taking advantage of hard-working, tax-paying whites and a threat to their well-being. People of color are assumed to be majority recipients of government benefits, undeserving ones at that (Gilens 1999; Neubeck and Cazenave 2001; see also Luttmer 2001). The purpose of such storylines was to drive a white rebellion against what was perceived as a coercive, redistributive tax state that pandered to minority interests. As Andrea Louise Campbell (2009) observes,

> Government was taking in a lot of taxes and spending a lot of money, but spending it on other people, many Americans seemed to think. The percentage of National Election Study respondents saying the government wastes 'a lot of money we pay in taxes' increased from 43 percent in 1958 to 78 percent in 1980. And the percentage of Gallup respondents saying their federal income taxes were too high grew tremendously during the 1960s, from 46 to 49 percent by the end of the decade, dropping to 58 percent in 1967, but rising again rapidly to 68 percent by 1980
>
> (p. 62).

Whites resented "big government" for its bureaucratic incompetence, inability to prevent fraud, and wasteful spending (Lo 1990). They raged with anger, and refused to be a slush fund for black interests. Research completed by Erzo F.P. Luttmer (2001), however, shows that whites express strong support for welfare spending when recipients are fellow in-group members. For these reasons, as well as persisting trends of economic uncertainty, tax reform resonated with public sentiment and garnered much voter support.

Reagan simply surfed into the White House from California on a wave of tax rebellions (Martin 2008; Prasad 2012). Once in office, he passed a number of major federal tax reforms (see Table 3.1 for an overview and brief summary). Among them was the most comprehensive tax cut in American

Table 3.1 Overview of Federal Reforms Downwardly Displacing Tax Liability, 1978–1983*

Legislation:	Regressive Reforms by Line Item:
Revenue Act of 1978 (Public Law 95-600)	• Individual Income Tax Reduction (decreased number of tax rates and widened brackets) • Corporate Tax Reduction (lowered top rate from 48 to 46 percent) • Standard Deduction Increase (raised standard deduction from $3,200 to $3,400) • Capital Gain Expansion (raised exclusion rate from 50 to 60 percent) • State/Local Tax Deduction Elimination (repealed state/local gasoline deductions for nonbusinesses)
Crude Oil Windfall Profit Tax Act of 1980 (Public Law 96-223)	• Excise Tax Implementation (created an excise tax on crude oil products until 1993) • Dividend Exclusion Increase (expanded dividend exclusion from $200 to $400 [joint filers], includes gained interest)
Economic Recovery Tax Act of 1981 (Public Law 97-34)	• Individual Income Tax Reduction (reduced marginal rates 23 percent over 3 years; decreased max rate from 70 to 50 percent) • Capital Gains Tax Reduction (decreased tax rate from 28 to 20 percent) • Marriage Income Credit Implementation (created a 10 percent exclusion for two-income couples, $3,000 cap) • Accelerated Depreciation Deductions (created faster write-off guidelines for business equipment [5 years for most items] and structures [15 years for most buildings]; repealed in 1982) • Income Tax Parameters Indexation (enabled standardized deductions and personal exemptions to adjust for inflation by 1985) • Gift and Estate Tax Exemption Expansion (created an unlimited marital deduction; expanded estate exemption from $175,625 to $600,000 by 1987) • Investment Incentivization (extended IRA eligibility to active employer pension plans) • Exclusion Expansion (replaced dividend exclusion of $400 with 15 percent deduction [joint filers], $900 cap; repealed in 1984)
Tax Equity and Fiscal Responsibility Act of 1982 (Public Law 97-248)	• Dividend Withholding Implementation (created 10 percent individual withholding provision on dividends or interest gained) • Employment Tax Expansion (increased federal unemployment tax wage base and tax rate; extended hospital insurance taxes to federal employees) • Excise Tax Expansion (increased rates on airport and airport trust fund taxes, cigarette excise taxes, and telephone excise taxes)

Legislation:	Regressive Reforms by Line Item:
Highway Revenue Act of 1982 (Public Law 97-424)	• Excise Tax Expansion (increased tax on gasoline products from 4 to 9 cents per gallon until 1987)
Social Security (Public Law 98-21)	• Social Security Income Tax Expansion (accelerated scheduled payroll tax increases; enabled taxation of certain Social Security Amendments of 1983 benefits, up to 50 percent if income surpasses $25,000 for single taxpayer or $32,000 for joint return)
Interest and Dividends Tax Compliance Act of 1983 (Public Law 98-67)	• 10% Interest and Dividend Withholding Repeal (replaced it with 'backup withholding') • Caribbean Basin Initiative (implemented tariff and trade benefits to particular Central American and Caribbean countries that serve American foreign policy interests)

Source: Public Record

* The summary provided represents a cursory analysis of all major federal tax reforms from 1978 to 1983 performed by the author. Due to space constraints, progressive reforms or reforms that apply to small segments of the population have been omitted (e.g., Railroad Retirement Revenue Act of 1983).

history, the Economic Recovery Tax Act of 1981 (ERTA). The new tax law caused a negative 5.7 percent change in federal receipts after its first year in effect, a 12.3 percent after its second year, 16.5 percent after its third year, and 18.6 percent after its fourth (Tempalski 2006). Despite populist framing of across-the-board tax relief for all Americans, most these tax reductions were upwardly distributed. Less than 10 percent of all tax benefits, according to Frances Fox Piven and Richard Cloward's (1982) estimates, went to households annually earning less than $20,000, even though this group comprised about half the population. Meanwhile, business and affluent interests gained most of the remaining tax relief.

Through a series of reforms initiated by Reagan but passed with bipartisan support, federal tax codes have replaced progressive taxes with regressive ones (see Figure 3.2). Consider data from the Office of Management and Budget (2010).[9] Whereas corporate taxes comprised nearly 2.5 to 3 percent of the Gross Domestic Product during the 1970s, these revenues declined to levels comparable to the pre-New Deal era once Reagan took office. Corporate taxes fell to 1.1 percent of the GDP in 1983, and aside from 2006 and 2007, have never rebounded to the levels they once were. Meanwhile social insurance taxes, which include Social Security and Medicare, have steadily risen. In the late 1970s, social insurance taxes hovered around 5.5 percent, but during the 1980s they climbed to nearly 7 percent. Individual income taxes, on the other hand, have remained constant. They have hovered around 8 percent in most years throughout the 1970s and 1980s. By the mid-1980s, the numerous tax reforms culminated to redraw

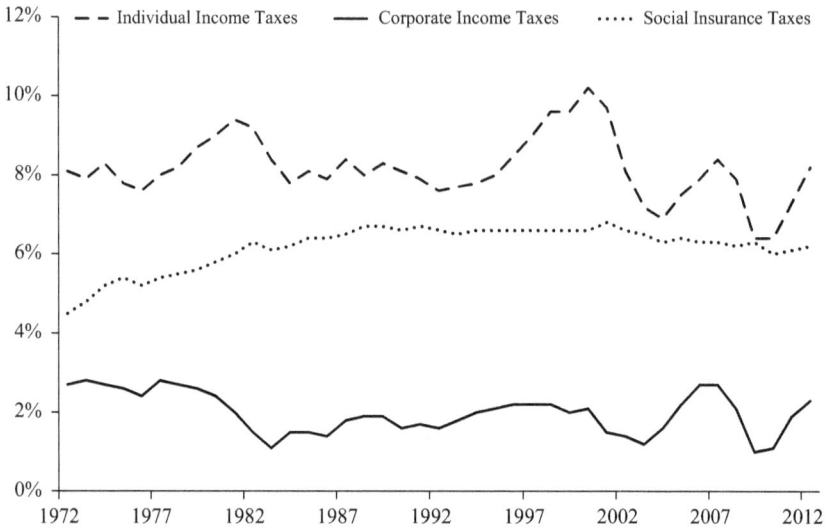

Figure 3.2 Federal Individual, Corporate, and Social Insurance Taxes as a Share of GDP, 1972–2012 (in percentages)

America's tax distribution. Whereas combined individual income and social insurance taxes generated only about 4–5 times the amount of money from corporate taxes, this figure gap doubled in the 1980s. This trend persists into the early 2010s, as individual income and social insurance taxes raise about 12 times what corporate income taxes raise.

Despite the uneven distribution of tax relief, tax reforms like the ERTA have elicited popular support among Americans. Unlike many partisan or controversial policies, as Monica Prasad (2012) points out, "the individual tax rate cuts at the heart of the ERTA have not been reversed by later administrations, or subverted by action at other levels of government. Instead, the popularity of ERTA has seen similar tax cuts repeated again and again" (p. 352).[10] Tax law like this represents a broader social trend in contemporary politics, in which tax burdens are shifting:

- "From corporations to individuals.
- From foreign corporations to domestic corporations.
- From foreign investors to American workers.
- From multinational companies to medium-sized and small businesses.
- From the federal government to state and local governments, whose taxes already fall most heavily on those in the middle and at the bottom" (Donald L. Barlett and James B. Steele 1994: 14).

An inevitable consequence of these new tax laws has been a severe reduction in state capacity altogether (Prasad 2012).

In light of these trends, among other political reasons, the federal government shifted more responsibility to lower levels of government since the 1980s; *especially in terms of services provided by the welfare state* (Piven and Cloward 1982). Pressure was placed by the federal on state governments, in terms of both administration and finance, to maintain public services historically satisfied by federal government (Brunori [2001] 2005). In doing so, numerous social programs—like Medicare and Medicaid, not to mention infrastructure upkeep like education, highway maintenance, and other services—were delegated from the federal to state government. Though the fiscal design of relying upon lower levels of government to satisfy public services expanded under the Reagan administration, it is important to note that the seeds for this design did not begin there. In large part, as Michael Brown (1999) argues, origins of such design can be traced to the fiscal conservatism of President Franklin D. Roosevelt's New Deal policies.

Rather than create a truly universal welfare state, one that was fully funded and administered at the federal level without means-tested restrictions, FDR's administration built an infrastructure that relied upon matching state funds to finance "unpopular" programs. In the words of Brown (1999),

> [Q]uestions of taxing and spending influence, and often determine, social policy choices. Since policymakers must worry as much about who will feel the tax bite as who will benefit from a new social policy, they are motivated to finance the welfare state with taxes that will minimize taxpayer resistance
>
> (p. 6).

New Deal programs deemed politically feasible, most of which catered to white recipients (e.g., Social Security),[11] were federally centralized and implemented, whereas those that served a disproportionate amount of racial minorities (e.g., Aid to Dependent Children),[12] were delegated to state and local governments to exercise broad discretionary administration (Katznelson 2005; Lieberman 1998; Quadagno 1994). This bureaucratic maneuver enabled unsupportive local and state governments to underfund racially stigmatized welfare programs, but it also endorsed the systematic exclusion of minorities through Jim Crow codes. States routinely provided welfare services to "qualified" and "deserving" beneficiaries who were overwhelmingly whites (Katznelson 2005).

Though various Civil Rights Acts have banned explicit racial exclusion from these programs, bureaucratic exclusion persists because the fundamental arrangement of the state has not changed (Bracey 2015; Moore and Bell 2010). Seen this way, the legacy of FDR's conservative fiscal design was merely extended one step further by Reagan's revolution of state devolution.[13] When federal funding for welfare programs was reduced across the board during the early 1980s, state and local governments were left to expand their commitment in providing the same levels of administration (Piven and Cloward 1982). This ultimately caused state and local governments to play a larger role in satisfying public services. All the while, James

O'Connor's autopsy of the state's fiscal crisis remains as true today as when originally written in 1973. Demand for public services continues to outpace the state's ability to pay for them (O'Connor [1973] 2002).

California, the Alabama of the 1970s

During the 1970s and 1980s, argue Thomas Edsall and Mary Edsall (1991), racial antagonism, resource competition, and *taxation* all became conflated into one interrelated issue. This transformation did not begin on the national political stage, though; it merely culminated there. For more than a decade prior, white-driven local politics campaigned against what they perceived as repressively out-of-control "big government" (Lo 1990; Warren 1976). Beginning in California with property tax revolts and later spreading throughout the country, mostly white lower- and middle-class suburbanites (and some business interests later on) spearheaded tax rebellions that would profoundly redefine American politics. According to Isaac William Martin (2008), it created "the permanent tax revolt."

The permanent tax revolt is about more than smaller government and lower taxes though. Throughout the 1970s in California, for example, pollster Mervin Field (1978) reports that most people did not want to downsize government or the public services they received. What they did have a problem with, especially the white voters, was government initiatives that allegedly catered to racial minorities. David Sears and Jack Citrin (1982) explain:

> [Government] services whose clienteles are most widely thought to be racial minorities tend to be favored least. Welfare, public housing, food stamps, and unemployment compensation are the obvious examples. . . . Californians are quite happy about supporting 'the elderly and disabled,' and support the status quo in spending on 'public assistance programs for low income families with dependent children,' to which a major portion of welfare funds is devoted. But they are less happy about the latter, presumably because of its image of black welfare mothers
>
> (p. 49).

In other words, white apprehension was not expressed toward "big government" in general. It was directed at racialized components of the state, often codified in symbolic language (e.g., government waste, welfare, etc.) that eschews racial reference (Lo 1990; Sears and Citrin 1982).

In 1978, Californians took to the ballot box to approve the People's Initiative to Limit Property Taxation, better known as Proposition 13 or the Jarvis-Gann Amendment. With nearly a 70 percent voter turnout, Californians passed the new law by a two-to-one margin. Perhaps unsurprisingly, the vote was split along race lines (see Figure 3.3). According to statewide polls before and after the election, the majority of support came from whites (Sears and Citrin 1982). In May 1978, for example, 66 percent of whites

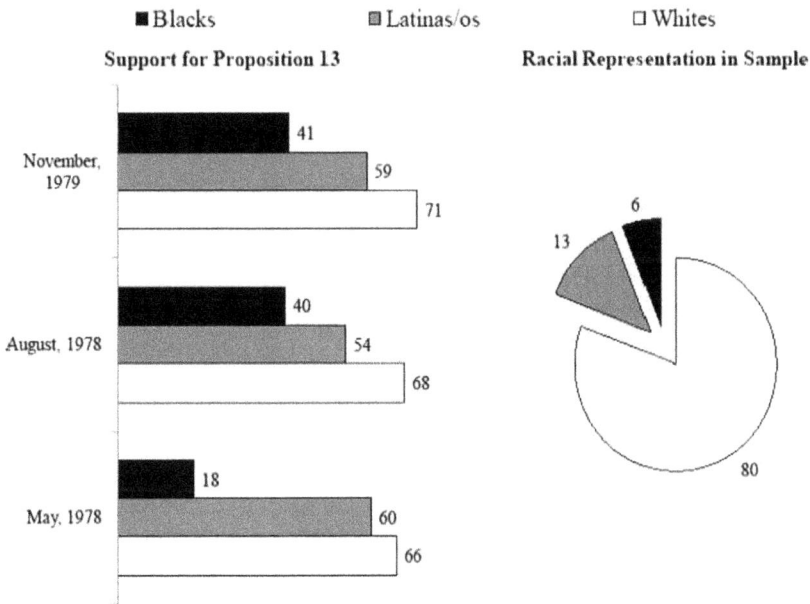

Figure 3.3 Who Supported Proposition 13? A Racial Breakdown (in percentages)*

expressed definite support for Prop. 13, compared to only 18 percent of blacks. Latinas/os fell in between this range, but a majority still supported the initiative at a 60 percent approval rate. Though these polls measure some variance of support, all confirm a persistent trend of support and opposition between racial groups.

Once passed, Prop. 13 became listed as Article 13A of the state constitution. It rolled back property assessments to 1975 levels, prohibited any new statewide property taxes, permanently reduced property tax rates to 1 percent or less of market value, and capped annual value assessment increases at 2 percent. Redeemers instituted similar initiatives after Reconstruction with the 1875 Alabama constitution (McMillan [1955] 1978). These changes in California provided across-the-board property tax reductions to *all* property owners. In just a decade, according to the U.S. Department of Commerce, the state's overall tax burden went from fifth highest in the union to thirtieth (Cox 1988). Property tax revenues declined by 57 percent after just one year, and the annual revenue for local government decreased by about $6 billion (Pfiffner 1983). These reductions were unequally distributed. Two-thirds of all relief went to business owners, while small homeowners got any remaining scraps (Sears and Citrin 1982).[14]

Taxpayers were, to quote the infamous words of leading tax crusader Howard Jarvis (1979), "mad as hell." They saw government not only as undemocratic but unrepresentative of their interests. So they took matters into their own hands. As Daniel Smith (1999) writes,

> According to these enthusiasts for cuts in taxes and government spend-ing, the people, not their elected officials, must be the ones who deter-mine how much a government may tax and spend. Ironically, the same rhetoric once used by the founders to bring forth a new form of govern-ance is being used by modern day tax crusaders to challenge the sys-tem of representative democracy. A more fitting declaration for many of these modern day tax crusaders, to paraphrase the Revolutionary maxim, might be *"No taxation, even with representation"*
>
> (p. 18, emphasis added).

An out-of-touch representative democracy was no democracy at all for these tax rebels. If a money-grubbing state goes unchecked, even despite the pres-ence of elected representatives, government inevitably descends its people, argues Jarvis, into "bankruptcy or dictatorship" (qtd. in *Time* 1978: 13). It leaves "the people" broke, while the government gets rich.

What Whites Talk About When We Talk About Taxes

In other words, these tax revolts were not simply about fiscal matters. They were symbolic battles "intrinsically tied to the ideal of democratic self-governance" (Smith 1999: 22; see also Kidder and Martin 2012). Just like when Samuel Adams and a band of patriots defied the British in the infa-mous "Boston Tea Party," contemporary tax rebels understood their actions as resistance against government policy gone wrong (Lo 1990; Sears and Citrin 1982; Smith 1999). No longer were they going to recognize the state as legitimate, especially since they saw it as overstepping its bounds and encroaching individual freedoms (Warren 1976). On the 1978 election night of California's Prop. 13, for example, Jarvis declared:

> Now we know how it felt when they dumped English tea in Boston Harbor! We have a new revolution. We are telling the government, "Screw you!"
>
> (qtd. in *Time* 1978: 21).

These modern tax rebellions paid homage to the "Sons of Liberty" and rebelled in the name of colonial revolutionary spirit, except these revolts were not directed against the British Crown. They were directed at their own government for going astray from the "people's" interests.

All they desired was restoration of America's promise, or at least how they envisioned it. Like their pro-Prop. 13 bumper stickers read, these tax rebels wanted to "Save the American Dream." Perhaps this includes the house, white picket fence, two-car garage, golden retriever, 2.5 children, and all the public services that come along with it. As Clarence Lo (1990) perceptively observes:

> The suburban life was no longer the easy life. Consumer electronics, furnishings, and apparel were only affordable at discount outlets, or at end-of-the season department stores, at half off. Consumers felt they could afford to pay even less than half for the public services that had contributed to the high quality of life in suburban communities
>
> (p. xiii).

For thousands of pissed-off white suburbanites, property taxes became an obvious target of their frustration. They were seen as the vehicle driving the coercive and redistributive tax state. Personal matters of how much money government took from their paychecks increasingly became seen as taxing the many for benefit of the few.

Fresh on their minds, as William Fischel (1989) argues, was the California Supreme Court *Serrano v. Priest* (1971) decision. In this case, the court found the use of local property taxes to finance public schools a violation of equal protection under state law. It guaranteed that de facto disparities in communities segregated by wealth and race would inevitably reproduce gaps in funding across school districts, and thereby institutionalize a state-sanctioned cycle of inequality. To remedy this problem, the court's solution was to divorce property taxes from local school spending altogether. According to Fischel (1989), this distressed taxpayers in middle-class and wealthy districts because they no longer saw a "bang for their buck."

Frustration among these taxpayers grew. On the surface, concerns about what schools get whose property tax dollars seem to have little to do with race. Some scholars, however, have unmasked how quite the opposite is true. Studies completed by Douglas Reed (1998) and Kent Tedin (1994), for example, reveal that many whites perceive school finance reform as unfairly favoring racial minorities (even when this is not empirically the case). Not wanting to sacrifice their own self-interests, these whites acted upon these false observations to oppose any efforts of reform. They saw their money being spent elsewhere on "other" people's kids, meanwhile their community schools were left to suffer. This was true in much of the country as well as California (see Figure 3.4).

These pictures were taken at various antibusing protests across the nation. Crowds of predominantly white parents and students gathered to resist desegregation efforts, as ordered by the U.S. Supreme Court's *Brown v. Board of Education* decision nearly a decade and a half earlier. As the signs show, crowd members claimed their schools were integrated, framed the state as coercive, and resented "wasteful" government spending. Such protests created a ready-made environment for antitax resentment to be expressed at ballot boxes across the nation.

1975
Dallas, TX

1976
Boston, MA

1976
Detroit, MI

These pictures were taken at various antibusing protests across the nation. Crowds of predominantly white parents and students gathered to resist desegregation efforts, as ordered by the U.S. Supreme Court's *Brown v. Board of Education* decision nearly a decade and a half earlier. As the signs show, crowd members claimed their schools were integrated, framed the state as coercive, and resented "wasteful" government spending. Such protests created a ready-made environment for antitax resentment to be expressed at ballot boxes across the nation.

Figure 3.4 The Nexus of White Racism and Antibusing Campaigns

Sources (Listed by Picture Order): From the collections of the State of Texas, Dallas History and Archives Division, Dallas Public Library, Photograph number PA83–42–1975–9–6–11; State of Massachusetts, Boston Public Library, Spencer Grant Collection, Accession number 11_07_002973; University of Michigan, Bentley Historical Library, Carmen A. Roberts Papers, Box 1, photographs. Reprinted with permission.

As animosity grew from year to year, so too did California's property tax bills. Many whites did not blame racial minorities for this trend, though. Instead they reserved this judgment for big business, suburban sprawl, and general economic growth (Martin 2008). For more than 10 years these disgruntled homeowners collectively organized to demand tax relief, and in some cases, even downward distribution (Martin 2008; Sears and Citrin 1982). Meanwhile others promoted property tax limitation through a progressive veneer, claiming it could keep houses affordable or protect low-income homeowners from displacement (Martin 2008; Martin and Beck Forthcoming).[15] Their pleas grew tired as they fell on policymakers' unresponsive ears. This all changed, however, when elites took an interest in tax reform (Lo 1990). Up to that point class conflict had prevented lower- and middle-class whites from forming alliances with pro-business interests, but it was racial antagonism that offered opportunity for what Derrick Bell (1980) called "interest convergence."

Whereas pro-business interests would reap more profits with reduced property tax rates, many small property owners would preserve a white, middle class lifestyle they saw being eroded away by the undemocratic imposition of property taxes (Lo 1990). Whiteness yielded ideological common ground that propelled a successful taxpayer revolt in 1978 (Edgar 1981). It served as social glue for smoothing over these dissimilar class interests and fostering white solidarity. Consider the words of Amanda Lewis (2004):

Whiteness works in distinct ways for and is embodied quite differently by homeless white men, golf-club-membership-owning executives, suburban soccer moms, urban hillbillies, antiracist skinheads, and/or union-card-carrying-factory workers . . . In any particular moment, however, certain forms of whiteness become dominant

(p. 634).

Along with white resentment of racial minorities, which is reinforced by social and spatial insularity, comes a host of shared repertoires of cultural groundings and symbolic boundaries (Bonilla-Silva et al. 2006; Hughey 2012; Lewis 2004; Lipsitz 2011). It was latent resources like these that facilitated a shared group disposition of white racial formation, and ultimately, helped mobilize white-driven taxpayer revolts of the 1970s and early 1980s.

White racism helped build the infrastructure of homeowners associations and taxpayers organizations that made the passage of California's Prop. 13 possible. It often blurred the conceptual boundaries between tax revolts and other race-explicit causes like the antibusing movements. Lo (1990) writes:

The antibusing movement and the tax protest were closely related. In Los Angeles, both were strong in outlying white suburbs such as the San Fernando Valley and the Harbor area. Activists from BUSTOP, a coalition of community antibusing groups, helped in campaigns to lower property taxes, as did two major leaders of the antibusing movement, Bobbi Fiedler and Roberta Weintraub. Conversely, anti-tax crusader Howard Jarvis was a founder of the Taxpayers School Reform Committee, formed in 1977 to campaign for an antibusing ballot initiative

(p. 57–58).[16]

White suburbanites campaigning for tax relief were often the same people protesting school integration efforts. One of Howard Jarvis' top aides who handled media and advertising, Roland Vincent, even ran the presidential campaign of segregationist George Wallace in California during 1976 (Furlong 1978). David S. Broder (1978), a columnist for *The Washington Post*, noted the similarities. He equated Prop. 13 with the Alabama governor's "in your face," "let's send a message" style of politics. Not only do these patterns imply that the underlying causes for protest were interrelated, but they attest to how they shared the same organizational base. What white racism helped facilitate, in other words, was movement building (see also Hughey 2015).

So Goes California, So Goes the Nation

When Election Day of Prop. 13 approached, a once dispersed coalition of community-based groups became a unified movement under a solid financial backing of monied interests (Lo 1990; Smith 1999). Rebelling against "big government" and its alleged coercive, redistributive fiscal program, white animosity channeled taxpayer revolt to the ballot box (Edgar 1981). California merely sparked the fire.

> 'Politicians all the way down the ladder, down to the school boards and water districts,' said Director of the National Taxpayers Union Charles Crawford, 'are going to hear footsteps behind them . . . they are going to realize what the Legislature didn't do first in California, they are going to have to do at their levels of government'
> (qtd. in "The Associated Press" 1978a: C12).

In a national poll of voters outside California, 51 percent expressed support for Prop. 13, 24 percent opposed it, and the remainder was undecided (Clymer 1978). These results were split along racial lines, and Democrats, liberals, women, and the poor were fairly split even. Meanwhile 78 percent of voters said government wasted too much money. Such sentiments spilled over into American politics, as reported in *The Sacramento Bee*, as many states followed "the golden state's" lead and passed similar tax-reduction measures shortly after (Cox 1988).

Without California's rebellion, the wave of tax revolts that spilled across the country likely would have not happened (Martin 2008). Shortly after Prop. 13 made it onto the ballot in 1978, as George Peterson (1982) documents, numerous other referendums popped up on ballot boxes from coast to coast. Between 1979 and 1981, for example, voters across the nation overwhelmingly approved more than 150 major reforms on state and local tax codes (see Table 3.2). The vast majority were some form of tax reduction or relief. In total, 104 new laws either limited property taxes or provided property tax relief, 30 reduced personal income tax rates, and 28 decreased

Table 3.2 Number of Local and State Tax Reforms throughout the U.S., 1978–1981

Tax Action			1978	1979	1980	1981
Property Tax						
	New Statewide Limitation on Levies, Rates, or Assessment Growth		7	9	7	4
	New Property Tax Relief		20	21	19	17
		Total Major Measures	27	30	26	21
Personal Income Tax						
	Reductions Indexation		3	4	2	0
	General Rates		4	6	2	3
	Specific Rates		3	3	0	0
		Total Major Measures	10	13	4	3
	Increases Indexation		0	0	0	1
	General Rates		2	0	0	0
	Specific Rates		0	0	0	1
		Total Major Measures	2	0	0	2
Sales Tax						
	Reductions Across-the-Board		1	0	0	1
	Base Contraction (food, drugs, or medical-exemption or reduced rates)		9	12	2	3
		Total Major Measures	10	12	2	4
	Increases Across-the-Board, Permanent		0	0	1	3
	Temporary and Extension of Temporary		1	1	3	3
	Base Expansion		3	1	0	3
		Total Major Measures	4	2	4	9

Source: Peterson (1982)

sales tax rates. Racial antagonism had become displaced onto taxation, and no longer did white voters sit idly by.

Taking it to the streets and the voting booth, these white-driven tax rebellions reconfigured America's tax composition at the state and local levels (see Figure 3.5). From 1972 to 2007, these transformations were most pronounced in property taxes. Prior to the taxpayer revolts, data from the U.S. Census Bureau's State and Local Government Finances shows that property taxes contributed about a quarter of all local and state revenues. In 1972, for instance, this figure was 25.6 percent. More than 100 major property tax reforms and 10 years later, this figure dropped about three-tenths to 17.9 percent. Property taxes continued their decline to 16.7 percent in 2007, effectively marking a negative rate of change by more than 35 percent over three and a half decades. What this trend represents is a withering of one of state government's most progressive and highest generating sources of revenue.

It was not the only type of taxation to decline in revenues. Select sales taxes, like those on food, drug, or other medical-exempted items, was another tax type frequently subjected to taxpayer angst. After more than 20 major tax reductions between just 1978 and 1981, this tax type saw the second most dramatic decline over the past four decades. Whereas select sales tax items generated 10.2 percent of all state revenue in 1972, this figure dropped to 7.2 percent by 1982 and even further to 6 percent by 2007. This percentage change represents nearly a 41 percentage drop in total share of local and state revenues. It was dwindling revenues from both property and select sales taxes that helped force the state's hand to devise new ways to generate money and remain fiscally solvent. Had no other alternatives

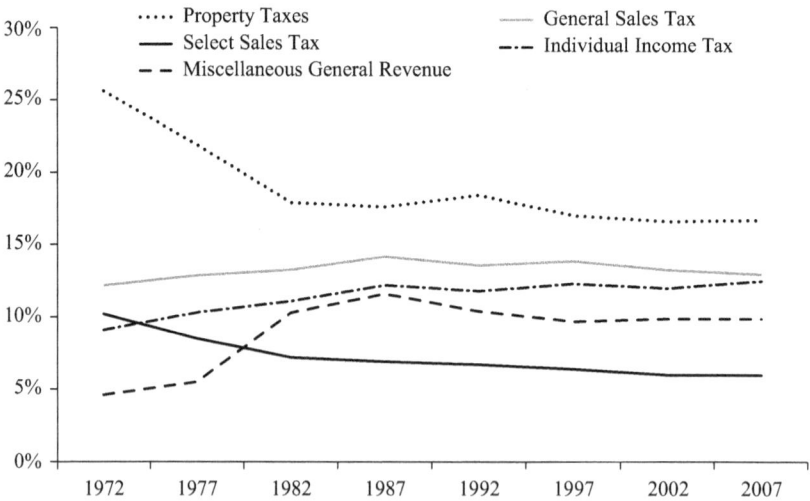

Figure 3.5 Sources of Local and State Revenue: Selected Years, 1972–2007 (in percentages)*

emerged for governments to generate money, many states' financial situation would have gone from bad to worse.

Fiscal Crisis and Prop. 13's Aftermath

Prop. 13 supporters downplayed the budget cuts it would cause, claiming reductions would not exceed 10 percent of the current budget (Bernstein 1978). They insisted that, by eliminating this 10 percent, government would be forced to eliminate waste and ax "non-vital" services. An implicit assumption here is that these non-vital services were racially stigmatized welfare programs (Gilens 1999; Neubeck and Cazenave 2001). Not only did most Californians agree with these sentiments, but most American voters did too. According to a national poll conducted by CBS News and *The New York Times*, 68 percent of voters said out-of-control welfare costs consumed a majority of local government revenues (Clymer 1978). The presumption here is faulty because property taxes have little to no relationship with federal spending. Excluding New York City, for example, 56 of the 57 largest cities in the U.S. allotted 4.1 percent of their local budgets to welfare in 1975. Nonetheless, when lies are repeated enough times, they can take on a life of their own and seem true. California's antitax poster child, Jarvis, and others in the movement, exploited these misperceptions. During a 1978 interview on "Meet the Press," for example, he argued that homeowners ought to finance police, fire protection, and the like—nothing else.

Even after the taxquake struck, a poll by *The LA Times* reported that 70 percent of California voters thought that Prop. 13 would cause no reduction in local services (*"Time"* 1978). They could not have been more wrong. News headlines across California said that the revolt had made beggars out of counties (see Figure 3.6). The legacy of Prop. 13 can be found in unfixed potholes, rarely open public libraries, closed-down hospitals or those that lack enough beds, overcrowded and run-down schools, downsized firehalls, and so on. Budgetary shortfalls required lawmakers to adopt a priority list, and decide which services to keep or do away with. Changes immediately discussed ranged broadly, from reducing staffing and hours across motor vehicle offices to the elimination of some departments to mass layoffs of state employees.

Employment Consequences

Lawmakers and experts warned voters of consequences before tax reform was passed. As Harry Bernstein (1978) of *The LA Times* reported, they estimated the 10 percent reduction Jarvis and others touted would translate into 120,000 lost government jobs. Others would experience drastic pay cuts. Once Prop. 13 did pass, Governor Jerry Brown (who was re-elected nearly three decades later and serves as California's current governor) performed damage control by freezing all hires of new state employees, which

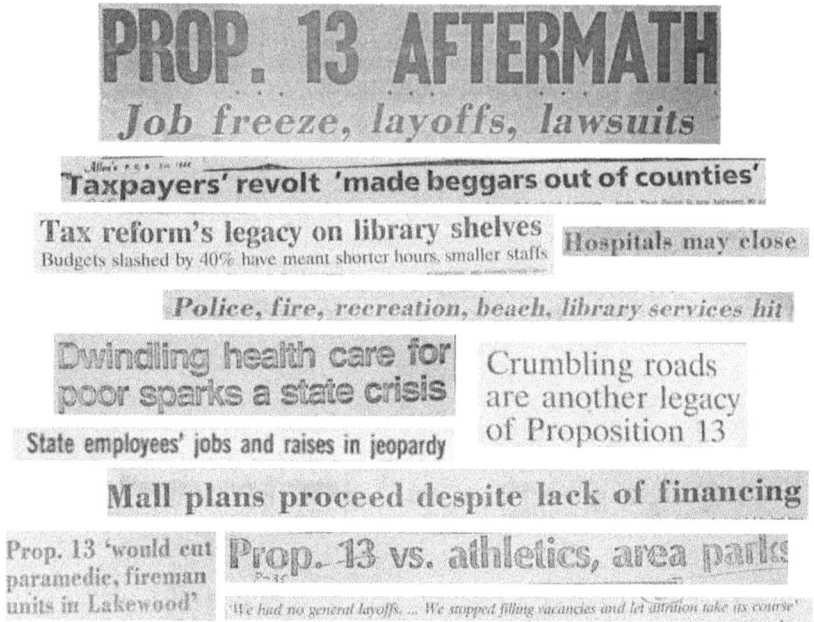

Figure 3.6 Local Headlines across California: General Consequences of Prop. 13

annually amounted to 12,000 jobs (*"Consumer Reports"* 1979). In Los Angeles County alone, city payroll was trimmed by 4,000 jobs over the next 10 years despite increased population (Will 1988).

Those who recently acquired niche occupations in the public sector, ones in which they had long been formally excluded (see also Steinberg 1981; Wilson 1997), would be the first let go. Maxine Waters, a representative in the state assembly, pleaded for local government officials to develop alternative ways of determining layoffs aside from seniority (*"Time"* 1978: 20). She knew that the "last hired, first fired" strategy would cause de facto racial consequences of mass layoffs. A report compiled by the Urban League estimated that Prop. 13 would reduce Los Angeles County's black workforce by 63 percent and its Latina/o workforce by 83 percent (*"The Independent"* 1978a). In the City of Los Angeles, Mayor Tom Bradley proposed layoffs for 8,300 city employees out of 49,000 (*"Consumer Reports"* 1979). Half of these would be trainees recently hired under the Comprehensive Employment Training Act, a federal program aimed at the unskilled unemployed— many of whom were black.

Healthcare Consequences

The problems created surpassed employment and extended into healthcare. As Prop. 13 dried up money spent on prenatal care, and California slipped down the rankings to 36th among states for infant mortality rate, experts predicted over 4,500 newborns would die before their first birthday in 1988 (Gray 1988). To be sure, this statistic cannot be attributed to property tax relief alone. Medical costs outpaced inflation. The uninsured population increased, as did the general population. You'd be a fool, claimed county managers across the state, to think Prop. 13 didn't contribute (Gray 1988). In Los Angeles County, the Chief Administrative Officer, Harry Hufford, expected to layoff 20,000 employees before Prop. 13 passed (*"Long Beach, California"* 1978b). Many of these were medical jobs, since about half the county's health budget derived from property taxes. These cuts would not be enough though. Hufford correctly anticipated some medical programs would be eliminated altogether, especially those not required by state law, like ambulatory care clinics and substance abuse centers.

El Cerrito Health Center, Long Beach General Hospital, and the Long Beach Health Department, all public services that catered to mostly minority communities, were already on an underfunded lifeline (*"The Independent"* 1978a). Prop. 13 essentially cut the line. These were the experiences of minority communities throughout the state, even though they were among the least likely to support it (*"The Independent"* 1978a). Compton, for example, rejected Prop. 13 by a margin of 78 to 22 percent. After the election, according to City Manager Allen J. Parker, its general budget went from $10.5 to $6.5 million and many public health services closed their doors. This left many folks with too pricey private healthcare, under-serviced healthcare, or none at all. Willie Brown, a representative in the state assembly, said the antitax crusaders did not explicitly endorse racism but their actions created the same result ("The Associated Press" 1978b).

Consequences from a County-Level View

In Contra Costa, an investigation by the *West County Times* estimated that one-third of local revenue derived from property taxes before Prop. 13 (Daigle 1988a). Afterwards local revenues nosedived from $82.6 to $37.4 million. Rather than downsize, recalls Contra Costa Auditor Donald Bouchet, vacancies were no longer filled and attrition took its course (Daigle 1988a). Small departments were consolidated into a general services one. Jail inmates were put to work, washing county cars once washed by public workers earning union wages. The county's $5 million library budget was slashed by 40 percent (Daigle 1988b). Full-time library positions declined to 137 from 192, and annual new book orders declined from one new book for every seven residents in 1978 to one for every 15 in 1987. Meanwhile, the budget for road maintenance declined by 88 percent in 10 years (Beaver and Daigle 1988). Because the money was never replaced, according to the county's Public Works Director Michael Walford, streets in unincorporated parts would revert to gravel in about 10 years. At Merrithew Memorial Hospital, bedpans were spread across the top floor to catch raindrops from a leaky ceiling (Daigle 1988c). Chronic shortages of foster homes and children's services, kids were sent to the county's overcrowded juvenile facility simply because there was no other place for them.

Much of the same occurred elsewhere in California. Alameda's budget plummeted from $142 to $47.8 million after Prop. 13 (Daigle 1988a). Immediately, 10 percent of the county's workforce was let go. About 45,000 sickly, and mostly poor, people were turned away from healthcare because there was no room to serve them (Cox 1988; Gray 1988). Monrovia saw its budget go from $5.5 to $1.75 million in one year (*"Time"* 1978: 16). This forced the city to let go 19 of its 185 employees, library staff reduced from six to two, and city council members lost their monthly stipends. Tehama County was the first of California's 58 counties to make headlines of going broke, closing its parks and relocating its single library to a vacant Safeway (Daigle 1988a). The public library in Oakley, operated by just one person, cut its hours to 17 per week (Daigle 1988b). Outside El Cerrito Library, kids lined the door before opening hours to get the books they wanted. Often, the good ones, like Nancy Drew, went fast because not enough were in circulation.

Schools Lick Their Fiscal Wounds in the Post-Prop. 13 ERA

Most Americans, let alone Californians, did not want to harm schools in the late 1970s. According to a 1979 CBS News poll, only 13 percent of the nation was willing to see a reduction in school funding (*"Consumer Reports"* 1979: 547). The bitter irony of Prop. 13, as well as the copycat legislation it shaped, is that it did just that. Schools are financed by local property taxes, so massive reductions to the latter will directly impact the former. Prop. 13 was one hell of a fiscal storm that wrecked California education (see Figure 3.7). School trustees of the Long Beach Unified School District vowed to eliminate 81 percent of administrative offices at its central office (*"The Independent"* 1978b), as well as lay off 1,330 teacher (*"Long Beach, California"* 1978c). Those left over would act as a skeleton crew capable of satisfying minimum requirements by law. Superintendent Vernon A. Hinze said that this was the trustees' way of showing the public that Prop. 13 was being taken seriously (*"The Independent"* 1978b).

The story of Long Beach was like many others throughout California. Los Angeles Unified School District Superintendent William Johnson said his schools would lose $700 million ("The Associated Press" 1978c). In Mt. Diablo, Associate Superintendent Lauren Fickett claimed her schools had a tough decision between cutting programs or maintenance (Weintraub 1988). She and her colleagues chose the latter, and the roofs quite literally began leaking across the district. Buildings, grounds, electrical, and sewage systems suffered as a result and showed signs of neglect. San Ramon Valley had one music teacher for every two schools in 1978, according to the *West County Times* (Weintraub 1988). Ten years later, the county had one for every 13 schools. Livermore shortened the school day from

Schools still licking their economic wounds from Proposition 13

L.A. school crisis anticipated

Crossing guards are fired

UC freezes some hiring, eyes tuition

'Prop. 13 didn't affect our books and paper. It affected ... the buildings, grounds, electrical systems, sewage systems. They were neglected'

Schools feel double pinch

Schools May Need State's Aid to Open on Schedule

Busing foe to support Prop. 9

$40 MILLION IN SCHOOL CUTS

Proposition 13's effect on schools 'devastating'

College District Is Double Loser

School administrative jobs slashed by 80%

Lack of summer school may delay would-be grads

Termination notices for 1,330 L.B. teachers

Figure 3.7 Local Headlines across California: Prop. 13's Consequences to Education

seven periods to six, and reduced the ratio of counselors to students from 1:375 to 1:450. For Richmond schools, it meant students were forbidden to write in workbooks and required to copy assignments on their own paper. It meant summer school was cancelled for Fontana schools (Mittelstaedt 1988). It meant average class sizes going from 26 to 35 students in the Redlands.

Schools in Richmond retreated from desegregation efforts and discontinued their busing program due to save money (Weintraub 1988). In Mt. Diablo, parents were required to pay for busing services that once were free. One year after the passage of Prop. 13, Governor Brown signed legislation calling for a special election. Atop the ballot were two items: a Constitutional Amendment banning "forced" busing and the "Spirit of 13" initiative known as Proposition 4. The former was an anti-desegregation measure against court-ordered busing, one that many voters hoped would persuade judges and politicians to rescind California's "student assignment plan." The latter represented the tax revolt's second wind and an extension of Prop. 13—one that placed spending limitations on local and state government (Bergholz 1979). Both measures passed with landslide approval, with 68 percent of voters supporting the antibusing amendment and 74 percent supporting Proposition 4. And for the moment, California had turned its back on interrelated matters of racial justice and education in favor of tax relief.

On many measures of education, California fell further behind most states in the union. Prop. 13 had prevented government from generating the necessary funds through property taxes. Whereas the state ranked 22nd in the nation for per pupil spending in 1978, it had slipped to 41st by 1982 (Will 1988). New York, for example, spent 49 percent more per pupil in 1977 (Mittelstaedt 1988). By 1987, it was spending 60 percent more than California. The golden state was $3.6 billion behind in building new schools by 1988. As for the old schools already in existence, they were neglected and under-maintained. Ten years after Prop. 13, the state had defunded its statewide summer school program, one designed to assist kids who need remedial help, from $120 to $40 million (Weintraub 1988). All these problems were not lost on Californians, though. Whereas tax relief was their chief concern in 1977, reports *The Sacramento Bee*, it was near the bottom a decade later (Cox 1988). Education had taken its place.

Californians applied growing pressure to state government for help, but Prop. 13 had placed lawmakers in a procedural straightjacket. It erected a procedural barrier that required a difficult-to-obtain two-thirds supermajority to pass tax increases. State government did what it could to alleviate fiscal crisis. According to *The Sun*, state aid accounted for 30 percent of school budgets before Prop. 13 (Mittelstaedt 1988). Ten years later, it accounted for 70 percent of school budgets. The money was not enough. Per pupil spending still declined at high rates (Will 1988). Many counties worked around Prop. 13, and like Ferguson, switched to piecemeal systems of generating revenue (Coin 1988; Lau 1988). These revenues derived from special fees and assessments, sales tax hikes, and other creative alternatives. At the state level, similar ingenuity was applied with the lottery. This implicit, voluntary tax became a major component of California's changing tax composition.

Lottery Formation in California

Chances of winning the lottery, reports journalist Molly Burrell (1978), drastically went up after June 8, 1978—the day voters weighed in on Prop. 13. How else would the state make up for the billions in property taxes that would no longer be collected? Predicting a landslide passage of property tax relief, policymakers like Robert Cline and Herschel Rosenthal, representatives of the state assembly, drafted a lottery proposal well in advance (Burrell 1978). They modelled it after the state of Illinois, and even attempted to entice others by handing out Illinois Lottery tickets the day of the vote ("The Associated Press" 1978d). Cline argued that a lottery could bring California at least double the revenues generated from the Illinois Lottery as well as other revenue sources like horse racing or liquor taxes ("The Associated Press" 1978d, 1978e). According to his estimates, the lottery was not a question of "if" but "when." He thought his proposal would be vetted through both chambers of California's legislature within weeks after

Prop. 13. Voters, in turn, would have the opportunity to voice their say in the upcoming November election ("The Associated Press" 1978e). Cline was right that California would eventually get its lottery, but his timing was wrong. A state lottery would not be approved for a few years.

Proposition 37, the referendum initiated a state lottery in California, passed comfortably by a 16-point spread, 58 to 42 percent, in the 1984 election (Geissinger 1984). Lottery tickets would be sold the following spring, and after the first year, an estimated $680 million (in 1984 currency), or 34 percent of all sales, was to be provided to ailing public schools. What took so long? The initial effects of Prop. 13 were not immediately felt because the state enjoyed a large surplus (Mittelstaedt 1988). California was able to temporarily plug its leaking lifeboat with this money for a few years. During the first two fiscal years alone, for example, the state provided more than $8 billion of "bailout" money to localities to make up for losses incurred from Prop. 13 ("*Consumer Reports*" 1979: 547). After the well went dry, and Californians became more conscious about their ailing school systems, lottery debates took a more serious tone.

In the county courthouse of San Joaquin, as reported in *The Stockton Record*, for example, directors of the County Taxpayers Association met to debrief the pros and cons of lottery adoption (Marsh 1982). Susan Harris, the association's vice president, insisted that the lottery could be one way to alleviate California's dire fiscal situation. Meanwhile opposition from Douglas Carter, the association's general manager, said that adopting the lottery would be like letting politicians off the hook. "[T]he lottery is the easy way out of dealing with Proposition 13 and financial priorities," he said. "It lets them (legislators) avoid making tough decisions" (Marsh 1982: 15). Over time, more Californians strayed toward Harris' position and away from Carter's. Editorials poured into local newspapers throughout California, offering the same question Mickey Gastwirth of Cypress (1978) asked when it was clear Prop. 13 would pass: "Are we too naïve or prudish not to adopt a state lottery?"

A lottery was not the end-all answer to fix California's finances, but it was a politically viable option within reach during the 1980s—a time when the state perhaps needed the money most. Politicians like Governor George Deukmejian ballyhooed the lottery as a godsend, boasting how it helped him deliver unprecedented amounts of new money into California's schools (Mittelstaedt 1988). Throughout the 1980s, for example, the lottery contributed about $500 million per year to schools. He attributed these contributions as part of a larger trend of reversing California's decline in per pupil spending. By 1988, per pupil spending was 25 percent above pre-Prop. 13 levels (Weintraub 1988). The subject was likely a sore one among educators. Like most other states, California's lottery money did not offer extra funding but simply substituted for other sources of revenue (Borg and Mason 1988, 1990).

Lingering Implications of Lottery Proliferation Across America

In short, the proliferation of state lotteries is a part of a broader trend in America's rearranging tax composition. This reconfiguration was caused, in part, by white-driven tax revolts. Once these rebellions culminated into numerous legislative reforms, state finance was forever changed. Since the traditional tax base of government has been eroded, policymakers cannot depend upon once reliable forms of revenue like property taxes. They no longer generate enough money to cover all the state provides. Confronted with massive budgetary shortfalls, governments have been compelled to entertain new ways to replace the missing revenue. Lotteries represent one viable alternative that helps make up the difference (Clotfelter and Cook 1989; Nibert 2000; Peppard 1987).

Looking to Figures 1 and 4, the expanding role of lotteries in state finance becomes evident. In 1972, only three lotteries had operated more than a year. It was this year that miscellaneous revenues, which include lottery proceeds among other sources of income, contributed only 4.6 percent of all local and state revenue. Over the next 15 years, however, lottery operations expanded nearly nine-fold from 3 to 26 states. During this same time span, miscellaneous revenues increased nearly 3 times to 11.6 percent. Expansion of lotteries continued during the next 15 years, as 13 additional states adopted their own. Despite this expansion, miscellaneous revenues remained relatively stable from 1987 on. They accounted for 9.9 percent of all local and state income in 2007, a figure that nearly doubles their share of the treasury 35 years prior. A total of 44 lotteries operated by the end of the 2000s, and all help state governments pay for public services.

What these trends indicate is national confirmation of case study observations made by Mary Borg and Paul Mason (1988, 1990). Lottery revenues tend to displace particular sources of state revenue, ones that tend to be more progressive in nature like property taxes. Displacing one form of taxation with another does not simply rid problems of fiscal solvency. Newspaper headlines about government expenditures exceeding revenues, hitting debt ceilings, driving over fiscal cliffs, and so on remain as commonplace today as they did 30–40 years ago (O'Connor [1973] 2002). What the emergence of modern state lotteries has done is fundamentally redefine the role and function of government. These regard matters of:

1) what is the general nature of lottery operations,
2) how much money do lotteries contribute to the state,
3) which public services do they finance, and
4) perhaps most importantly, from whom does this money come?

Unfortunately, these questions have not been fully answered by many analysts. Yet they have profound implications for how state monies are collected and public services are financed. It is these subjects that we turn our attention to next.

Notes

1 An earlier iteration of this chapter appeared as a journal article in *Georgetown Journal of Law & Modern Critical Race Perspectives* (see Henricks 2014).

2 While minority inclusion was met with resistance, it is worth noting that gains for people of color during the 1970s and 1980s were modest at best. Socioeconomic measures for virtually every indicator available show that whites remained overrepresented atop socially desired positions, while people of color, blacks in particular, were losing relative ground (Harris and McCullough [1973] 1998). Most poor blacks actually experienced declines in quality of life measures (Phillips 1990). Widespread institutional discrimination persisted in major institutions, from housing to education to employment and so on, ensuring that exclusion remained central experiences for people of color throughout America (Pinkney 1984).

3 For many readers, the historical review we offer should resonate with modern political movements so much that it seems like déjà vu. Participants of contemporary Tea Party Movements, for example, deploy narratives similar to those observed during the late 1970s and 1980s. Members of both revolts connect taxation to exploitation and a loss of personal freedom. See Jeffrey Kidder and Isaac William Martin (2012) for a thorough analysis of these historical continuities and the moral politics of contemporary tax discourse.

4 We should qualify that not all racially exclusive opportunities sponsored by government have resulted in white backlash. When federal "white wealthfare" subsidized homeownership opportunities and exacerbated segregation to unforeseen levels (see Oliver and Shapiro [1995] 2006), whites across the nation did not take to the streets in outrage and protest. These policies were never subject to the politics of racial inequality (Quadagno 1994). Instead, they were framed as sound economic policy (Katznelson 2005). And many whites benefitted from them. FHA- and VA-sponsored programs—ones that sponsored low-interest loans, expanded loan amortization, and guaranteed mortgages—assisted nearly 27 million white households migrate from central urban areas to racially homogeneous suburbs between the 1930s and 1960s (Massey and Denton 1993). By conservative estimates, this solidified a newly formed white middle class by enabling them to amass more than $100 million in unprecedented equity (Massey and Denton 1993).

5 To frame Latinas/os, like those of Mexican descent, as foreigners exemplifies a case of historical amnesia. After all, many members of this group have origins in American territory that predate European colonization and U.S. annexation, yet they are often deemed strangers in their own land (Takaki 1993).

6 These sentiments are not restricted to a high-profile Harvard academic like Huntington. Various researchers (e.g., Kefelas 2003; Kidder and Martin 2012; Wilson and Taub 2006) show that many whites share these views. In an interview conducted by Kidder and Martin (2012) for example, one research participant commented: "[W]e throw away millions and billions of dollars a year on health care for people that don't pay any taxes, aren't even citizens. And, it's not just the health care, it's other things they get. They get schooling; they get housing. And, now they're trying to dip into the social security, which they've never paid a dime into, all these millions of illegals" (p. 133).

7 Whites of all class positions gain from Latinas/os' subordination, especially those without citizenry. In his work on undocumented Mexican laborers, Nicholas de Genova (2005) describes the consequences of living with the never-ending threat of deportability. It renders members of this group in a perpetual position of vulnerability. Due to the fear of deportation, many accept harsh labor conditions and pay that is below minimum wage without resistance. Keeping the

group stigmatized as "an immigrant problem" serves capitalist interests because it ensures non-negotiable, low labor costs. It also benefits lower- and middle-class whites by reducing consumer prices.

8 Though the analytic focus here is drawn to Reagan, such racial rhetoric is not exclusive to the Republican Party. The language offered here by Reagan in many ways aptly foreshadows the same discursive maneuvers used by later Presidents George H.W. Bush, Bill Clinton, George W. Bush, and Barack Obama. It is further worth noting that these rhetorical devices are not merely political rhetoric, but they represent elements of the dominant ideology most everyone subscribes (Bonilla-Silva 2001).

9 Issued by the Office of Management and Budget, these data derive from a collection of budgetary documents issued by presidential administrations with regard to how the federal government fiscally operates from year to year.

10 Recent examples of similar tax policy include "the Bush Tax Cuts." Signed into law by President George W. Bush, these pieces of legislation are the Economic Growth and Tax Relief Reconciliation Act of 2001 and Jobs and Growth Tax Relief Reconciliation Act of 2003. It is further worth noting that these laws were extended under President Barack Obama in the Tax Relief, Unemployment Insurance Reauthorization, and Job Creation Act of 2010 and American Taxpayer Relief Act of 2012.

11 Agricultural laborers and domestic servants, two occupations where black people were relegated and concentrated, were excluded from benefits by a Southern-controlled Congress even though these workers paid taxes (Quadagno 1988). Many of these restrictive provisions were slow to expand and did not incorporate agricultural laborers and domestic servants until 1976. Similar racial exclusions of Social Security persist to the present day. For undocumented Latinas/os, many pay Social Security taxes for services they will never receive due to their noncitizen status. In 2005, for example, the Social Security Administration identified thousands of unauthorized workers who contributed US$7 billion that could not be credited properly to the appropriate beneficiaries (Porter 2005). Despite stereotypical tropes that undocumented Latinas/os drain social services, their Social Security contributions show that quite the opposite is true. They are contributing to a program that may never return anything to them.

12 "Aid to Dependent Children" and "Aid to Families with Dependent Children" are the same federal program. Under President John F. Kennedy's Administration in 1962, the name changed to include the words "families with" out of racialized concerns that the program discouraged marriage (Brown 1999). Under President Bill Clinton's Administration in 1996, the program became replaced by the more restrictive program entitled "Temporary Assistance for Needy Families" (Neubeck and Cazenave 2001).

13 It is further worth noting that even the Great Society did not overturn the fiscal conservatism found in FDR's New Deal policies. Brown (1999) writes: "In the 1960s, as in the 1930s, liberal aspirations were mediated by race and money. But whereas southern defense of Jim Crow and labor-market discrimination were the underside of Roosevelt's fiscally circumscribed social policies, in the 1960s federal tax and budget policy formed the crucible in which Kennedy's and Johnson's responses to America's racial crisis were forged. Neither Johnson nor Kennedy set out to reshape the relationship between the public and private sectors, and both men designed their policies and made budget decisions so as to preclude extensive intervention in private labor markets and to avoid a greatly expanded public sector" (p. 208).

14 According to Los Angeles County Supervisor Ed Edelman, property taxes would be reduced by $7 billion but only $2 billion of these savings would go to homeowners ("Long Beach, California" 1978a). The remainder would benefit commercial,

industrial, and apartment owners. In Los Angeles County, the owner of a $60,000 home would see her or his tax bill decrease by $1,530 under Prop. 13. The tax reduction for THUMS Long Beach Co., a field contractor formed by Exxon, Mobil, Shell, Texaco, and Union, would drop from $11.8 to 5.6 million.

15 After the passage of Prop. 13 in California, Myers (2009) finds that white homeowners enjoy greater tax savings than their minority counterparts; specifically compared to Asians, blacks, and Latinas/os. Meanwhile Martin and Beck (Forthcoming) complete a national-level study that shows white homeowners disproportionately benefit from tax limitation amendments (see also Goodman 2006). According to their models, white homeowners accrue $36.8 billion in property tax savings as a result of property tax limitations. About $3 billion of this figure represents excess savings over what would accrue if tax relief with distributed across racial groups in an unbiased fashion.

16 It is further worth noting another instance of the overlapping convolution between property tax revolts and white backlash. Even the "Yes on 13 Committee," which was put together by Jarvis in 1978 with the explicit purpose to raise revenue, had its media and advertising operations headed up by Roland Vincent. Prior to this commitment, Vincent had spearheaded the 1976 presidential bid in California of former Alabama Governor, and staunch segregationist, George Wallace (Smith 1999).

4 Dissecting the Evolution of Lotteries and Their Racial Implications[1]

> "I have never played the lottery in my life and never will. Voltaire described lotteries as a tax on stupidity. More specifically, I think, on innumeracy."
>
> ~Daniel Tammet[2]

According to National Geographic (2005), the odds of being struck by lightning in a person's lifetime are 1:3000. On the other hand, the odds of winning the largest jackpot to date in the United States are 1:176,000,000 (Shur 2012). On March 30, 2012, three winning tickets allowed residents of Illinois, Kansas, and Maryland to split a Mega Millions prize amounting to $656 million. Doing the math, this means that the likelihood of getting struck by lightning is nearly 58,667 times greater than hitting this particular jackpot. Such a figure looms so large that for many it is a challenge to grasp just what it means in practical terms.

To illustrate just how absurd odds like these are, *The Huffington Post* (2012) posted an article that listed 15 other occurrences that are more likely to happen than winning the lottery. It included the following:

1 Dating a Supermodel (1:88,000)
2 Becoming President (1:10,000,000)
3 Becoming a movie star (1:1,505,000)
4 Picking a perfect NCAA bracket (1:13,460,000)
5 Birthing identical quadruplets (1:13,000,000)
6 Becoming an astronaut (1:12,100,000)
7 Dying by a hornet (1:6,100,000)
8 Dying from being left-handed (1:4,400,000)
9 Drowning in a bathtub (1:840,000)
10 Getting a royal flush in a first hand of poker (1:649,740)
11 Being murdered (1:18,000)
12 Dying in an asteroid apocalypse (1:12,500)
13 Finding a four leaf clover (1:10,000)
14 Losing an appendage to a chainsaw (1:4,464)
15 Be an author who writes a *New York Times* bestseller (1:220)[3]

And if this list does not illustrate just how unlikely it is to win one of those seemingly unreal jackpots, one lottery insider puts it into perspective. In an interview with CNN, the founder of lotterypost.com, Todd Northrop, told one reporter that winning record-level jackpots of Mega Millions "is akin to getting struck by lightning at the same time you're being eaten by a shark" (Hanna and Johnston 2013: ¶ 16). These statistics mean little to the individual lottery player, though. As Alan J. Karcher (1989) points out, a past television commercial sponsored by the Michigan Lottery suggests as much. In the commercial, one cynic argues he has better odds of being struck by lightning than winning the lottery, and then seconds later, he is hit by a lightning bolt. Flabbergasted, the man says: "One ticket, please" (Karcher 1989: 83).

Few other social phenomena can generate such media frenzies, long lines at ticket counters, and even twitter shout-outs from the general public. It is as though lotteries have assumed a commonplace role, one that is comparable to a favorite leisure activity like following sports or watching movies. Perhaps Americans cannot help but indulge in fantasies of what could be. Lottery themed entertainment like the motion picture *It Could Happen to You* or TLC's television show *The Lottery Changed My Life* only add fuel to this fire. And in one news article after another, journalists report storybook dreams as to what those unlikely winners would do with the money. Inevitably, it is some variation of "We're going to Disneyland," "I'm paying off the house," or "Tell my boss to shove it." Stories of "lottomania" have gained a foothold in everyday conversation throughout America. When jackpots reach into the hundreds of millions, it seems that everyone becomes a player.

Where Does Lottery Money Go? Down to the Penny

State lotteries are a big business, so much so that they rank among the highest in gross sales among all U.S. businesses (Karcher 1992). Consider the words of satirist John Oliver (2014) from his show *Last Week Tonight*:

> $68 billion [in 2013 lottery sales], that's more than Americans spent last year on movie tickets, music, porn, the NFL, Major League Baseball, and video games combined . . . which means Americans basically spent more on the lottery than they spent on America
>
> (Episode 24, November 9).

One poll reports that about half of American adults purchased a lottery ticket within the past year (Jones 2008). Lottery sales do not compare to the levels of revenue generated by income or sales taxes, but this does not mean they are insignificant. Putting per capita lottery sales into perspective, they surpass the typical amount of money spent on prescription drugs, medical supplies, and reading materials (Clotfelter and Cook 1989).

By our own estimates of data derived from the U.S. Census Bureau's 2011 State Government Finances dataset, per capita sales for the 222 million persons legally eligible to purchase a lottery ticket in 2011 were about $247.[4] In the highest grossing states of per capita sales, Massachusetts peaked the charts at $813 worth of lottery tickets. Delaware followed in second with $652; meanwhile, Rhode Island landed in third at $610. (See Figure 4.1 for a glimpse of how uneven lottery purchases are across states; it overviews the five states with the highest and lowest per capita sales.) Statistics like these show that lotteries are among America's most popular form of gambling (Gillespie 1999).

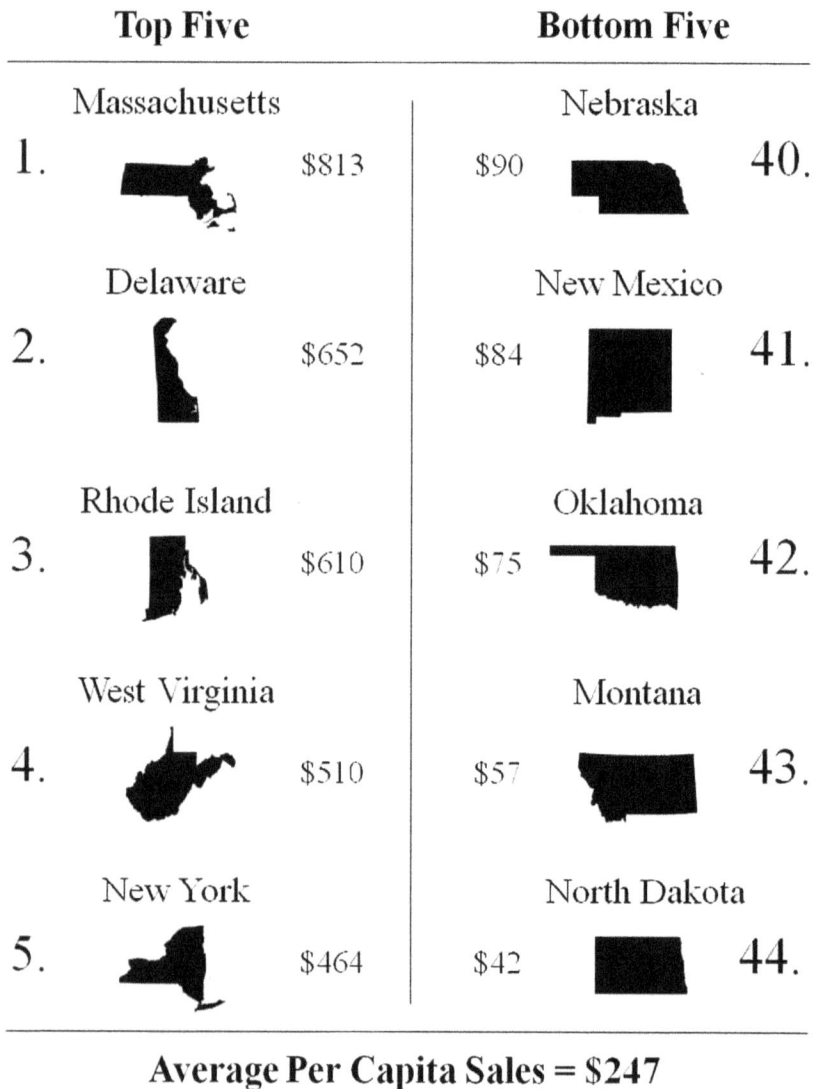

Top Five

Massachusetts

1. $813

Delaware

2. $652

Rhode Island

3. $610

West Virginia

4. $510

New York

5. $464

Bottom Five

Nebraska

$90   40.

New Mexico

$84   41.

Oklahoma

$75   42.

Montana

$57   43.

North Dakota

$42   44.

Average Per Capita Sales = $247

Figure 4.1 The Five Highest and Lowest States of Per Capita Lottery Sales, Fiscal Year 2011

Another way of measuring the popularity of the lottery is to look at the national sales trends (see Figure 4.2). Since the first modern one was initiated in New Hampshire, lotteries have gradually expanded in scope. Inflation held constant, players spent an estimated $2 billion on lottery tickets in 1973, $18 billion in 1987, and $34 billion in 1997 (Clotfelter et al. 1999). In 2011 alone, gross lottery sales surpassed $55 billion in total revenue ("U.S. Census Bureau" 2011a). These sales ranged broadly across different states, of course. The New York Lottery accounted for nearly about $7 billion, or 13 percent, of all national sales in 2011; meanwhile, the North Dakota Lottery sold about $22 million. Still, the average lottery state in America fell well in between these extremes and generated about $1.3 billion in sales. (See Tables A.1 and A.2 of Appendix A for a full listing of each state's gross sales for fiscal year 2011, as well as descriptive information like total prize winnings, administrative costs, and proceeds transferred to public services, among other items.) So where does all this money go?

Lottery revenues are redistributed along three general categories: operations, prize winnings, and public finance (see Figure 4.3). Each of these is discussed in greater detail below, but first we offer a national overview of lottery budgets. About 5 percent of all lottery money, or $2.7 billion, is spent on day-to-day expenses of running the operation. These include commissions to retail outlets as well as other costs like the creation and marketing of lottery products. Once these costs are covered, well over half the revenues are returned to players in the form of prize winnings. In 2011, this figure represented 61.6 percent, or $33.9 billion, of all lottery revenues. The

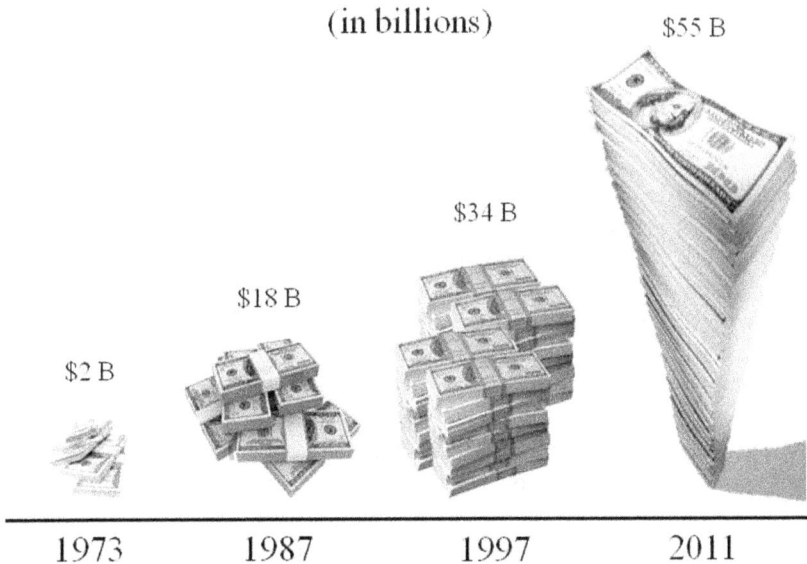

(in billions) $55 B

$34 B

$18 B

$2 B

| 1973 | 1987 | 1997 | 2011 |

Figure 4.2 Select Years of Gross Lottery Sales Across the United States*

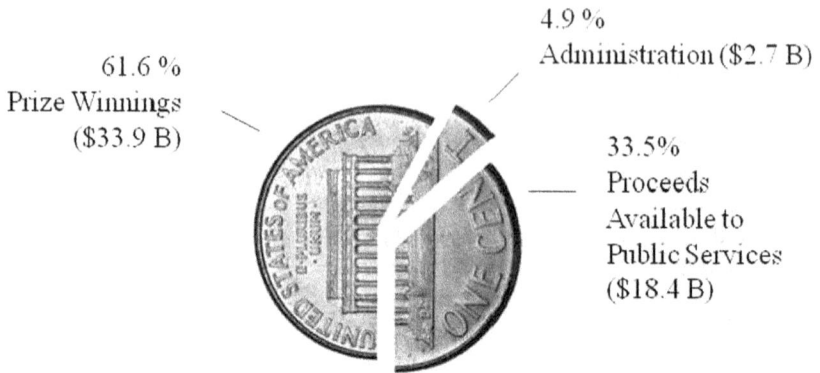

4.9 %
Administration ($2.7 B)

61.6 %
Prize Winnings
($33.9 B)

33.5%
Proceeds
Available to
Public Services
($18.4 B)

Figure 4.3 National Breakdown of State Lottery Expenditures, Fiscal Year 2011*

remainder of lottery sales is leftover for state finance. For fiscal year 2011, this means that approximately $18.4 billion was left over for states that use this money for about every public service imaginable.

Operations: How Do State Lottery Machines Work in America?

By our own estimates, the average lottery in 2011 cost 5.8 percent of a state's total sales. Of course some states ran their lottery above this standard while others ran it below, but this variation did not necessarily result from disparities in bureaucratic functionality. State lotteries follow an economy of scale (see Figure 4.4), meaning that some states spend more money on operating costs than do others (Clotfelter and Cook 1989). This is because the expenses for running a state lottery are, relatively speaking, a fixed cost. States that sell high volumes of tickets will, by default, run a more efficient lottery than states that do not. A majority of the most populous states ran their lottery at an efficient cost of 4.4 percent of total sales in 2011; meanwhile, it took nearly 10 percent or more of total sales to operate lotteries in less populated states. One can imagine the cost advantage of daily lottery operation this presents to densely populated states like California and New York, compared to smaller scale states like North Dakota or Montana. Nonetheless, these daily operations cannot solely be carried out by states on their own.

Though states may own a monopoly on lottery operations, and even introduce a new consumer product where there once was none, they cannot supply lottery products by themselves (Karcher 1989). Independent state agencies are created to carry through daily lottery operations, with an oversight committee and director typically being appointed by the governor. Legislatures grant these agencies exclusive rights to sell lottery tickets, but

Total Operating Costs (in dollars)

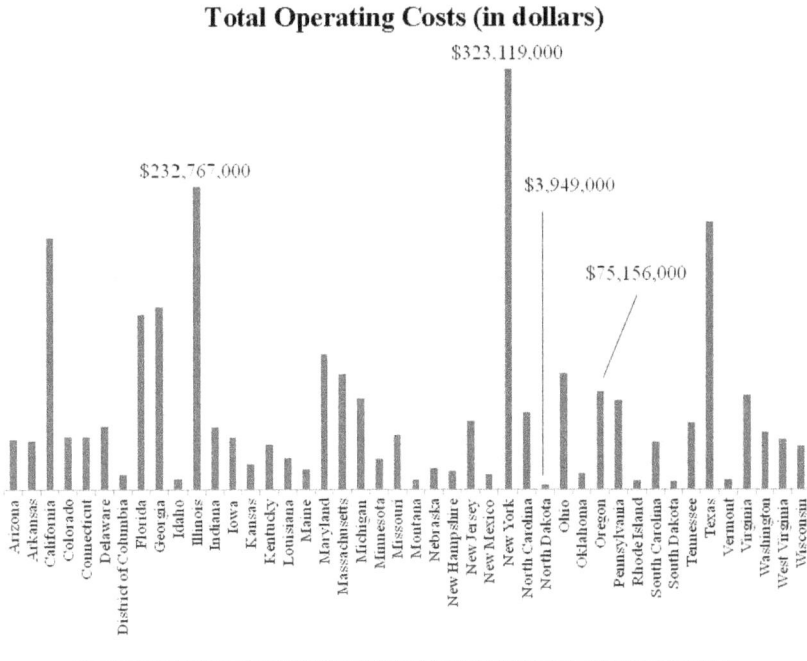

Figure 4.4 A State-by-State Overview of Lottery Operating Costs, Fiscal Year 2011*

these agencies do not have the legal authority to produce these commodities and they do not directly sell lottery products to the public. Instead, their activities are entrenched within a vast network of product developers and vendors. The product developers include companies, like Scientific Games Corporation,[5] that ultimately provide state lottery agencies with game design, marketing advice, and the actual tickets sold by vendors. To be able to sell these tickets, retailers must be granted a license by the state. Acting as a mediator, retailers like gas stations, grocery markets, and liquor stores, among others, are the ones that process monetary transactions between the state and lottery players. They receive small but significant returns for their efforts, which usually translate into less 5 percent of all lottery sales, according to census records. Of course what these vendors are selling has evolved tremendously over the years, as lottery tickets can have many faces.

Evolving Lottery Games and Their Many Faces

Virtually all lotteries in the United States follow a simple formula. They provide players with the opportunity of buying randomized opportunities to win prizes. These prizes can range broadly. Some might translate into sums of cold, hard cash, while others could be a voucher or coupon that can be exchanged for more lottery tickets. That said, modern lotteries have expanded this simple formula into four general lottery products: passive drawings, scratch-off games, numbers, and lotto (Borg et al. 1991; Clotfelter and Cook 1989). These four types of games represent an evolution in consumer demand and what lottery products have "worked" best, by which we mean they have bolstered lotteries in their seemingly endless pursuit of fattening the bottom line. Each of these lottery products is unique in its own way.

PASSIVE SWEEPSTAKES

The first modern state lottery came about in New Hampshire in 1964, but its operation was comparable to most colonial American lotteries (Clotfelter and Cook 1989). Its game of choice was the passive drawing. Essentially, it was a sweepstakes raffle, in which a stub from each ticket was stripped and placed into a drum and a winner was drawn from all the tickets purchased (Shaw 2000). The game was a proven success in New Hampshire during its first year, helping the state generate $58.6 million in sales. This standard could not withstand the test of time, though. After the first year of operation, America's first modern lottery experienced a five-year wane in sales. Some lottery scholars like Clotfelter and Cook (1989) have pointed to the general nature of passive drawings as the root of the problem.

New Hampshire's drawings were held infrequently during the operation's beginning, with winners being announced only about two times a year (Borg et al.1991; Vyse [1997] 2014). This setup killed momentum, prevented opportunity to generate buzz, and preemptively deflated any sustained following. It was as though lottery players got bored with passive drawings. Perhaps New York learned from some of these mistakes. When its representatives created the second modern state lottery in 1967, they, too, had their own version of passive drawings but they boosted the frequency of drawing to once per month (Blakey 1979; Borg et al. 1991). New Jersey followed in these footsteps, too, once legislators had initiated their own state lottery in 1971. Lottery operators there held weekly and, eventually, daily drawings (Nibert 2000). Still, many early state lotteries experienced lackluster sales and were not an overnight success. This caused many in the industry to take risks with their operations, often through modifying or adding items to their product line (Vyse [1997] 2014). Really, they had no choice.

Passive drawings more or less became obsolete by the 1980s, but techno-logical innovations in printing allowed for a new lottery breakthrough in "scratch-off" tickets (Borg et al. 1991; Clotfelter and Cook 1989). Devel-oped by John Koza of Scientific Games, a prominent private business in the gaming industry, tickets for these games are printed with a set of pre-determined numbers, letters, or symbols hidden from plain view by vinyl covering. Players then rub off this covering to determine whether their ticket possesses a certain combination of characters. If the combination is right, then those tickets are "instant" winners. These games offer a level of engagement, however simplistic, that is absent from passive drawings.

With scratch-off tickets, no longer is it necessary to play the anticlimactic "waiting game" like in the early lottery days of New Hampshire, where players might wait four, five, or six months to hear results. The immedi-acy of scratch-off games allows players to find out for themselves whether they hold winning or losing tickets. And unlike passive drawing lotteries, scratch-off players have higher odds of winning lower payments that can be cashed in immediately at approved lottery vendors (Hansen 1995; Price and Novak 1999). The success of these games, argues Koza, lies in their ability to entertain players or at least not to bore them (Stevenson 1977). Espe-cially for winners, scratch-off games allow players a type of suspense that compares to other joys in life, such as opening the mailbox during holiday season, discovering a good parking spot, or checking Facebook comments on your birthday. All state lotteries had some version of these games by 1982 (Clotfelter and Cook 1989).

DAILY NUMBERS GAMES

Alongside the introduction of scratch-off games came daily numbers games. These games were not original, though. In many ways, they are carbon cop-ies of illegal numbers games that were long been played in urban areas like Chicago and New York (see Drake and Cayton 1967, [1945] 1993). When state lotteries introduced these games, they were able to capitalize off an already-established consumer base (Haller 1979). The timing was perfect. These games boosted sales in a number of states where political commitments to keep a lottery stood in question. Arguably, it was these numbers games that silenced lottery critics and revealed lotteries' true revenue-generating potential (Clotfelter and Cook 1989). A perfect example can be found with the Illinois Lottery, which is discussed at length in the next chapter.

Table 4.1 Bets on Three-Digit Numbers Games and Their Corresponding Payouts*

Type of Bet		Description of Bet	Odds of Winning	Illustrative Bet	Examples of Winning Combos	Typical Payoff
Straight		Three digits in exact order	1:100,000	246	246	$500
Box						
	3-Way	Two identical digits in any order	1:333	122	122, 212, 221	167
	6-Way	Three digits in any order	1:167	123	123, 132, 213, 231, 312, 321	83
Front Pair		First two digits in exact order	1:100	12X	120, 121, 122, 123, 124, 125, 126, 127, 128, 129	50
Back Pair		Last two digits in exact order	1:100	X12	012, 112, 212, 312, 412, 512, 612, 712, 812, 912	50

Source: Adapted from Clotfelter and Cook (1989).

*   All bets are assumed to be $1.

As the name of this "new" lottery product implies, numbers games offer players the opportunity to select their own numbers. This illogical logic allows some to believe that if certain skills are developed, then the jackpots are theirs for the taking (Borg et al. 1991; Clotfelter and Cook 1989; Guryan and Kearney 2008). "[P]layers feel like they have some control," argue Borg et al. (1991), "over their chance of winning since they choose their own numbers" (p. 7). Most often, players pick three or four digits, and if drawn, they receive a payout. These payouts range, of course, depending on the type of numbers game, how many digits were correctly guessed, and the order in which they were guessed. (See Table 4.1 for an overview on bets for three-digit numbers games and their payouts.) Generally speaking, payouts for these games are considerably larger than instant games but significantly smaller than passive drawings (Nibert 2000). Unlike passive drawings, though, numbers are typically announced several times a week if not every day.

THE LOTTO

The most recent, and successful, product introduced by state lotteries is "the lotto." In fact, no other lottery game, or perhaps gambling games in general, rival the money it has generated. Following a logic that synthesizes numbers games with bingo, keno (a typical casino game), and other features of illegal numbers games, the lotto allows players to pick their own numbers but the range of winning combinations ranges much more broadly (Clotfelter and Cook 1989). This decreases the odds of winning, but when someone does, these lotto jackpots often dwarf the size of prizes offered by scratch-off tickets and numbers games combined. Consider Mega Millions, for example. It is a version of the lotto that requires players to choose six numbers from 1 to 75 (Lazarus 2013).[6] With this particular variation, the odds of winning the jackpot are about 1 to 259 million. That said, these typical jackpots are often in the hundreds of millions range.

Two features that make the lotto unique from other lottery games are that it is played across states and has a jackpot that accumulates over time. Operators of lottery states have come to realize that there is more money to be made through collaboration rather than independence (Borg et al. 1991; Nibert 2000). Especially for smaller states, jackpots can only grow so big, so fast because their sales growth is constrained by finite consumer bases. Interstate lotteries like Powerball or Mega Millions get rid of this problem. They expand the base of potential lottery players, and in the process, exponentially boost how much money can be generated. When no winner is drawn in these games, prize winnings roll over until a winner is selected. One can imagine the type of snowball effect this setup can have. Compound that fact with extremely low odds of winning, and jackpots can soar into the $400, 500, and 600 million range in a short amount of time. And when this occurs, it is a winning combination for broader consumer base and players buying even more tickets (Oster 2004).

Prize Winnings: Is the Lottery a Sucker's Bet?

It is no secret that the odds are stacked when it comes to the probability of winning the lottery, but just how much of a losing bet are they? Earlier we compared the odds of winning a multi-state lottery jackpot of $400 million or more to being struck by lightning while being eaten by a shark. As blunt as this analogy is, it does not illustrate how these odds unravel over the long haul. To give an idea of what these odds look like, Clotfelter and Cook (1989) offer simple computer simulations of 1,000 hypothetical lottery players (see Table 4.2). These players place bets on three-digit numbers games over a five-year period. A random-number generator selects "winners" of these hypothetical bets, which inevitably follow two common betting patterns. These patterns do not represent actual lottery players, but they are consistent with much survey data on lottery play.

The first betting pattern ("Pattern A") consists of daily bets of $1 dollar on a straight three-digit number and $1 on a six-way box. This assumes a $500 payout for an "exact" match on the former bet, and $80 payout for an "any-order," three-digit match on the latter. Over five years, these players would have bet $3,120. Only two percent of them, however, would have cleared a net gain. The remaining 98 percent would have lost money.

Table 4.2 How Much of a Losing Bet Is the Lottery? 1,000 Simulations of Betting
        Patterns on a Three-Digit Numbers Game over Five Years

	Betting Patterns*	
	A	B
Amount Wagered	$3,120	$520
Percent of Simulations with a Net Gain	2.0%	17.6%
Largest Net Gain	$1,520	$855
Largest Net Loss	–$2,960	–$520
Percentage of Simulations where Over Half Wager Lost	58.1%	49.9%

Source: Adapted from Clotfelter and Cook (1989).

* *The betting patterns are as follows:*
A: *$1 a day on a straight bet and $1 a day on a six-way box six days per week.*
B: *$1.50 per week on a three-way box and 50 cents per week on a front pair.*

Of the luckiest of lucky players, the largest payout would have amounted
to $1,520. As for the unluckiest of the unlucky, the largest loss would have
been $2,960. In total, about 58.1 percent of all trial players would have lost
half or more of their bets.

The second betting pattern ("Pattern B") is one that is considerably more
modest and infrequent. It consisted of betting $2 per week, with $1.50 on
a three-way box and $.50 on a front pair. This assumes a $250 payout on
the former bet, and $25 on the latter. Bets made like this over five years
would have amounted to $520 on lottery tickets. Payoffs in this simulation
are much greater than the previous betting pattern, with 17.6 percent of
all trial bets amounting to some sort of net gain. Of course, these gains do
not compare in magnitude, though. The luckiest of the lucky would have
won $855, while the unluckiest of the unlucky would have lost $520. And
49.9 percent of all trial players would have lost half or more of their bets.
Betting patterns like Pattern B amounted to higher odds of winning lower
jackpots compared to Pattern A, but still do not alter the fact that "the
house always wins."

*How Much Do Lotteries Give Back? A State-by-State Overview
of Prize Winnings*

The key to successful lottery design is meeting an adequate, if not delicate,
balance between developing a lottery that sustains high levels of participation and operating a lottery in order to generate revenue for already worn
thin treasuries. Compared to other forms of gambling, lotteries do not
pay out nearly as much. Whereas most states, for example, require about
80 percent of all wagers to be returned at horse races (Benson 1991), our
own analysis shows that the average lottery state returned only 57.9 percent

Top Payout State

Massachusetts

Total Payout: $3.2 B

Payouts as a Percent
of Gross Sales: 76.8 %

Bottom Payout State

West Virginia

Total Payout: $120 M

Payouts as a Percent
of Gross Sales: 16.2 %

Summary Statistics of Total Operating Costs

	Absolute Value of Payouts	*Payouts as Percent of Gross Revenue*
Mean	$ 770,116,577	57.9 %
Median	327,085,000	62.5
Minimum	119,410,000	16.2
Maximum	3,967,672,000	76.8
Quartile Distribution		
25	127,478,000	56.1
50	327,085,000	62.5
75	1,283,438,750	66.3
N		44

Figure 4.5 A National Overview of State Lottery Prize Winnings, Fiscal Year 2011*

of lottery sales back to the players themselves through prize winnings. This is about $770 million in absolute terms. (See Figure 4.5 for a general overview.) Of course, the more money that is returned to players, the less there is for the state.

Some states keep very large portions of lottery sales to themselves, as evidenced by low payout rates. In fact, five states returned well under half of all lottery revenues during 2011. These included West Virginia (16.2 percent), Delaware (16.8 percent), South Dakota (19.3 percent), Oregon (24.9 percent), and Rhode Island (28.2). On the other extreme stands Massachusetts, one of the highest grossing lotteries in the union. It stood second only to New York despite its relatively small population size, at nearly $4.2 billion in sales for 2011 alone. This is no anomaly. "The bay state" consistently ranks above other states when it comes to generated revenues (Clotfelter and Cook 1989). Part of the reason sales do so well in Massachusetts is that payout rates stand at 76.8 percent. The players' odds are so good it keeps a steady stream of ticket purchases pouring in.

The Lottery Leftovers: Money for State Finance

If you turn to the literature to learn how lottery revenues are spent across the country, mostly inconclusive answers will be found. This is because the question has long been overlooked by lottery scholars (Borg, Mason, and Shapiro 1991; Henricks 2014). Some recent scholarship diverts from this trend, but most studies are limited to case studies of particular states or large metropolitan areas (e.g. Borg et al. 1991; Henricks 2014; McCrary and Palvak 2002; Stranahan and Borg 2004). Few studies have yet to show how lottery revenues are spent on a national scale. Such an omission is problematic given the broader historical trends of state finance. Lottery revenues have injected new cash flows into state treasuries that can no longer depend upon traditional sources of revenue. Along the way, they have assumed larger roles in state finance and helped reconfigure the financial mechanisms that make public services possible. In fact, each lottery dollar spent represents a dollar that may have otherwise come from some other tax revenue stream.

Lotteries have proliferated across the nation on the promise that proceeds would be directed toward noteworthy causes, but these causes vary tremendously from state to state. In the early years, most states allocated lottery proceeds to an all-purpose fund (Clotfelter and Cook 1989). Once this money is placed here, it becomes part of a general pool of tax money from other sources like motor vehicle taxes and federal subsidies, among others. State legislatures are empowered with great discretion on how to spend this money, so that lottery revenues can be distributed according to their perceptions of the state's most pressing needs. This means that lottery expenditures can vary over time, but frequently they do not. Variation in spending from year to year is subtle by most measures. If unearmarked lottery money is dispersed to public education one year, for example, the odds are that similar spending patterns will occur the following year. For this reason, a simple analysis of how lottery money is spent in 2011 paints a reliable picture of how this process works.

A number of states still allocate their lottery revenues to an all-purpose fund, 17 to be exact, but most have moved in the direction of earmarking lottery funds for specific causes. As of 2011, 33 lotteries transferred the majority of their proceeds to earmarked public services. When states take this route, the process operates similar to how excise taxes for gasoline work. A predetermined percentage is reserved for some designated public service. Whereas gasoline excise taxes tend to go toward services like road construction and maintenance, lottery proceeds are often earmarked for a much broader range of public services like education, senior services, and environmental conservation.

Often, the purpose of earmarking is to help bolster the lottery's general appeal. Consider the words of Edward J. Powers (1983), for example, the New Hampshire Lottery's first director:

> It seems preferable from the lottery viewpoint to earmark the funds for a special purpose. By doing this, the benefits derived can be more readily measured and recognized. For example, it is very impressive to read

in the annual report of the Pennsylvania Lottery of the $267 million distributed tax rebates and free transportation for senior citizens, with appropriate photographs

(p. 28).

Such tactics can readily be seen at a couple strokes of the keyboard and a few clicks of a mouse in the information age. On many states' websites, like Arizona's and New Hampshire's (see Figure 4.6), pictures of lottery beneficiaries are placed front and center under headlines like "how the money helps" or "where the money goes." Of course one of the recurring patterns of these promotional messages is stressing the exact dollar amounts of how much lottery money was returned to the people through public services.

As mentioned above, the lottery generated well over $18 billion for public services in 2011. For the average state, this transfer amounted to about $419 million, or 35.4 percent of gross sales, to the treasury. (See Table 4.3 for a state-by-state overview for all lotteries across the nation.) The final contributions varied significantly across states, though, and it is important to investigate these trends because larger lotteries tend to translate into larger revenues from other tax sources lost (Borg et al. 1991). By our own measure, the bottom quarter of all lottery states allocated less than 27 percent of these sales to their treasury. Meanwhile, the top quarter allocated more than 37 percent. Arkansas and Massachusetts represent the outliers that

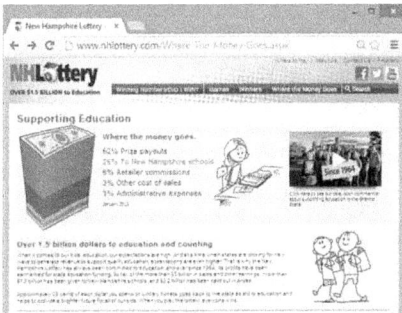

Since its inception, the New Hampshire Lottery Commission has generated over $5 billion in sales, of which $1.5 billion has been given to the state's primary and secondary schools.

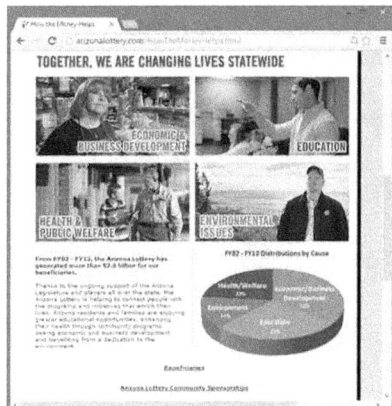

From 1982 to 2012, the Arizona Lottery generated more than $2.8 billion for the state legislature. Most this money was expended on environmental initiatives, primary, secondary, and higher education, business development, healthcare programs, and general public welfare.

Figure 4.6 Promotional Messages of Earmarking on Select State Lottery Websites

Table 4.3 A State-Level Overview of Lottery Proceeds Allocation, Fiscal Year 2011

Lottery States	Proceeds Transferred as a Percentage of Gross Sales %	Absolute Value of Proceeds Transferred (in thousands)$
Arizona	26.6	144,776
Arkansas	21.1	92,483
California	39.8	1,385,264
Colorado	23.3	111,809
Connecticut	31.1	298,298
Delaware	72.3	326,236
District of Columbia	40.6	94,122
Florida	31.4	1,186,992
Georgia	27.3	848,072
Idaho	26.9	36,480
Illinois	29.3	663,446
Indiana	26.2	192,488
Iowa	26.6	72,275
Kansas	30.2	66,083
Kentucky	31.9	214,505
Louisiana	37.3	134,969
Maine	25.2	51,017
Maryland	29.2	467,686
Massachusetts	21.1	879,064
Michigan	32.7	700,227
Minnesota	25.9	122,679
Missouri	30.6	300,297
Montana	25.2	10,928
Nebraska	24.5	30,294
New Hampshire	28.9	62,415
New Jersey	37.4	931,136
New Mexico	31.9	41,421
New York	38.6	2,695,497
North Carolina	32.2	437,070
North Dakota	27.5	6,016
Ohio	30.6	747,381
Oklahoma	43.7	92,381
Oregon	66.2	554,766
Pennsylvania	30.2	877,962
Rhode Island	70.5	356,331
South Carolina	27.6	268,076
South Dakota	75.9	106,645
Tennessee	40.2	445,701

Lottery States	Proceeds Transferred as a Percentage of Gross Sales %	Absolute Value of Proceeds Transferred (in thousands)$
Texas	28.0	1,006,330
Vermont	34.9	31,379
Virginia	31.9	445,683
Washington	29.0	138,978
West Virginia	78.6	586,694
Wisconsin	35.5	178,430

Sources: 2011 State Government Finances.

transferred the lowest portion (21.1 percent) of lottery sales to their treasuries, while West Virginia transferred the highest (78.6 percent). In terms of total dollars transferred, New York ($2.7 billion), California ($1.4 billion), and Florida ($1.2 billion) round out the top three states that generated the most lottery money for public services, and Nebraska ($30.3 million), Montana ($10.9 million), and North Dakota ($6 million) represent the bottom three states that contributed least.

Lottery proceeds were spent on a variety of public services that include but are not limited to: gambling treatment, economic development, construction initiatives, recreational facilities, libraries, education, environmental conservation, health and human services, law enforcement, military and veterans affairs, research, public servant pensions and retirement, as well as general tax relief. (An exhaustive list of public services financed by lottery funds is available in Tables A.3 and A.4 of Appendix A.) Though this list represents a broad range of public services that show just how pervasively entrenched lotteries are in state finance, our analysis reveals that states tend to prioritize lottery funds for some public services more than others. (See Figure 4.7 for a frequency distribution of how states spend lottery funds.)

More than any other public service, 29 states relied upon lottery proceeds to help finance K-12 public education. The trend makes intuitive sense given the historical link between education finance and property taxes (see Kozol 1991). The majority of money for K-12 education comes from property taxes, but since the racialized tax revolts, these property tax revenues have significantly dwindled. They comprised about 10 percent less of state and local budgets today than they did 40 years ago (see Chapter 3). Herein lies a prime example of how lottery revenues have substituted for other sources of state income, sources that are often more progressive in their tax structure. Since state lotteries have assumed a larger role in America's tax structure and they are, more or less, here to stay, a big question remains: From whom does this money come?

Public Servants (e.g., Pension, Retirement)   1   Number of States
Public Debt   2
Tax Relief or Offset (e.g., Motor Vehicle,...   3
Senior Services   3
Parks and Recreation   3
Child and Family Services   3
Veteran's Services   4
Pre-K or Adult Education   6
Public Building Construction and Maintenance   7
Health and Human Services   9
Public Safety, Judicial, or Corrections   11
Economic or Business Development   11
Conservation and Environmental Services   11
Gambling Treatment   14
General Fund / Other   17
Higher Education   21
K-12 Education   29

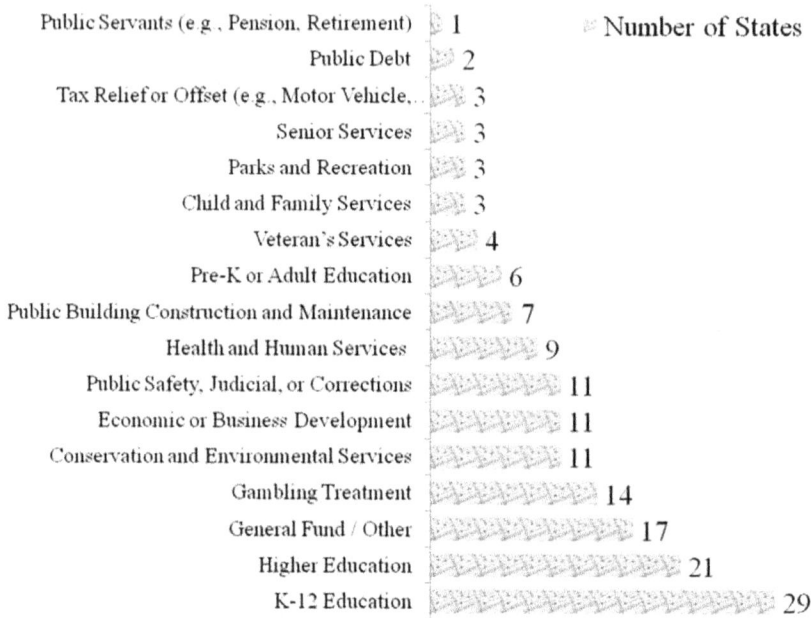

Figure 4.7 Frequency Distribution of How States Spend Lottery Funds, Fiscal Year 2011 (*N* = yes)

Robbing Percy and Pablo, Not Peter, to Pay Paul: How Lotteries Redraw Tax Liability Along Racial Lines

Common knowledge may lead many to believe the lottery is a tax on the poor. Maybe, maybe not.

From the literary overview we provide in Chapter 2, the jury remains out. Some scholars provide evidence indicating that most lottery sales come from those with less education (Brown et al. 1992; Price and Novak 1999) or income (Borg et al. 1991; Hansen et al. 2005; Miyazaki et al. 1998; Pirog-Good and Mikesell 1995), while others provide evidence showing that those with more education (Hansen 1995; Ludwig 1999) or middle-to-high income levels spend more on lotteries (Mikesell 1989; Ludwig 1999; Stranahan and Borg 1998). The picture becomes even more blurred when matters of race and ethnicity are introduced. Studies completed by McCrary and Palvak (2002) and Stranahan and Borg (1998), for example, suggest that no differences exist between racial groups when it comes to the frequency of play. That said, these same studies do yield evidence that blacks spend more money on lottery tickets compared to other groups. Still other studies, like those completed by Hansen (1995) and Price and Novak (1999), suggest that Latinas/os spend more money than other groups on lottery tickets, especially when it comes to scratch-off games. In light of these discrepancies and conflicting claims, one safe conclusion to draw is that it is unclear from whom lottery money comes.

Questions like these have great importance for understanding just who bears the burden of this new means of public finance. Who plays the lottery, and how much, says much about how tax liabilities are undergoing revision, and possibly being redistributed along racial lines. In what follows, we provide an analysis that discerns exactly who plays the lottery. The nationally representative dataset we draw from is the *Gambling Impact and Behavior Study, 1997–1999* (henceforth *GIBS, 1997–1999*).[7] Though the dataset is over 10 years old, it remains the most comprehensive one on gambling to date. Participants were asked a host of questions regarding behavior and attitudes associated with the lottery, and gambling in general, but our focus is limited to describing who plays the lottery, how much money they spend, and what is their frequency of participation.

The goal is to utilize this data to offer an analysis that straddles the line between general and specific. First we sketch a general profile of lottery participation, and then we narrow our attention to distinguish heavy players from occasional ones. Throughout this process, our emphasis is placed on race, given that our argument is race-centered, but we also pay close attention to other socio-demographic factors that many lottery scholars have uncovered as important predictors of lottery play. The implications of this analysis permit us to assess who lottery players are, so that we can determine who carries the burden of this new distributional impact.

Not everyone plays the lottery, but most have at some point in their lifetime. In fact, lotteries have considerably broader participation than most other forms of commercial gambling (Clotfelter and Cook 1989). According to Pareto's ([1906] 1971) principle, otherwise known as the 80/20 rule, we can expect 80 percent of lottery revenues to come from 20 percent of the population. When analyzing data from the *GIBS, 1997–1999*, the specific numbers of this formula are wrong, but the crux of Pareto's point remains true (see Figure 4.8). An overwhelming majority of people, 71.8 percent, report playing the lottery at least one time in their lives, but it is the frequent lottery players who comprise the real consumption base. When asked how recent the last time they played the lottery was, 71.6 percent said within the past year, 39.8 percent said within the past month, and 36.1 percent said within the past week (see Figure 4.9). Still, most lottery sales are generated from a small fraction of the general lottery playing population.

Participation can be defined in many ways, but it is the weekly players who end up spending the most money on lottery tickets. They represent a group that can be considered the heavy bettors, relatively speaking. For simplicity sake, we define those who played within the past week as "frequent lottery players." These players tend to treat the lottery as though it is

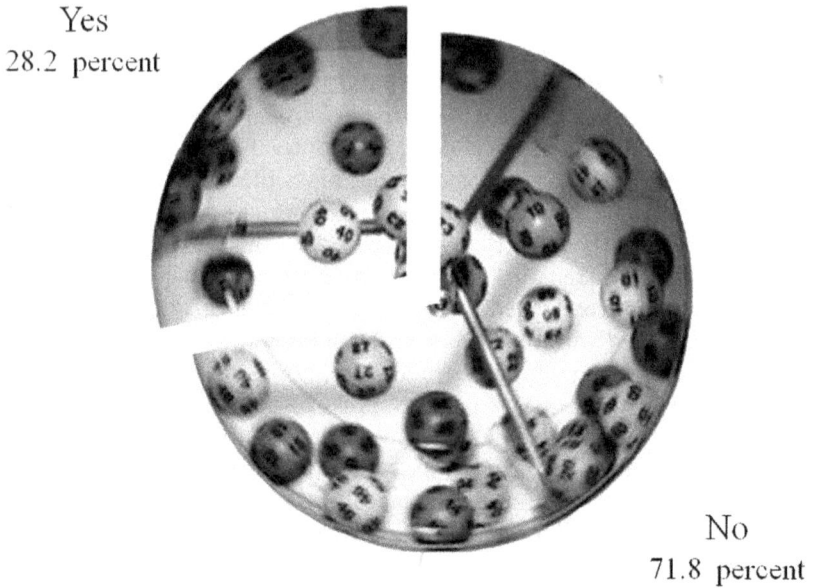

Figure 4.8 General Lottery Participation during a Person's Lifetime

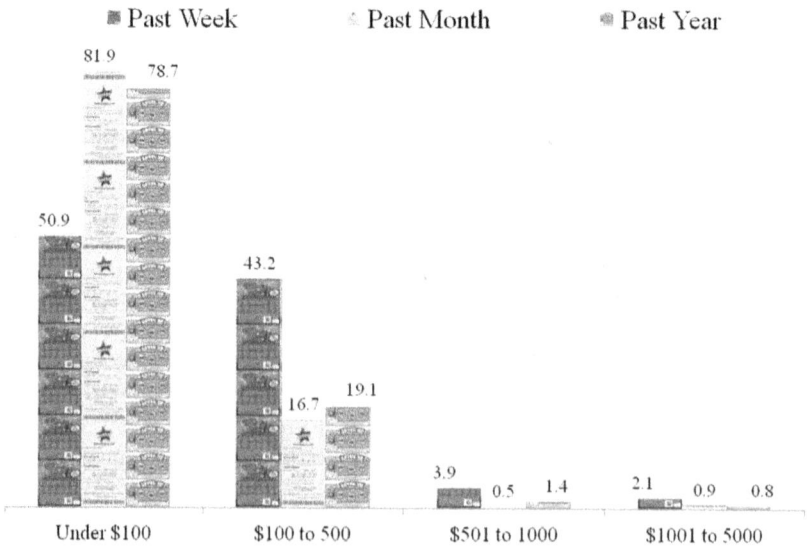

Figure 4.9 Dollars Lost on Lottery by Frequency of Play

a planned and regular activity, one that is routinized alongside other activities of daily life like filling up at the gas station or shopping for groceries. Compared to those who play more infrequently, members of the "weekly players" group lost the most money during the past year.[8] They are, in other words, much more likely to be "in the red" and report net losses of considerably more money than their counterparts (see Figure 4.9).

From Whom Does Lottery Money Come?

Do certain groups play the lottery more than others? Our focus here is on discerning exactly from whom lottery money comes, with a keen eye toward readily observable socio-demographic characteristics. Starting our analysis, we begin with a simple two-way crosstabulation to compare the frequency rates of play among different racial groups.[9] This type of analysis offers a general picture of any differences that may exist between races, but it does not account for other factors (e.g., income, education) that may explain away any observed differences. Nonetheless, these bivariate statistics offer a starting basis for generalizing patterns of lottery play. When we crosstabulate those who are frequent lottery players with measures of race, it becomes apparent that certain groups play more than others (see Figure 4.10). In terms of being frequent lottery players, nearly a 15-point gap separates

Played Last Week?

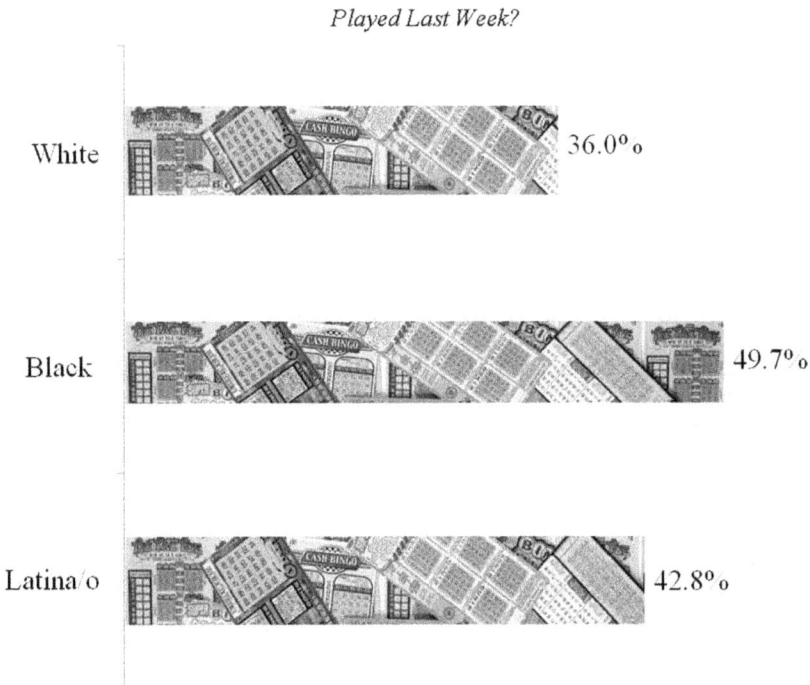

Figure 4.10 Racial Differences Between Frequent Lottery Players (in percentages)

whites and blacks while more than 5 points separate whites and Latinas/os. Whites report the least frequency of play (36.0 percent), blacks the most (49.7 percent), and Latinas/os fall in-between (42.8 percent).

Do these observed racial differences hold constant when other factors are considered? A skeptic of the argument that we have advanced thus far may say that these observed differences could be attributable to some other unknown factor. Consider how income might affect lottery play, for example. Because racial minorities tend to earn less money than whites, this may prompt more desperation in them to purchase lottery tickets. And if this is the case, the racial differences we observe would not really be a matter of racial differences at all. They would be a matter of income differences. To account for arguments like these, we incorporate a statistical analysis commonly used among social scientists to consider multiple factors at once: binary logistic regression.[10] Doing so permits us to measure the simultaneous and independent effects of race on frequent lottery play, as well as the impact other variables have on this outcome. (See Table A.5 in Appendix A for descriptive statistics and coding schemes of all the variables we consider.)

Given that the thrust of our analysis is race-centered, we begin with a simple "race-only" model. Then this model is supplemented by two others that progressively "subtract" other covariates that could account for observed differences between racial groups. Variables for these other models have been selected for substantive reasons. Namely, they preoccupy the lottery literature most and have been found to carry the most predictive value. The second model contains variables of household income and education attainment, while the third one includes individuals' employment status; unemployment, disability, or SSI receipts; Social Security, pension, or annuity compensation; welfare or public relief receipts; marital status; sex category; age; student status; religiosity; and spatial proximity to lottery vendors. (See Table 4.4 for the results of our statistical models.)

Table 4.4 Binary Logistic Regression of Frequent Lottery Players (Played During Past 7 Days)

		Model 1		Model 2		Model 3	
		SE	OR	SE	OR	SE	OR
Race/Ethnicity Dummies (Reference Group: White)							
	Black	.283[†]	**1.544**	.285[†]	**1.518**	.295[†]	**1.524**
	Latina/o	.233*	**1.972**	.239*	**1.720**	.248*	**1.754**
Driving Socioeconomic Measures							

	Model 1		Model 2		Model 3	
	coef	OR	coef	OR	coef	OR
Annual Household Income			.094	1.062	.101	1.077
Education Attainment			.078**	.786	.080*	.778
Other Variables						
Employment Status					.257	1.093
Unemployment, Disability, SSI Recipient					.359	.763
Social Security, Pension, or Annuity Compensation					.296	.957
Welfare/ Public Relief Recipient					.844	.508
Marital Status					.199	.825
Sex Category					.169**	1.501
Age of Respondent					.085**	1.266
Currently Attending School					.326	1.384
Importance of Faith in God					.095	1.000
Purchase of lottery Ticket in Neighborhood					.207†	1.452
Constant	089**	.463	.260	.814	.643*	.262
Pseudo R^2(Nagelkerke / Cragg & Uhler's)		.018		.037		.079
Change in Pseudo R^2		—		.019		.042
-2 Log Likelihood		927.918		917.781		894.705
Change in χ^2		9.809		10.137		23.076
Count Correct (In percentages)		65.7		66.8		68.2
Change in Count Correct (In percentages)		0		1.1		1.4
N		742		742		742

Note: OR = Odds Ratio (in bold).

† $p < .10$, * $p < .05$, ** $p < .01$ (two-tailed tests)

Race

Can differences in lottery play between racial groups be explained away by other factors? All three binary logistic models confirm that race likely plays a role in predicting lottery play (see Models 1, 2, and 3 in Table 4). Model 1 shows sizeable and highly suggestive differences in frequent lottery play between racial groups. Compared to whites, blacks are about one and a half times more likely (154 percent) to be frequent lottery players while Latinas/os are nearly twice (197 percent) more likely. When covariates of socioeconomic status (i.e., household income and education attainment) are introduced in Model 2, the odds ratios of racial differences reduce slightly but retain similar value. Holding measures of socioeconomic status constant, this model estimates that blacks are about one and half times (152 percent) more likely than whites to be frequent lottery players. For Latinas/os, the odds indicate that they are about one and three-fourths (172 percent) more likely than whites to be frequent lottery players. These odds stay about the same in Model 3, even when a host of other measures are included.

Socioeconomic Measures

Many scholars are preoccupied with socioeconomic factors when it comes to explaining who plays the lottery (e.g. Borg et al. 1991; Brown et al. 1992; Garvía 2007; Hansen et al. 2005; Miyazaki et al. 1998; Pirog-Good and Mikesell 1995; Price and Novak 1999), but measures of income and education yield mixed results. According to our analysis, annual household income had little statistical value in terms of predicting frequent lottery play. This observation suggests that no relationship exists between income and lottery participation, and also counters conventional claims that the lottery preys upon the poor (e.g. Borg et al. 1991; Hansen et al. 2005; Miyazaki et al. 1998; Pirog-Good and Mikesell 1995).

Players' level of education attainment, however, is statistically significant. The frequency of lottery play decreases with additional years of schooling (see Model 3 in Table 4). Those who have attended graduate or professional school, for example, are:

- 22.2 percent less likely to have played the lottery within the past week than those who've attended four years of college,
- 44.4 percent less likely than those who've had some college or technical school,
- 66.6 percent less likely than those who've completed 12th grade,
- and 88.8 percent less likely than those who have not completed high school or its equivalent.

Results like these corroborate what others (e.g., Brown et al. 1992; Price and Novak 1999) have argued. People with less education play the lottery more than their counterparts, even after a number of variables have been considered.

Other Influential Variables

Perhaps the evidence in Table 4 confirms the obvious, but weekly lottery players were more likely to identify as men, report older age, and live near lottery vendors. We estimate that men are about one and half times more likely (150 percent) than women to play the lottery weekly. Generally speaking, this trend mirrors the same patterns observed for education. Though men play the lottery more than women, this gap is much smaller compared to other forms of gambling such as casinos or horse racing (Clotfelter and Cook 1989). In terms of age and its impact on lottery play, older people are more likely to play the lottery weekly than are younger people. The *GIBS, 1997–1999* study categorized respondents into five age brackets: 18–29 years, 30–39 years, 40–49 years, 50–64 years, and 65 or above. Climbing these brackets increases the odds of playing the lottery by 127 percent. All else being equal, this means, for example, that a 60-year-old person is about 4 times (or 381 percent) more likely than a 20-year-old to play the lottery weekly. In addition to sex and age, patterns of lottery play are influenced by a convenience factor. Those who typically purchase lottery tickets in their home neighborhood are about one and half times more likely (145 percent) to play weekly than those who buy their tickets outside their neighborhood.

Summarizing from Whom Lottery Money Comes

All these binary logistic models offer evidence that confirms which groups most frequently play the lottery, but they also raise deeper implications about the nature of state finance.[11] Questions of "who plays" help to answer questions of "who pays" larger tax burdens of state finance, especially given that lottery money represents larger shares of contemporary budgets. Our analysis helps discern this question of who. By our count, some play the lottery more frequently than do others. This is especially true in terms of race, education, sex, age, religion, and location. It is these variables that remained statistically important predictors of lottery play for those in our nationally representative sample, even when a number of other common factors were considered.

Perhaps more so than all other variables, however, the lottery is a racially regressive source of revenue. Measuring among the greatest magnitude levels, our analysis reveals that most frequent lottery play does not come from whites but blacks and Latinas/os. These patterns we uncover offer a useful framework for understanding exactly from who lottery money comes, and which groups are taking on this new tax liability for financing public services provided by state government. They also say something about who directly benefits from a tax infrastructure designed in such a way.

Lotteries As a Reverse Robin Hood Tax, With Racial Implications

Who plays the lottery, and how frequently, has deep implications for the overall tax structure of a state. These implications vary significantly across the country, however, because different regions tend to follow their own styles of taxation. Recent work by Katherine Newman and Rourke O'Brien (2011) show that states in the southern and western parts of the United States have historically relied more heavily on regressive taxation, such as the sales tax, to keep their governments running. Meanwhile states in the New England area, for example, tend to place higher premiums on property taxes. This makes their state-level government not only more reliant on them, but highly vulnerable to tax losses when this revenue is no longer available due to property tax revolts and reforms.

The magnitude of the lottery's effect on a state's collected revenues largely depends upon these preexisting tax structures (Borg et al. 1991), and likely has more regressive consequences in some states compared to others. Assuming our national results of who plays the lottery are fairly consistent at the state level, states that have steadily replaced property tax revenues with lottery money are likely to have regressively redistributed tax liability along racial lines compared to those states that already had regressive tax structures to begin with. The tax-side of the lottery is but one-half the issue. Another half regards how this money is spent.

Along with the steady march of tax reform over the past 40–50 years, the growing reliance on lotteries in state finance has produced, to appropriate David Cay Johnston's (2003) words here, "not trickle down economics, but Niagara up" (p. 2). What we currently have (and have long had) is a fiscal system that limits tax liability in ways that add up to a "hidden wealthfare" state that privileges the already privileged (Howard 1997). Tax liability is limited to the extent that it reduces what some would otherwise owe to the government. People tend to not see it this way, however, because playing the lottery is a choice. Therefore, they can keep their money, they think, by not playing. To adapt the words of Isaac William Martin and Kevin Beck (Forthcoming), the process "disguises a racially based public subsidy as private property" (p. 5). Meanwhile, lottery money, which comes from select groups, is used to finance public services in which we all partake.

A common thread that ties all state lotteries together is that they are state-sanctioned mechanisms for hoarding some groups' capital and redistributing others'. Much variation exists in how states carry through these tasks, though. Some might designate most of their lottery money for K-12 or higher education. Others might reserve this money for environmental conservation. It is beyond the scope of our study to measure the variance of such distributional effects, and how these might be racialized in uneven ways, but comparative studies of this nature could yield new ways for understanding the reverse Robin Hood nature of lotteries.

We expect that some lottery operations transfer greater amounts of capital from marginal to mainstream racial groups than do others. One can imagine, for example, how this would play out in states that earmark lottery money for higher education compared to states that use these same dollars for conservation. Lottery-sponsored scholarships to college would build upon existing racial disparities in higher education access in ways that lottery spending on conservation could not, leaving minority groups to subsidize college expenses for white students. The fine print of the lottery tax provides a window for seeing how states preserve inequitable distributions of capital.

On paper, racial groups are not required to pay different sets of taxes. This does not change the fact that taxation carries implicit biases and disparate consequences. The lottery tax represents a form of institutionalized racial discrimination if not by intent then certainly *by effect*. Since the proliferation of state lotteries throughout the nation, black and brown tax dollars have steadily displaced white tax dollars. Then this money becomes spread across all groups who benefit from public services. What makes this process so pervasively insidious, however, is that it is accomplished in ways that are institutional, covert, and racial in almost every way but name.

Notes

1 An earlier iteration of this chapter appeared as a journal article in *Georgetown Journal of Law & Modern Critical Race Perspectives* (see Henricks 2014).
2 Quote taken from: Tammet, Daniel. 2009. *A Tour Across the Horizons of the Mind: Embracing the Wide Sky.* New York: Free Press.
3 Please buy more of these books; they are a great gift for any (perhaps every) holiday.
4 Per capita sales is calculated as total lottery revenues as reported by the U.S. Census Bureau's 2011 State Government Finances dataset divided by 2010 Census records of total state populations who are legally permitted, as determined by age, to purchase a lottery ticket. Lottery tickets can be purchased in a majority of states by those 18 years of age and older, though some outliers deviate from this trend. The minimum age in Louisiana and Nebraska is 21 years and 19 years, respectively.
5 Scientific Games Corporation is among the largest lottery product providers in the United States. During the early years of modern state lottery proliferation throughout America, representatives from this company routinely provided state politicians with persuasive public relations information, like lottery revenue projections and expert testimonies, to influence lottery adoption (Nibert 2000). Amy Bayer (1990) reports that in California, this company spent an estimated $2 million in lobbying efforts. Once a lottery was approved, the California state government awarded the company a contract worth over $20 million.
6 Prior to 2013, numbers could be selected only from 1 to 56.
7 *GIBS, 1997–1999* is a public-use dataset made available by the Inter-university Consortium for Political and Social Research at http://www.icpsr.umich.edu/icpsrweb/SAMHDA/studies/2778. Here, one can also find an in-depth summary of the study and its design.
8 This is a correlative relationship confirmed beyond the 0.01 level.
9 Asians are omitted here due to limitations of the data. Once cases that included missing information were excluded from our analysis, the sample size of Asians became too small for nationwide generalization. This empirical absence is not to suggest that Asian lottery play is insignificant, though. On the contrary, it is an area of study that will likely yield potent findings given the broad levels of lottery participation and rich lottery histories in Asian communities.

10 Binary logistic regression is a statistical classification model that calculates probability. In our case, it allows us to predict the likelihood, or odds, that racial minorities play the lottery more frequently than white people while a number of other factors are held constant.

11 We also measured interaction effects in attempt to expand model efficiency. Ultimately these interaction variables did not significantly improve levels of explained variance, and therefore, they are omitted from the final analysis.

5   Who Plays? Who Pays?
A Case Study of Illinois[1]

In many ways, Illinois is your typical lottery state. We have chosen it as a case study not only to transition our focus from the general to the specific, but because this particular case embodies many of the matters that have dominated our analysis so far. The legalization of the Illinois Lottery represents a process from which a certain form of gambling went from prohibition to state-sanctioned in the historical blink of an eye. This whole process did not unravel without political conflict, though. What became a nearly decade-long battle over lottery adoption seemed only to delay the inevitable. The state of Illinois got its lottery in 1974, and it began with a boom.

As lottery supporters proposed, the Illinois Lottery delivered the sales it promised—if only for the first two years. Then, like most other lotteries, sales went south and desperation crept in. This is when operators of the Illinois Lottery went back to the proverbial drawing board, and ultimately redefined how it did business. They placed bets on tapping into a preexisting consumer base made possible by an illegal gambling infrastructure with deep historical roots. Of course the mantra of lottery proponents throughout this whole process was of the "do it for the kids, their education, and our state's future" variety.

The Illinois Lottery was passed on the promise of money for education. In this way, it became a revenue stream for a state strapped for cash. The lottery had assumed a new role in public finance, but it soon became clear that the lottery did not deliver what was promised. Its revenues merely replaced other money streams of public finance, and consequently, altered the tax distribution of who is liable for funding education. Of course, it is not just anyone who plays the Illinois Lottery either.

Most revenue comes from people of color. Nonetheless, lottery dollars are typically framed as a boon to education finance. In Illinois, this framing is paired with state politicians who pride themselves in having progressive finance policy that gives extra aid to poor districts. What becomes problematic with policy like this, however, is that it does not consider lottery money, and from whom it comes, at all. This has great potential to leave "progressive" education policy financed by a racially regressive lottery tax, countering whatever good intentions policymakers started with. For reasons like these, among others, the Illinois Lottery serves as a launching point for understanding a more intimate knowledge of how lotteries operate in general.

Do You Hate Law-Abiding Citizens? The Common 'Man'? The Children? If Not, Then Support the Illinois Lottery

Turn on WGN America Midday News or open up an issue of *The Chicago Tribune*, and odds are that the Illinois Lottery will be featured. If we were betting men, our prediction is that you might see some sort of ritualized announcement of the daily winning numbers and perhaps even some cliché advertisement like "you can't win if you don't play." What would not be seen are negative messages about the Illinois Lottery. Journalists of these media outlets, as well as a number of Republican politicians, were among the most vocally opposed to the state adoption of a lottery (Gribbin and Bean 2005).

When a lottery bill was introduced into the 1972 legislative session of the Illinois House, it was Republican State Representative George Hudson of Hinsdale who condemned the idea. He argued that a lottery would not generate the money the state needs because it taxed those who could least afford it (Elmer 1972). This is not to say, however, that Hudson's arguments were motivated out of empathy for those in poverty. After all, he would often go on to say that it would be only a matter of time that the welfare state would be expanded just so poor folks could buy their lottery tickets (Seslar 1972). A number of editorials in *The Chicago Tribune* echoed some of these sentiments (Clotfelter and Cook 1989) and went further to censure state politicians for even bringing up the idea (Gribbin and Bean 2005). Some columnists saw the lottery as a superficial distraction that diverted attention from the very politicians who created Illinois' fiscal problems in the first place.

The bill's sponsor, Democratic state representative E. J. Giorgi of Rockford, countered these criticisms by appealing to values shared by most. He argued, as did other lottery proponents, that a lottery would help the innocent, vulnerable children of Illinois (Seslar 1972). Since the state was failing to meet its obligation to finance public education, surely it could entertain alternatives to generate all the money it could get. Meanwhile, other politicians had few or no solutions to offer. Giorgi's support of a lottery squarely addressed some of the most pressing social problems of the time. As economist Glenn Fisher (1969) has outlined:

1 The population size of school age children (age 5–17) had nearly doubled between 1942 and 1965 from one-and-a-half million to well over two-and-a-half million,
2 per child expenditures had increased nearly twofold from \$258.46 to \$437.74 between 1950 and 1960, signifying a deliberate commitment to improve the quality of education,

3   and the state had expanded its presence in education finance between the early 1940s and late 1960s by doubling its contribution from 12.8 to 24.0 percent of all costs.

These transformations were further complicated by the broader social forces discussed at length in Chapter 3, like the 1970s wave of antitax hysteria that swept the nation as well as fundamental shifts in the political economy.

Efforts by the National Taxpayers United in Illinois, a Chicago-based organization now known as Taxpayers United of America, spearheaded a meat-ax approach to tax reform. Actually these efforts remain ongoing (Lindall 2015). Borrowing from the 1970s California playbook, the organization demanded across-the-board cuts to about every tax imaginable; property, sales, and income taxes—you name it. It delivered some success stories too. The organization's president (and economics instructor at Elmhurst College), James Tobin, boasted in *The Chicago Tribune*:

> In the past three years we've saved Illinois taxpayers more than $500 million in new and added taxes. . . . We've opposed tax increases in 51 separate elections, and we won 49 of them. Last November we had tax cuts on 23 ballots in 9 counties. Twenty of these passed
>
> (qtd. in Mabley 1981: 4).

He and other members of the backlash movement took aim, in racially coded language (Edsall and Edsall 1991), at public sectors seen as catering to minority interests, such as desegregating public schools and occupational niches where black-white parity was a stated goal (see also Steinberg 1981; Wilson 1997). In an "Angry Taxpayer Action Committee" campaign, Tobin (1981) circulated a call to action (and a donation request) whereby he alleged that the Illinois government was throwing tax dollars down the drain on "waste," incompetence, and corruption. Teachers' unions, school districts comprised by mostly minority students, and those sponging off "non-vital" public services were among those singled out.

Meanwhile, changes like deindustrialization, deregulation, privatization, and globalization helped erode the Illinois tax base, so much so that expenditures on education exceeded the tax dollars that residents were able to contribute (see Wilson 1996). Per pupil spending increased at much faster rates in Illinois, for example, than did increases in real income (Fisher 1969). Still, many refused to let their children's education be the victim of these broader social forces. Much like many Americans of the time, they wanted to "pay less for more"—or at least pay the same taxes and keep the current services (Sears and Citrin 1982). It was Giorgi's political rhetoric that spoke to these sentiments. He understood that Illinoisans were in a real time of need, and he asked people to support his lottery so that the state could bring struggling schools up to standard.

It would be overly simplistic, however, to say that Giorgi's strategy was only of the "do it for the children" variety. He framed the lottery in the image of "the common man," too (Seslar 1972). The implementation of a lottery would not only turn workers into millionaires, but it would curb illegal gambling and help end "seedy" games of the underground economy.[2] The strategy of these lottery proponents was to engage in moral politics and reframe the debate (Lakoff 2004). It diverted attention from their opponents' criticisms that a state-sponsored lottery would be unethical, and ultimately achieved some success in mobilizing popular support and minimizing dissent. Messages like these forced lottery opponents to debate the lottery on their terms, which proved quite difficult to direct challengers. After all, who wants to be the politician that argues against the interests of working people and innocent, vulnerable children in Illinois? Two months of debate later, it seems that most state representatives agreed with pro-lottery arguments (or at least remained desperate for new state revenue streams and unwilling to consider alternative tax hikes). Giorgi's bill passed the House by a vote of 100 to 64. The fight did not end here.

At least one prominent politician agreed with Hudson's anti-lottery position, Republican Governor of Illinois Richard Ogilvie. He slowed the bill's momentum once it entered the Illinois Senate by threatening a veto (Clotfelter and Cook 1989). After less than a month of debate, the lottery bill died. A slim majority of state senators voted against it in June of 1972, by a vote of 22 to 20. Though the battle was lost, the proverbial war had just begun. Less than a year later, the idea of a state lottery was reincarnated and given new life. Only this time four new factors worked to lottery proponents' favor.

First, Governor Ogilvie was replaced by someone sympathetic to the passage of a lottery, Democratic Governor Daniel Walker (Clotfelter and Cook 1989; Gribbin and Bean 2005). Second, Chicago mayor Richard J. Daley threw his political support of the lottery into the ring (Clotfelter and Cook 1989; Gilbert 1973).[3] Third, a number of expert testimonies tempered the critics' arguments by projecting that Illinois could expect about $50 million dollars in net annual state revenue (Gribbin and Bean 2005). And fourth, politicians began entertaining tax alternatives, much to the public's dismay, like increasing the state's sales tax (Clotfelter and Cook 1989). These factors taken together helped make the inevitable occur. Governor Walker signed a lottery into state law on December 1, 1973, and the first tickets became available in June of the following year. Illinois had become just the tenth state in the union to adopt a lottery.

Boom-Bust-Boom, Early Years of the Illinois Lottery

The first Illinois Lottery tickets were sold July 30, 1974. With Ralph Batch being appointed as the lottery's first Superintendent ("Illinois Lottery" 2013), about 7,500 vendors, which included food markets, liquor stores, gas stations, and convenience outlets, participated in the inaugural year (Clotfelter and Cook 1989). Wanting to encourage broad participation and make it a "lottery of people," operators of the Illinois Lottery avoided precedents set by high-priced lotteries of New Hampshire and New York and instead followed in the successful footsteps of New Jersey. Tickets were priced at $0.50 a ticket, and prizes ranged from $1 to 20 million. Like many other lotteries, the first years were booming, revenue projections were satisfied, and former critics became fans. Even journalists of *The Chicago Tribune*, which represented some of the strongest, most outspoken opponents of a state lottery, jumped on the bandwagon. The Illinois Lottery had become, more or less, a political nonissue and seemingly immune from criticism.

Journalists wasted no time diverting their attention to other stories readers wanted—"human interest" articles that left them with warm fuzzies. One story that captured the heart of the people early on regarded the Illinois Lottery's first "big" winner, a welder with a chronically ill child (Keegan 1974). The winner of $300,000 received a personal call from the governor, and was even invited to a ceremony in his honor at the capital. When asked what he would do with the money, he said he would donate a good portion of it to Easter Seals Disability Services and the hospital that provided most of his child's care. It is likely that stories such as these contributed to overall lottery sales. The Illinois Lottery had already sold its 100,000th ticket by December 31, just four months after the first one was sold ("Illinois Lottery" 2013). About $128 million in lottery revenues were generated the first fiscal year, and nearly $163 the second (Clotfelter and Cook 1989).

As the old adage reminds us: what goes up must come down. The Illinois Lottery followed the patterns of most other state lotteries, with an initial boom in sales followed by a bust. Sales slipped for the next few years, with the real value of sales declining by over 60 percent between 1976 and 1979 (Clotfelter and Cook 1989). Lottery officials provided a variety of excuses to explain away the sales slump, even citing heavy snow as a reason. A second Superintendent, Richard Carlson, was introduced in 1977 ("Illinois Lottery" 2013), but excitement surrounding his tenure dwindled fast. It is worth noting that Carlson did mimic successful strategies already deployed by New Jersey and Massachusetts, in which he instituted a new Illinois Lottery game (Pick 3) where players could choose their own numbers (Clotfelter and Cook 1989). This move would pay large dividends in the long run, but sales continued to decline in the short run. Governor James Robert Thompson even went on record to suggest that the Illinois Lottery could be phased out if change did not occur (Clotfelter and Cook 1989).

Out of desperation, he appointed the Illinois Lottery's third Superintendent, Michael J. Jones, in 1981.[4] Jones continued what Carlson started by adding another numbers game (Pick 4) to the products the lottery offered ("Illinois Lottery" 2013), and initiated aggressive advertisement campaigns to generate publicity (Clotfelter and Cook 1989). Ultimately the new tactics worked. Between fiscal years 1981 and 1982 gross sales had increased by

62 percent, and on November 5, 1984, Governor Thompson announced a milestone in Illinois Lottery history ("Illinois Lottery" 2013). It had finally generated its first billion dollars in sales after seven years of operation, but more impressively, it took only 18 months thereafter to generate its second billion. To place these trends in relative perspective, lottery sales contributed about only one percent of the total state budget in its first years but about 5 percent by 1986 (Clotfelter and Cook 1989). It was the numbers games perhaps above all else that fundamentally altered the course of the Illinois Lottery's history.

What's Race Got to Do With It? A Lot

The introduction of "numbers" games represents one way the Illinois Lottery tapped into a ready-made gambling infrastructure. They capitalized off a booming underground economy of illegal lotteries, whereby similar "policy" games were commonplace—particularly in predominantly black neighborhoods of Chicago (Drake and Cayton [1945] 1993). A typical game would require players to place bets on combinations of numbers, usually three, chosen between the range of 1 to 78 (Haller 1979). Once bets were placed, a blindfolded person hand selects numbers from a drum, or "wheel," that whirls around. If a player who wagered 10 cents, for example, happened to have all three of her or his numbers picked, then s/he would have won a "gig" worth 10 dollars (Lombardo 2002). Players whose ticket had only two of the three correct number won a "saddle" that yielded winnings that were worth four or more times the original purchase price. Though the "you pick 3" numbers game was most popular, other variations that followed the same logic, like "you pick 1, 2, or 4," also existed (Drake and Cayton 1967). These games would foreshadow what we know as modern lottery products.

One of the factors that led to the introduction of the Illinois Lottery's numbers games, aside from dwindling sales, was an Illinois House of Representatives report written nearly 10 years earlier (1975) by the "Policy Numbers Game Study Committee." The committee, which was comprised by notable figures like Harold Washington (Chicago's first and only black mayor) and Brenetta Howell Barret (Director of the Governor's Office of Human Resources), concluded that these games needed to be legalized and administratively restored to the hands of black communities. Too long they had received nothing more than "petty cuts" from illegal gambling syndicates (Drake and Cayton [1945] 1993). Without instituting a state-sanctioned lottery numbers game, as Barret argued in the report, white gangsters could freely continue their intrusion into black communities, plagiarize black gambling games, and keep the profits for themselves. After all, surveys completed in Chicago's "traditional black belt" (the south and west sides) during the early 1970s reveal that nearly 40 percent of neighborhood residents played "numbers" ("Illinois House of Representatives, Policy Numbers Game Committee" 1975). Three years after their introduction of

Illinois Lottery's version of numbers, sales for these games nearly tripled (Clotfelter and Cook 1989). It was illegal numbers games turned legal that helped return the state to booming sales, and ultimately, lay to rest any suggestions that the lottery should be ended. These are the types of games that attest to the enduring popularity of lottery games in the United States.

It would be mistaken to assume that everyone in Chicago's black communities welcomed the lottery with open arms. This resentment boiled over during the early part of 1986, especially on the city's west side, and became among the top news cycle stories for outlets like *The Chicago Tribune* and *The Chicago Sun-Times* (e.g., see Cronin 1986; Koziol and Schneidman 1986). What prompted these short-lived protests, and ultimately a boycott, were predatory advertisements that crossed a line. One billboard located in a black ghetto read:

> "How to go from Washington Boulevard to Easy Street.
> Play the Illinois State Lottery."

Located at 2300 W. Washington Blvd., a location surrounded by racialized poverty, it was quite clear to community leaders like Rev. Thomas O'Gorman and other local religious figures whom these messages were targeting (Brodt 1986; Congbalay 1986; Formanek 1986). Ads like these, according to their perspective, taunted those with little discretionary spending and encouraged them to squander away their milk money. To illustrate his point, O'Gorman took a collection of losing lottery tickets one Sunday as opposed to the typical tithing (Formanek 1986). He drew the equivalent of upwards of $5,000 in losing tickets and pleaded that the money would have gone to better use if spent on food and heat.

Of course lottery officials denied any bad intentions behind the ads, and redirected attention to the continued contributions the Illinois Lottery makes to education (Koziol and Schneidman 1986). Despite these 1986 protests, a similar lottery campaign ensued in Chicago years later. One of these ads reads as follows: "This could be your ticket out." Of course such a statement begs the question: a ticket out of where? When one scholar, Robert Goodman (1995), further examined the locations of these ads, the answer became quite apparent. These winning lottery tickets were tickets out of the ghetto, as these ads were placed in predominantly black, impoverished areas. The billboard messages, themselves, resonate with people's desperation. It's as though the lottery is the only path these folks have to becoming a millionaire, or at least escaping their own situation. Protests in this case, however, were not heard.

Wait, What About the Kids? False Promises of the Illinois Lottery

Had the Illinois Lottery made good on its promise to deliver additional funds, it might be considered by some measures as a progressive alternative to the public policies in place. This is because even regressive taxes can bolster and enhance public services in ways that progressive tax structures have not. Consider France, for example. This country has a welfare state that is far more robust and comprehensive compared to what's available in America, but it is made possible not through progressive income taxes but a tax structure comprised of highly regressive consumptive taxes (Morgan and Prasad 2009). Such a case complicates crude Marxist interpretations that progressive tax structures are automatically linked to progressive spending practices, and vice versa when it comes to regressive tax structures. Notwithstanding, the history of France does not parallel the history of Illinois.

It may be unsurprising to some the Illinois Lottery did not make good on all its promises. This is especially true as it relates to the kids of Illinois and additional funds for their education. Economists Mary Borg and Paul Mason (1990) have shown that real net expenditures on public education declined for a ten-year period after the Illinois Lottery's initiation. Whereas the annual education budget totaled about $3.2 billion in 1975, it had declined to less than $1.8 billion by 1984. Some of this downward trend can be attributed to other factors, such as lower student enrollments, but lower student enrollments offer only so much of an explanation for declining education budgets in education. For most years between 1975 and 1984, dwindling expenditures on public education outpaced declining enrollments by rates that were frequently double, triple, or even more (Henricks 2014). The greatest disparities occurred in the early 1980s (see Table 5.1), an era marked by great divestment from public services throughout most of America (Piven and Cloward 1982).

Table 5.1 Illinois Public Education Expenditures and Enrollments, 1975–1984

	Rates of Decline in Percentages	
	Real Net Education Expenditures	Total Public Education Enrollments
1976	− 3.1	− 1.2
1977	− 4.8	− 1.5
1978	− 1.7	− 2.6
1979	− 5.2	− 3.4
1980	− 4.5	− 3.4
1981	− 16.2	− 3.0
1982	− 13.6	− 3.1
1983	− 5.3	− 2.3
1984	− 2.8	− 1.5

Sources: The Illinois' real net education expenditures were drawn from Borg and Mason (1990), and the Illinois' total public education enrollments were drawn from ISBE (2004).

Perhaps it was figures like these that prompted legal reform, so that the original promises of a lottery (e.g., additional funds for education) could be held accountable. Part of the problem with existing Illinois Lottery Law (1973) was that it directed net lottery proceeds to the General Revenue Fund rather than the Common School Fund. This meant that no mechanism was in place to ensure lottery money would go to education, and instead legislatures could effectively spend these funds however they saw fit. The Illinois Lottery Law was amended in 1985 to prevent this from happening, as it explicitly required net lottery proceeds to be "earmarked" to the state's Common School Fund. Even with this addition, the Illinois Lottery has not added funding but displaced alternative sources of revenue that once financed public education (Borg and Mason 1988, 1990). The lottery tax represents a regressive turn of education finance, whereby lottery revenues have essentially replaced progressive forms of taxation like corporate, property, and income taxes. Illinois is no anomaly however. On the contrary, it is a symbolic example of the situation confronting many states across America (Borg and Mason 1990).

The ways in which lotteries are framed as a boon to education finance can cause unforeseen adverse consequences. Because they were initiated to supplement school funds, many people may be led to believe that schools are now swimming in more lottery money than they know what to do with. Though this is hardly true, sometimes facts do not matter as much as perception. James Smith, a former Belleville, Illinois, School Superintendent, knows this lesson all too well. In an interview for *Time Magazine*, he complained that he could not "get a bond issue authorized because local officials think that schools are rolling in the lottery money" (Donoghue 1989: 19). The Illinois Lottery's real financial benefit to schools has been, at best, negligible from a budgetary standpoint. Nonetheless, when distorted information is acted upon as though it were accurate and truthful, then this false information becomes real in its consequences (see Thomas and Thomas 1928). In the case of Illinois, it is the institution of education, and all those people embedded within it, that are most detrimentally affected. Many of these schools are in extreme need of resources and bare necessities, yet lotteries have ways of painting pictures that suggest just the opposite.

How Much Lottery Money Are We Talking About?

Year after year in the 2000s, the Illinois Lottery boasted record-breaking sales ("Illinois Lottery" 2010). So much so that the later years of the 2000s amounted to sales surpassing the $2 billion mark. In any given year, about a third, or $600 million, was allocated to the Illinois Common School Fund—the primary source of funding for the state's public primary and secondary schools ("Illinois Lottery" 2005, 2009). In 2011, the Illinois Lottery's contribution to education approximated $668 million and represented nearly 10 percent of the state's education budget ("State of Illinois" 2011). The remanding money was designated to cover prize winnings, operating costs, and other expenses. Over $1.3 billion (60.3 percent) was reserved for prize winnings. About $161 million (7.1 percent) went to retailers or vendors. And approximately $72 million (3.2 percent) was spent on other expenses like advertising. (See Figure 5.1 for a breakdown of how each lottery dollar was spent in 2011.)

While lottery proceeds are spread across Illinois, most of this money was generated from one area of the state: Chicago. To illustrate this further, we turn to data from the 2010 Census and integrate them with 2011 records obtained from the Illinois Department of Revenue. The latter information was collected by performing an audit that followed guidelines of the state's Freedom of Information Act (FOIA), or §5–140 of the Illinois Compiled Statutes.[5] Most states have adopted freedom of information laws like these, which are commonly referred to as "sunshine" laws among journalists and legal scholars, so that members of the public can access a broad range of government documents and records. These include the various budgetary items that drive this study. According to records collected from the Illinois Department of Revenue, nearly 70 percent of the over $2.1 billion in lottery sales for fiscal year 2011 came from tickets sold within the Chicago Metropolitan Statistical Area (see Figure 5.2). This means that a vast majority of the lottery tickets sold in Illinois came from eight of the state's 102 counties.[6]

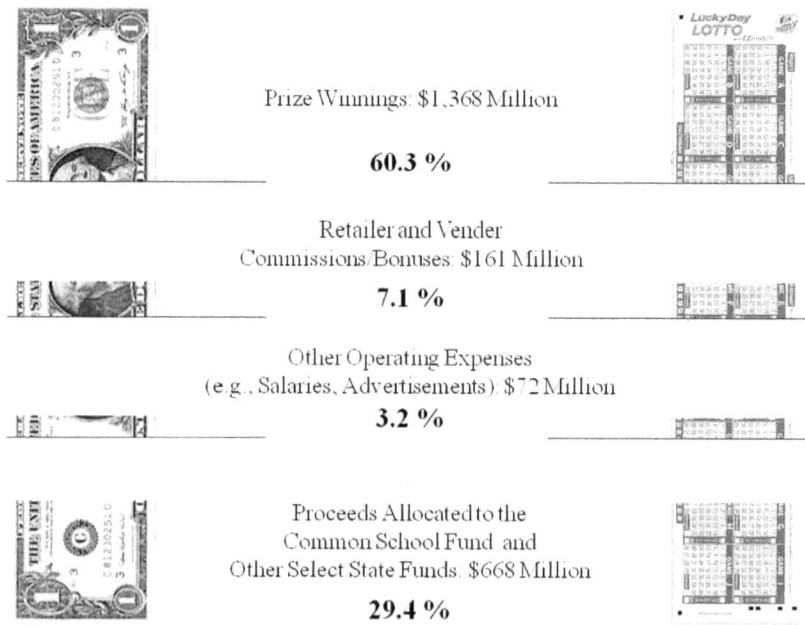

Prize Winnings: $1,368 Million

60.3 %

Retailer and Vender
Commissions/Bonuses: $161 Million

7.1 %

Other Operating Expenses
(e.g., Salaries, Advertisements): $72 Million

3.2 %

Proceeds Allocated to the
Common School Fund and
Other Select State Funds: $668 Million

29.4 %

Figure 5.1 Where Does Illinois Lottery Money Go? A Breakdown for Fiscal Year 2011

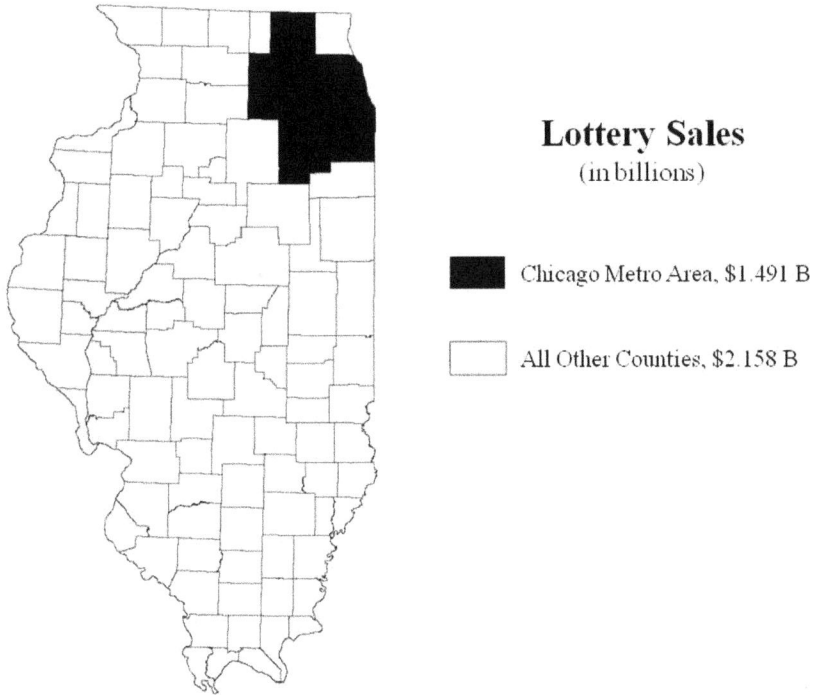

Lottery Sales
(in billions)

■ Chicago Metro Area, $1.491 B

☐ All Other Counties, $2.158 B

Figure 5.2 From Where within Illinois Do Illinois Lottery Revenues Come? A Comparison of the Chicago Metropolitan Statistical Area and All Other Illinois Counties

When taking a closer look at the zip codes that comprise the Chicago Metropolitan Statistical Area, it is apparent that most lottery money comes from certain pockets of Cook County (see Figure 5.3). These pockets represent communities within the densely populated city limits of Chicago, especially those on the South- and West-Sides. In 2011, for example, it was not uncommon for many of these zip codes to generate over $10 million in lottery sales. Meanwhile, the further one gets from the city, the fewer lottery sales are generated. Sales for zip codes at the outer edges of McHenry, Kane, and Will Counties, for example, struggled to surpass $2 million in annual lottery sales.

The Lottery Tax, Generated from Whom?

According to our analysis in the previous chapter, the lottery is like a reverse Robin Hood tax with racial implications. It swindles money from marginal groups, and then spreads it across all groups by financing public services most people are entitled to. Does this observation hold up at the local level,

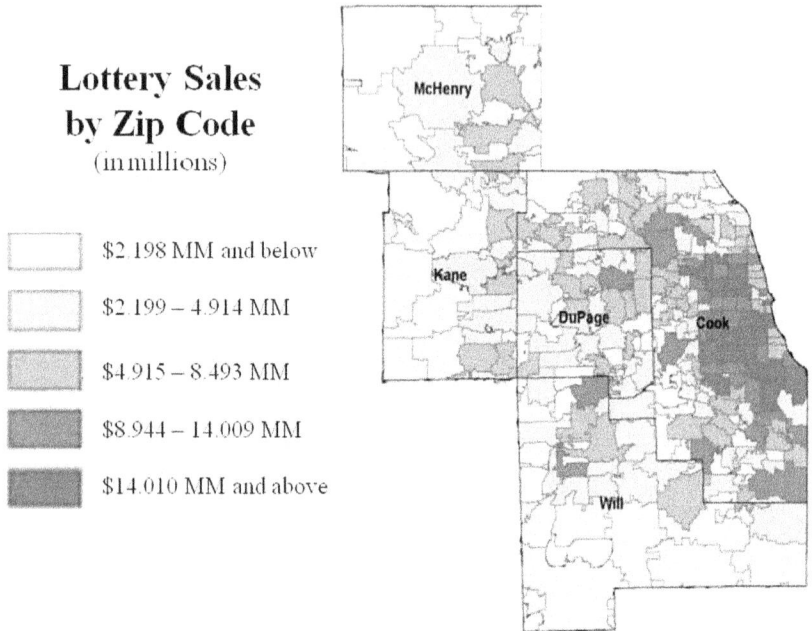

Lottery Sales by Zip Code

(in millions)

☐	$2.198 MM and below
☐	$2.199 – 4.914 MM
☐	$4.915 – 8.493 MM
■	$8.944 – 14.009 MM
■	$14.010 MM and above

Figure 5.3 Where Did Illinois Lottery Revenues Come from during Fiscal Year 2011? An Overview of Lottery Sales for Zip Codes in Select Counties of the Chicago Metropolitan Statistical Area*

though? To measure whether this is the case, we rely upon the Chicago Metropolitan Statistical Area as a case study. Our intent is to estimate the extent to which lottery revenues disproportionately come from communities comprised of people of color compared to those consisting mostly of whites.[7] Therefore, the approach we take is inherently both a racial and a spatial one. Race and space are inseparably linked in our analysis because the Chicagoland area remains among the most segregated places in the entire country (Henricks et al. 2014; Massey and Denton 1993). By a few measures, it can even be characterized as hyper-segregated.[8] (See Figure 5.4 for a spatial overview of segregation patterns in the Chicago Metropolitan Statistical Area.)

The unit of analysis for comparing lottery sales between communities is a zip code tabulation area. This is a census unit generalized from areal representations of the United States Postal Service zip code service areas. In total, the Chicago Metropolitan Statistical Area is comprised by about 300 zip codes. Most of these are neighborhoods that people call home, but a slim minority consist of airports, business districts, or other restricted areas where next to no one lives. Once these sparsely populated areas are omitted for statistical reasons, we are left with 285 zip codes for our final analysis. (See Table 5.2 for a descriptive summary of the socio-demographic

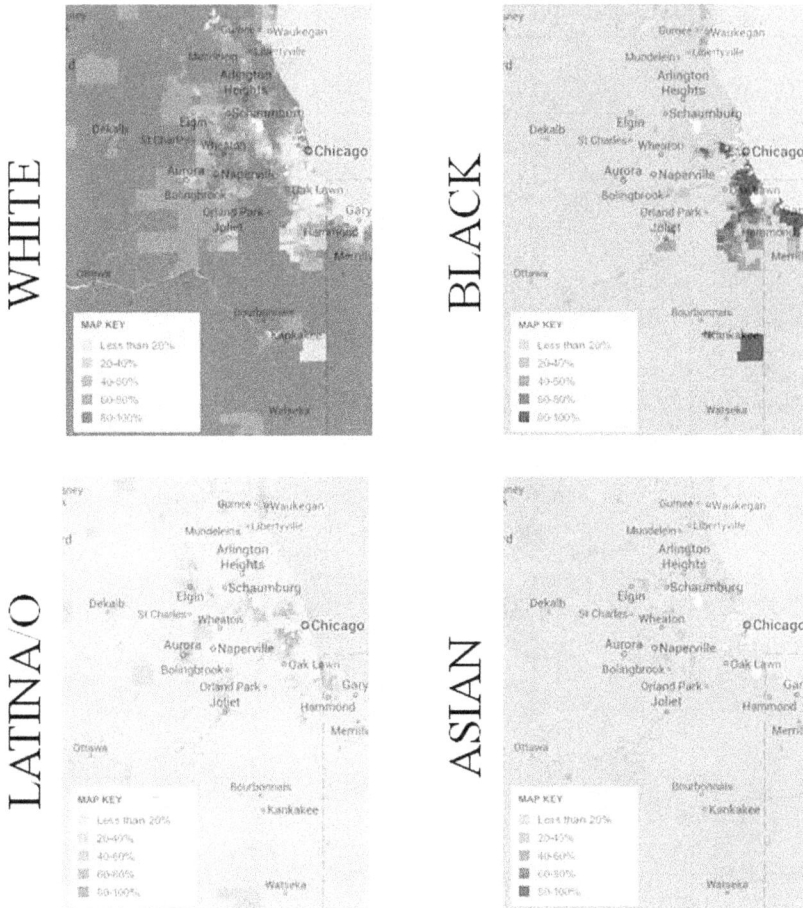

Figure 5.4 How Segregated is the Chicago Metropolitan Statistical Area? A Spatial
Overview by Racial Group*

characteristics regarding these zip codes.) Total lottery revenues generated
by these zip codes in 2011 ranged from a low of $35 thousand to a high of
nearly $27 million. The average zip code, however, amassed about $5.2 in
lottery sales.[9] When lottery revenues are further examined by a community's
racial composition, considerable variation becomes obvious.

Predominantly nonwhite communities, by and large, generate millions of
dollars more than do communities comprised predominantly of white people.[10] Compare the five highest and lowest grossing communities in 2011,
for example (see Figure 5.5). At least $19 million in lottery sales separate
these communities. The five communities that sold the least number of lottery tickets were majority-white spaces. Four of these five communities
consisted of populations that were 90 percent or more white. At the other

Table 5.2 Who Lives in the Chicago Metropolitan Area? A Socio-Demographic Overview by Zip Code

		Mean	Min.	Max.	Std. Deviation
Lottery Revenues					
	Sales for Fiscal Year 2011	5,233,105	35,192	26,805,228	4,758,807
Racial Composition					
	Percent of White Residents	61.7	0.3	96.8	27.9
General Demographics					
	Total Population	27,454	493	113,916	20,712
	Median Years of Age	37.4	23.8	57.0	5.0
	Percent Over 17 Years Old	75.6	63.1	97.4	5.9
	Mean HH Size	2.7	1.5	4.1	0.4
Housing Characteristics					
	Percent of Vacant Units	7.8	1.3	75.0	5.9
	Percent of Renter-Occupied Units	29.2	4.4	75.6	18.0
N (ZCs)					285

* Note: *The data presented here draw from the 2010 Census and audits of the Illinois Department of Revenue.*

end of the spectrum, the highest grossing communities were those where mostly people of color lived. Two of the highest grossing zip codes, which respectively sold about $27 and $21 billion worth of lottery tickets, had black populations of 96.8 and 94.2 percent. The third highest grossing zip code has a black population of 62.2 percent and a Latina/o population of 33.9 percent, while the fourth highest grossing zip code was predominantly Latina/o (75.9 percent).

Though comparing the five highest and lowest grossing zip codes along with their racial compositions offers a quite suggestive interpretation regarding from whom lottery money comes, it remains limited as a form of analysis. Namely, it accounts for only two variables at once, but other

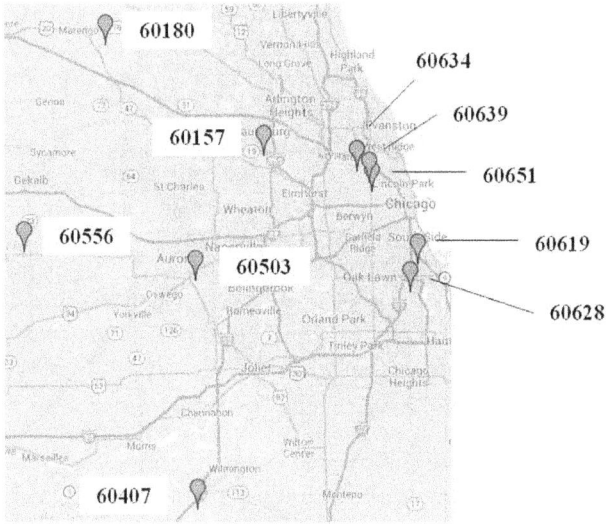

	Total Sales	Percent White	Percent Black	Percent Latina/o
Five Zip Codes with the Lowest Sales				
1. 60503	35,192	61.2	8.8	12.4
2. 60157	39,106	90.6	0.1	5.3
3. 60180	104,899	93.4	0.3	4.1
4. 60407	113,454	93.6	0.5	3.1
5. 60556	123,394	90.2	1.1	5.7
Five Zip Codes with the Highest Sales				
1. 60619	26,805,228	0.5	96.8	1.1
2. 60628	20,964,146	1.2	94.2	3.3
3. 60651	20,036,300	2.8	62.2	33.9
4. 60639	19,844,372	7.1	15.2	75.9
5. 60634	19,333,370	60.1	1.0	33.5

Figure 5.5 How Do Lottery Revenues Range by Zip Code and Racial Composition?*

factors might explain the trends we observe. It is quite possible, for instance, that the communities with the highest grossing sales are also those with the largest population size. If this is the case, then these communities would likely have a larger base of potential tickets buyers and it would make good sense that sales are higher. To account for potential criticisms like these, and to better show the direct impact a community's racial composition has on lottery sales, we perform a linear regression (i.e., ordinary least squares) analysis.[11] Like our logistic regression analysis in the previous chapter, this permits us to gain a more nuanced understanding of how multiple variables simultaneously and independently affect lottery sales. A linear regression analysis yields several results that are of interest to us. Most importantly, it permits us to measure the effects of independent variables, disassociated from other independent variables, on the dependent variable of lottery sales. It also allows researchers to assess how race operates alongside other variables, since social factors do not exist in an isolated vacuum.

We begin with a race-only model, given that our analysis is race-centered, and from there, we supplement this model with two others that progressively subtract other variables that might explain away any observed racial differences. In this analysis, however, race is measured differently since our unit of analysis is a spatial not an individual unit. It is measured by the percentage of white residents within a zip code, which permits us to estimate how much lottery sales increase for each percent increase of white residents. In addition, we want to note that a significant difference between this analysis and the one in the previous chapter is that a linear regression predicts a numerical rather than a probabilistic outcome. In other words, a linear regression analysis allows us to predict how many lottery sales a community might generate given that community possesses certain characteristics. The characteristics we consider include most of those available in the 2010 Census, which include measures of racial composition, population size, age, household size, and various housing attributes.[12]

The main entries listed in Table 5.3 include unstandardized regression coefficients. These represent the predicted change in the dependent variable associated with a one-unit change in a particular independent variable, when all other independent variables are held constant (Lewis-Beck 1980). According to our final model (Model 3), each one-percent increase in a community's white residents decreases sales by $44,746. This is the effect race has on a zip code's lottery sales, when holding constant all other factors. These factors include the total population size, median years of age, percentage of residents over 17 years of age, mean household size, the percentage of vacant units, and the number of renter-occupied units in a community. Below the main entries are various other statistics that summarize the model. Namely this includes the R^2 statistic, which refers to amount of variance the model explains. Essentially, this statistic is a comparison of the actual observations versus predicted observations. It "tells you what proportion of the variability of the dependent variable is 'explained' by the regression model" (Norušis 2008: 43). For the final model, the R^2 statistic is .72. This means that Model 3 explains 72 percent of the variation among annual lottery revenues.[13]

Substantively, what do our models illustrate? They paint a picture of how race independently and simultaneously "colors" annual lottery revenues. For instance, lottery sales per zip code decrease by:

- $894,920 when a community consists of 20 percent white residents,
- $1,789,840 when a community consists of 40 percent white residents,

Table 5.3 What Determines Lottery Sales within the Chicago Metropolitan Area? A Linear Regression Model per Zip Code, Fiscal Year 2011*

		Model 1	Model 2	Model 3
Racial Composition				
	Percent of White Residents	−92,799 (8,515)	−56,477 (6,864)	−44,746 (8,778)
General Demographics				
	Total Population		156 (8)	157 (9)
	Median Years of Age		74,122 (35,819)	131,809 (43,863)
	Percent Over 17 Years Old*		207,955 (57,160)	167,744 (57,955)
	Mean HH Size*		433,489 (828,774)	964,309 (917,903)
Housing Characteristics				
	Percent of Vacant Units			94,748 (34,410)
	Percent of Renter-Occupied Units			15,143 (17,943)
Constant		10,962,162 (576,655)	−15,219,203 (6,491,707)	−17,705,592 (6,914,284)
Model Summary				
	R^2	.30	.71	.72
	N (ZCs)			285

Note: *The main entries listed are unstandardized regression coefficients (β), and the entries listed in parentheses are standard errors. No measures of statistical significance are presented because these data are comprised of population counts.*

- $2,684,760 when a community consists of 60 percent white residents,
- $3,579,680 when a community consists of 80 percent white residents,
- and $4,474,600 when a community consists of 100 percent white residents.

What the evidence from our regression analysis confirms is that our original observation remains true. Most lottery revenues are not generated by predominately white communities. Rather they tend to come from predominately black and Latino/a communities. Given this fact, the Illinois Lottery can also be understood as a racially regressive source of revenue for the state's primary and secondary education system.

Progressive State Finance? Or Robbing Percy and Pablo to Pay Paul? How Lottery Money Is Distributed in Illinois

Following Illinois Public Act 90–548, proceeds from the Illinois Lottery are directed to the Common School Fund. Once there, the Illinois Department of Revenue draws upon this revenue to finance the Illinois State Board of Education who then determines funding levels for school districts across the state ("Illinois State Board of Education" 2011; "State of Illinois" 2009). Alongside the lottery money in this pool are sums of cash generated from other sources, which can broadly range from private sector money to money from the state and federal governments (Johnson 1999; "State of Illinois" 2009). Placement of money in this common fund makes it difficult, if not impossible, for analysts to "follow the money" and trace how lottery dollars are spent. Similarly to how money laundering schemes work, the way Illinois government finances education obscures the origin of how expenditures for this public service originate. This lack of transparency could be demystified, however, if the state created a ledger to show where lottery money is spent with respect to where it originated. As is, no such document exists. We wish we could say this is uncommon.

It is not. The state of Illinois is similar to the rest of the country in how it pays for education. Drawing money from a common fund, the amount of money a school district receives is largely dependent on three criteria: district property taxes, student enrollment, and average daily attendance (McKoy and Vincent 2006). These criteria are outlined in the General State Aid formula, which is provided in Figure 5.6. The first criterion

EVA		Eva stands for Equalized Assessed Value, which refers to local wealth. This is measured by local property taxes. The wealthiest districts receive a flat rate, while impoverished districts are appropriated more money.
ADA		ADA stands for Average Daily Attendance, which is defined by the prior year's best attendance rate during any three-month span. Higher ADA rates translate into higher state appropriations. The wealthiest districts, however, receive a flat rate.
+	High Poverty	The high poverty criterion refers to an additional provision that provides supplemental funding for districts confronted with significant levels of poverty. This is measured by two factors: 1) the number of low-income residents per district and 2) the ADA of a district's pupils.
	$$$$$	

Figure 5.6 General State Aid Formula: How the Illinois State Board of Education Finances Primary and Secondary Schools

requires funding to be based upon measures of local wealth. This primarily consists of money from property taxes, which is also known as Equalized Assessed Value. Depending upon levels of wealth, each district is allotted a foundational level of funds. Impoverished districts are allocated more money than the wealthiest districts, which receive a flat rate. The second criterion accounts for ADA. Districts with high attendance rates receive more money, while those with lower rates receive less money. The wealthiest school districts, however, are capped by this criterion and receive a flat rate for high attendance. The third criterion considers an additional provision for poverty-stricken districts. Districts with high poverty counts can receive additional state funding, which is determined by the number of low-income residents and the average daily attendance of the district's pupils.

At face value, it seems as though the GSA formula embodies an education finance policy that is both race-neutral and economically progressive. Each district's financial ability, without regard to race, is considered before state aid is appropriated. The three criteria outlined above show the state's attempt to ensure that districts that lack resources, as determined by the property tax base, have a basic level of funding, while more affluent areas are obligated to fund their own district's education. For those that do not have ample resources, the state intervenes to make up the difference and guarantee a minimum level of funding. As stated on the Illinois State Comptroller's (N.d.) website, "The formula is designed to distribute more aid to poorer districts and a minimum amount to wealthier districts" (¶ 1). Progressive intentions, however, do not translate into progressive outcomes.

Because the GSA formula guarantees only a basic level of funding, inequities remain due to compounding factors of segregation and disparate wealth gaps across districts. Critics like Gary Orfield and Chungmei Lee (2005) as well as Pamela Walters (2001) argue that such a formula relies too much on local property taxes, and this perpetuates de facto disparities between communities and what they can contribute to education. Residential segregation by race (and class) inevitably leads to "inequalities in tax revenues among school districts [that] produce inequalities in educational resources, facilities, programs, and opportunities" (Walters 2001: 44). Wealthier districts, which are disproportionately white, can often pour more money into education than poorer districts, even when they receive substantially less state aid.

Progressive intentions are further displaced when lottery revenues are redistributed without considering from whom they originated. Roughly 70 percent of all lottery money comes from the Chicagoland area, which means that lottery players in this area contributed over $438 million of the total $668 million allocated to the state's common fund for education. That said, our regression analysis shows that this money is not generated equally across communities. In the Chicagoland area, nonwhite communities contribute considerably more money to education via the lottery than do white communities. Such unequal contributions offset a finance scheme intended to be race-neutral and economically progressive. Because marginalized communities are the primary source for lottery revenues, the formula ends up circulating this money out of these communities and spreads it across all communities.

It is the Illinois State Board of Education's omission of any lottery criterion—like from where and whom this money comes—for determining state aid for education that mobilizes minority money out of minority communities. In a worst case scenario, racially marginalized communities end up subsidizing public education, a service to which all state residents are entitled. The formula permits such an outcome to occur when it does not consider lottery revenues (and from where they come) as a criterion for funding each district. Nonwhite communities could collectively contribute more capital to education through the lottery (in addition to other sources of earmarked revenues for education) than predominantly white communities. When this occurs, financing public education becomes more of a racially inequitable obligation—regardless of progressive intent.

The Illinois Lottery: State-Sponsored (re)Production of Inequality?

During Reconstruction, students of color began enrolling in public schools at unprecedented numbers, but they faced much resistance from whites who refused to fund education for laboring classes, let alone racial minorities (Anderson 1988). White elites responded by restructuring education finance and shifting the burden to people of color. In their view, as Du Bois ([1935] 1992) noted, it was "an unjustifiable waste of private property for public disaster" (p. 641). Not only were blacks levied taxes that paid for general public education, but their schools were self-supported without tax contributions from the white population (Anderson 1988; Du Bois [1935] 1992). Such practices were standard throughout the South, but also spanned much of the nation.

What type of education did their money buy? It bought an education that was subpar and grossly inferior (Anderson 1988). Black students, and other students of color, attended schools that were segregated and underfunded. Such schools were often overcrowded, lacked qualified instructors, and provided inadequate learning materials. Much of the curriculum came to emphasize a vocational focus that presupposed that blacks occupy a position of political and economic subordination (Anderson 1988; Du Bois [1935] 1992). In the words of Du Bois ([1935] 1992), "every cent spent on [these schools] was taken from Negro rents and wages, and came back to property-holders tenfold in increased opportunities for exploitation" (p. 665).

What has changed in education since Du Bois' days is that racial inequalities persist in pervasively insidious ways that are institutional, covert, and seemingly nonracial, but no less effective (Bonilla-Silva 2001). The institution of education remains not a democratizing institution but one that sustains social control and constrains opportunity for mobility (Lewis 2003). Contemporary problems of segregation (Orfield and Lee 2005), tracking (Lewis 2003), high stakes standardized testing (Brennan et al. 2001), among many others, culminate in outcomes of disparity. How schools are financed is another contributing factor, but most scholars have yet to study how the lottery supplements these other discriminatory mechanisms to maintain racial inequality. When it comes to financing public education, lotteries exemplify old perfume in a new bottle.

In the case of Illinois, the lottery did not provide additional funding to education as promised but displaced other progressive sources of tax revenue (Borg and Mason 1988, 1990). Such infrastructural redesign quintessentially frees elite interests of their fiscal responsibility to public finance, all the while displacing the tax burden of public education, a service that helps make capital accumulation possible, onto those who play the lottery most: people of color. It is crucial to understand who this money comes from to understand how fiscal responsibility has been shifted from some groups to others. The evidence we offer shows that reliance on the lottery for education finance discretely shifts the tax burden onto groups marginalized by their racial status. Public education is increasingly supported by regressive taxation of the lottery, which exacerbates racial inequality when it transfers resources from marginalized to mainstream communities. Under the worst circumstances, such communities are burdened with subsidizing public education. This is especially true when lottery tax contributions eclipse other sources of money used to finance public education. When lottery-generated revenues are distributed in such a way, inequitable distributions of economic capital by race are preserved. One community's enrichment comes at the expense of another's impoverishment. It represents a state-sponsored money exchange that captures one mechanism for the reproduction of racial inequality.

Notes

1 An earlier iteration of this chapter appeared as a journal article in *Race Ethnicity and Education* (see Henricks 2014).
2 Whether illegal gambling needed to be curbed, or whether it should have been labeled a social problem, is open to debate. Skeptics of this provision might point to a number of positive effects of the so-called seedy gambling games, such as promoting economic competition among local "runners" (absence of a state monopoly), keeping money within the community, and having higher, untaxed payout rates (Clotfelter and Cook 1989).
3 It is worth noting that Mayor Daley's support of the lottery may have come with strings attached. Though the lottery legislation did not explicitly state that any of its generated revenue would be directed to the newly created Chicago Regional Transportation Authority, in effect this is exactly what happened (Gilbert 1973).

State legislature approved an annual budget of $171 million for the RTA, money that would ultimately come from the same funding pool (the General Revenue Fund) where lottery revenues would be allocated.

4 This is the same Jones who was (re)appointed as Superintendent of the Illinois Lottery by former Governor Pat Quinn in 2011.

5 For those interested in performing their own FOIA request, or auditing and verifying the information presented in this book, a duplication of the formal request we made is offered in Figure A.1 of Appendix A.

6 The counties comprising the Chicago Metropolitan Statistical Area within the state of Illinois include: Cook, Dekalb, DuPage, Grundy, Kane, Kendall, McHenry, and Will.

7 A brief comment on the race and class debate over housing is warranted here. Some attribute the persistence of segregation to economic, not racial, forces (e.g., Wilson 1987), while others show how racial minorities, particularly blacks and some Puerto Ricans, are relegated to live alongside other minorities regardless of class status (e.g., Massey and Denton 1993). Our stance differs from both positions. It is not the salience of class over race, or vice versa, but the convergent nature of how race shapes class that maintains segregation. Consider the work of Oliver and Shapiro ([1995] 2006), for example. Strictly comparing whites and blacks, they show how blacks are more likely to: 1) be discriminated against in "open" housing markets, steered to poverty-stricken, heavily black-concentrated neighborhoods, 2) be denied loans despite comparably equivalent measures of credit-worthiness, 3) be charged much higher interest rates once these loans are approved, 4) reside in homes that appreciate value at significantly lower rates than white counterparts, 5) and transfer significantly less accumulated wealth through inheritance to succeeding generations.

8 Residential segregation, which generally refers to the tendency for racial groups to live apart, can be divided into five distinct geographic dimensions: unevenness, spatial isolation, clustering, centralization, and concentration (Massey and Denton 1993). If four of these dimensions are evident, then hypersegregation, or segregation at much exaggerated levels, is present.

9 Based on our analysis in the previous chapter, it is assumed that most lottery purchases are made in the lottery players' local neighborhoods.

10 Our intent here is not to overgeneralize nonwhite communities by utilizing the white/nonwhite binary. This choice is motivated by methodological and substantive concerns. Methodologically speaking, our analysis relies upon aggregate statistics of zip code areas. This approach prevents us from accounting for racial differences at the individual level within these spatial units. Substantively speaking, the white/nonwhite focus is in line with our findings from Chapter 4 and more squarely addresses power differentials between whites and all other groups. That said, our references to nonwhite communities mostly refer to areas comprised by black and/or Latina/o residents. This is due to Chicagoland's demographic profile and race-based spatial arrangement (Henricks et al. 2014). Asians are the next largest minority group in the region, but most are concentrated within a few zip code areas on the City of Chicago's near west side.

11 Given the tendency for nearby neighborhoods that share similar social attributes to cluster in space, or what spatial analysts refer to as spatial autocorrelation, a risk of biased parameter estimates in linear regression is present. To test whether spatial autocorrection was present, we relied upon Moran's I statistic to test the residuals in our linear model. Because positive spatial autocorrelation was present, we supplemented our original analysis with moving average spatial regression models. These models are omitted here, however, for two substantive reasons: 1) the results they yield do not significantly deviate from the results of

our linear regression models, and 2) our intent in writing this book is to present material with a level of sophistication that does not alienate the potential audience.

12 Measures of income and education as predictors of lottery sales are omitted for practical and substantive reasons. First, these measures are not available in the 2010 Census since this survey was substantially shortened (i.e., to a 10-item questionnaire) compared to past decennial censuses. Second, our own analysis in Chapter 4 as well as other analyses (e.g., Clotfelter and Cook 1989) show that income has little to no effect on lottery sales. And third, income and education are less important than race in our spatial analyses for two reasons: 1) racial minorities are more likely to live alongside one another regardless of socioeconomic status and 2) whites are highly likely to be spatially insulated from all other groups (Henricks et al. 2014).

13 All models have been tested to determine if the assumptions of ols regression were violated, and little evidence is available to indicate the model specifications are problematic.

6   The Hidden Mechanisms of Racism

Placing Lotteries in Broader Contexts of How Race Works in America

"It can be said that the first wisdom of sociology is this: things are not what they seem. . . . It ceases to be simple after a while. Social reality turns out to have many layers of meaning. The discovery of each new layer changes the perception of the whole."

~Peter L. Berger[1]

The words of Peter L. Berger (1963) in the opening chapter of his famous book, *Invitation to Sociology: A Humanistic Perspective*, offer an appropriate conclusion for *State Looteries*. Berger's contribution to sociology was to remind us just how important the field of sociology is to understanding how our lives—our very understanding of the social world in which we live—are guided by larger social forces. It is often the case that we accept the world as less complicated than it really is. We tend to minimize, or perhaps dismiss altogether, the influence that institutions have over us, or the fact that social inequality (e.g., racism, sexism, classism, etc.) occurs not only at an individual level but is (re)produced at the structural level. Debunking social systems allows us the opportunity to "see" what really goes on behind closed doors.

As with anything else in life, some institutional curtains are more transparent than others. We do not have to look hard to capture a more rounded picture of the political, economic, or even social realities of what Berger (1963) labels the "informal power structure." For example, one could think about the latent functions of media that go beyond their role as purveyors of information or entertainment to the public. While we certainly do not mean that studying the media from a sociological point of view is a simple task, it is also our understanding that for the most part people are savvy enough to recognize that the media is also an outlet for political agendas, advertisements, or even satire. On the other hand, when compared to the media, issues of state taxation may be more difficult to untangle, as the curtain may be a bit more opaque. Yet, the ties between the media and taxation further complicate our understanding of power and privilege in the United States.

Perhaps the lottery represents one form of taxation whose curtain is hardest to peer through—the ominous brick wall from which deep inequalities remain safe from discovery. Our hope in this book is that we have provided some clarity to readers as to not only the historical underpinnings behind state lotteries, but also the social, economic, political, and racial implications that are largely hidden from the public. At the very minimum, we trust that we have conveyed the fact that playing the lottery is not simply a matter of individual choice to gamble in hopes of "winning it big." Rather, playing the lottery represents a hidden taxation with insidious consequences for people of color, blacks and Latinas/os specifically, and the poor generally. Thus, it is our intention to make transparent the opaque so that the invisible can be seen. Even though we have only scratched the racial surface on "separate and unequal" state finance of the lottery tax, our hope is that we have allowed some light to shine from behind the curtain.

Behind the Curtain: Taxing without "Taxation"

How can a country with such a rich resistance to taxation (e.g., "no taxation without representation") also be so quick to fuel the lottamania craze that has swept across America? Part of the answer lies in the fact that lotteries represent an anomalous form of taxation (Beckert and Lutter 2009; Clotfelter and Cook 1989; Nibert 2000). Unlike other taxes, people are not legally obligated to pay the lottery tax. Instead, they do so willingly. This mode of taxation permits lotteries to escape the stigmas often attached to other taxes. "The estate tax," for example, is often portrayed as a "death tax" that penalizes success and economic pursuits of the American Dream (Graetz and Shapiro 2005). On the contrary, the lottery is a tax often glorified as a means to transform the American Dream into reality—hence advertisement messages like "All you need is a dollar and a dream" (Heberling 2002). If media representations are any indication, winners happen every day. In this way, as the late media scholar and social critic Stuart Hall (1997) pointed out, effective media messages appear to reflect the very reality that they are constructing. Meanwhile, lottery losers fade into the shadows, as do their tax dollars.

In fact, lottery revenues are rarely, if ever, referred to as tax dollars. Not only does the state avoid advertising the lottery as a tax, but we live in a culture where those who purchase lottery tickets are not referred to as lottery taxpayers but as lottery players. Of course, this language is partly due to the lottery's peculiar position as a state agency. It must accommodate an activity once declared illegal, sanction a product that generates revenue for state treasuries, and stimulate sales to ensure its own existence (Clotfelter and Cook 1989). What this type of framing does is leave people to think of lotteries narrowly in terms of gambling or entertainment. The act of purchasing lottery tickets becomes seen only as a recreational activity, and this obscures (or even disguises) how lottery ticket transactions formalize a particular financial arrangement between social groups. It does so, however, through routinized practices hidden in plain view. Each lottery ticket purchase enacts a particular social relationship between taxpayers, lottery tickets, and through repeated transactions, this relationship becomes solidified as part of the broader social structure—one that is highly organized by race.

State Looteries: Fiscal Policy That Taxes Racial Inequality

Throughout *State Looteries*, we have explored a number of the deeply seeded racial implications, and general social ones too, behind states' tax structures. We argue that the proliferation and maintenance of modern state lotteries in America cannot fully be understood unless seen through the lens of race. It was the implicit and explicit racial politics of taxation, conflicts regarding whom this money is expended upon, and struggles over who carries their fair share of tax burden that set the historical backdrop of lottery proliferation from the 1960s onward (Edsall and Edsall 1991). It was tapping longstanding racialized customs of gambling games (i.e., "the numbers") that transformed lotteries from a fickle form of finance to a money-generating machine (Drake and Cayton [1945] 1993). It has been racially manipulative advertisements, tempting those in minority-concentrated ghettos with wealth beyond their dreams or co-opting Dr. Martin Luther King's "dream" with lottery-laced images, that have sustained lottery revenues over time (Heberling 2002). And perhaps the point most important to our study, the proliferation of lotteries in America represents a racialized reallocation of tax liability and a fundamental redesign of state finance. A common thread that runs throughout *State Looteries* is that the lottery tax functions as a state-sanctioned mechanism for generating, concentrating, and redistributing capital.

Although there are variations in how politicians and lottery agents manipulate "taxplayers" into parting with their money, all states rely upon lotteries for tax revenues that derive from those on the margins. This is important because it ultimately means that vulnerable populations are faced with higher burdens of taxation, while financial relief is afforded to those who need it least. These revenues have substituted for other taxes—ones that are more progressive in structure (see also Borg and Mason 1988, 1990)—meaning that black and brown tax dollars are steadily displacing white tax dollars through the lottery. Matters are only made worse when we consider where and how this lottery money is spent. From the data and analysis we offer, it becomes clear that these revenues are frequently redistributed across the general population not in a trickle-down but a Niagara-up manner. This is why labeling the lottery as "a reverse Robin Hood tax, with racial implications" is an apt analogy. It is the states' most vulnerable populations who are assuming a larger role in financing services most everyone is entitled to. They are the ones assuming a growing financial role in satisfying basic levels of sustenance, which includes a seemingly endless list of infrastructure investments like public education, roads and highways, parks and recreation, and hospitals, among many others. Undoubtedly, this type of lottery spending exacerbates existing socioeconomic disparities between racial groups.

Stereotypes Justify the Lottery Tax, the Lottery Tax Justifies the Stereotypes

The most insidious and egregious outcomes of modern state lotteries—at least in our view—are the racial implications. Many vulnerable populations such as the elderly and the poor are affected by state lotteries, but it is racial minorities that are impacted most. Not only do black and brown folks get much less in return for what they are contributing, but sometimes they end up subsidizing programs that disproportionately benefit whites. This is especially true, for example, in states that earmark lottery dollars to scholarships in higher education (see also McCrary and Palvak 2002; Stranahan and Borg 2004). Although racial minorities bail out finance systems in dire straits, they are often subjected to a victim-blaming ideology that scapegoats them for their own disadvantage (see Ryan 1971). In what Eduardo Bonilla-Silva ([2003] 2014) describes as "cultural racism," minorities are often criticized for lacking "personal responsibility," subscribing to a defective culture, and becoming caught up in a "tangle of pathology."[2] It is as though they are too lazy to pull themselves up by their bootstraps, and would rather take the easy way out in life—perhaps through welfare programs seen as being made possible by white tax dollars (Neubeck and Cazenave 2001).

Of course notions of cultural racism are distortions of fact, but they nonetheless do an effective job of blaming the victim. They provide justifications for the lottery being a tax on those who are impulsive, self-delusional, or mathematically illiterate. Meanwhile, these very narratives hide the lottery from being exposed for what it really is: an additional tax burden that fosters even greater racialized economic inequality. They divert people's attention from larger questions of the lottery tax, fair distributions of tax liability, and fiscal solvency in government. But they do more than distract. These victim-blaming narratives operate in a self-reinforcing way, so that the stereotypes justify the lottery tax and the lottery tax justifies the stereotypes. [3] It is not just that the lottery tax is shaped by an ideology of cultural racism. Rather, the cultural racism framework is intertwined with and embodied in the very tax itself. For these reasons, among others, state lotteries offer a window for seeing how racial hierarchy is preserved through highly infused ideology and practice. More specifically, they lend a means for understanding the "nuts and bolts" of how the racial structure operates.

Structural Racism as a Fluid, Endemic Feature of the Social World

In his landmark article entitled *Rethinking Racism: Toward a Structural Interpretation*, Bonilla-Silva (1997) paved new ways for thinking about how racial hierarchies are preserved in variegated ways over time (i.e., systems of white supremacy). He challenged students and scholars of race to move beyond outdated theories that confine racism to prejudiced attitudes held by individuals.[4] Instead, he argued, we need to understand racial conflict as a structural phenomenon that is materially grounded in practical matters of the everyday—one that is a fluid, yet endemic feature of the social world. Put differently, he argued that we need to grasp racial dynamics within the framework he labels a "racialized social system" (henceforth RSS). The theory is further elaborated by Bonilla-Silva (2001) in his book *White Supremacy and Racism in the Post-Civil Rights Era*. Here, he notes that "[a RSS] refers to societies in which economic, political, social, and ideological levels are partially structured by the placement of actors in racial categories or races" (p. 37). This is not to say that racial groups are real in any natural sense.

The Essential Social Fact of Race

Race may be a biological fiction, but it is a social fact (Bonilla-Silva 1999). It derives from political struggles rooted in everyday practical matters, including what makes American taxes so taxing, who pays these taxes, and what this money buys. Once a previously racially unclassified social relation, practice, or group takes on racial meaning, or becomes racialized (Omi and Winant [1986] 1994), a set of racial formations occurs and develops the ability to shift over time. Though these processes were initiated by power interests of Europeans (e.g, capitalists, planters, colonizers) over non-Europeans, racial categories have the capacity to take on an independent and autonomous life of their own in shaping social structure (Bonilla-Silva 1997, 1999). What constitutes this structure, to be more specific, is the systemic culmination of racialized ideas and practices across multiple, interlocking institutional domains (Bonilla-Silva 1997, 2001).

Despite the essential social fact that race assumes an autonomous and independent role in shaping how social rewards and penalties are distributed, racial dynamics shift over time because racial domination is neither complete nor totalizing (Bonilla-Silva 1997, 2001, [2003] 2014; Lewis 2004). Rather, differently positioned groups within the racial order act in ways to promote their own collective interests. Most members of the dominant group develop ideas and practices to sustain the racial order, whereas many subordinated group members develop ideas and practices to resist it. Though racial conflict is anchored in concrete battles over resources fought on uneven ground (Feagin 2006; Feagin and Elias 2013), its ongoing presence means that opportunities for undermining, if not challenging, the racial rule remain within the realm of possibility (Bonilla-Silva 1997, 2001; Lewis 2004).[5]

"A Change Is Gonna Come": The Emergence of New Racism

Just like the late "King of Soul" Sam Cooke said, "a change is gonna come."[6] So long as racial conflict remains ongoing and unresolved, changes in how racial domination manifests itself should be expected as a "normal" historical outcome (Bonilla-Silva 1997, 2001, [2003] 2014). According to Bonilla-Silva and Amanda Lewis (1999), ideas and practices of today's racial structure ("new racism" for short), which are often more subtle and sophisticated in nature, have emerged to displace those that typified the Jim Crow era. No longer is it politically feasible, for example, to maintain the racially explicit tax laws that W.E.B. Du Bois (1901, [1935] 1992) pointed out a century ago. In the so-called post-racial era, government can no longer impose different sets of taxes on the basis of race. Black people (and other folks of color too) cannot be subjected to paying Jim Crow taxes like the dog or poll tax that escaped whites altogether, nor can they be subjected to paying higher rates of property taxes (Stephenson [1910] 1969).[7]

Instead, today's racially regressive ideas and practices, just like those embodied with the lottery tax, occur in ways that are covert and indirect. New racism is comprised of at least five elements: 1) racial discourse and practice are increasingly covert, 2) direct racial terminology is avoided and many whites claim to experience "reverse racism," 3) political matters with inherent racial agendas are elaborated without direct racial reference (e.g., individual rights, personal responsibility, antistatism), 4) most mechanisms that reproduce racial inequality are rendered invisible, and 5) racial practices characteristic of Jim Crow have been revised, not abandoned (Bonilla-Silva 2001, [2003] 2014; Bonilla-Silva and Lewis 1999). Taken together, these elements represent new ways that white dominance is preserved and minorities are "kept in their place." The way this stratification occurs, however, has been rendered invisible through hidden mechanisms of social control. We argue that the lottery tax represents one component to the ongoing reorganization, which remains partial and incomplete, of the broader racial structure.

From a High- to Middle-Range Sociology: Anchoring The Racialized Social System Framework

Whereas the RSS framework offers a broad-sweeping, highly abstract explanation of how a racial structure acquires autonomy and changes in patterned, resilient ways over time, our goal throughout *State Looteries* has been to empirically anchor this macro-oriented theory within the specific world of the lottery tax. The RSS theory offers a set of logically interconnected propositions that can be scrutinized and verified through observations of empirical uniformities. In this regard, *State Looteries* represents our attempt to learn more of the general (i.e., RSS) through attention paid to the specific (i.e., the lottery tax), and in the process situate the empirical within the theoretical. The orientation of this type of work places data and theory on equal footing, so that any gaps between the two can be bridged. Our study of the lottery tax should not be seen as an end in itself, but as a means of connecting with high-level theory (or theories) so that it can be tested, revised, and if necessary, supplanted. Such an endeavor inherently falls into the realm of what has been labeled as middle-range sociology.

A primer to understanding the scope and purpose of middle-range sociology is offered in Robert K. Merton's ([1949] 1967) *On Theoretical Sociology: Five Essays, Old and New.*[8] He defines it as:

> intermediate to general theories of social systems which are too remote from particular classes of social behavior, organization, and change to account for what is observed and what is observed and those detailed orderly descriptions of particulars that are not generalized at all
>
> (p. 39).

While *State Looteries* is, in part, informed by this approach, it is important to note where we depart from Merton (and others who engage in middle-range sociology). Merton ([1949] 1967) equates totalizing systems of theory with empty explanations of bare nothingness, [9] and in the process, he preemptively squashes any attempt to understand the wholeness of the social world.

According to Peter Hedström and Richard Swedberg (1996, 1998), Merton's vision of a middle-range sociology was to assert it as the discipline's entire platform. Yet dismissal of the notion of totality is problematic because it closes off what questions can be asked. It leaves those of us who have interests in using middle-range sociology to offer clarity to "big picture" theories of racial structure with a conceptual partiality that can address only isolated aspects of this oppression. Fredric Jameson (1981) warned of this very problem in his critique of post-modern theory, but his words can be adapted here: "Without a conception of the totality (and the possibility of transforming a whole system), no socialist politics is possible" (p. 355). Totality is a concept that makes radical change possible, because it permits understanding the fundamentals of a problem and going to the root of it.

In contrast to Merton's ([1949] 1967) position, our strategy engages in middle-range sociology with the purpose of advancing high-level theory. What we offer with our analysis of the lottery tax is an advancement in understanding the dynamic processes at play in the everyday reproduction of racial structure. *State Looteries* offers more than sensitizing readers' interpretive abilities to the racial implications of state lotteries. Our work deepens the explanatory power of the RSS framework, in ways that are direct and fine-grained, toward a more precise, durable, and encompassing high theory that can consolidate the empirical attention to detail we have offered. In this way, *State Looteries* can be seen as a link between what can be theoretically explained and empirically observed through the sociological record.

The Hidden Mechanisms of Racial Oppression: Placing Lotteries in Context of How Race Works in America

The theoretical worth of the RSS framework lies in its ability to orient researchers to conceptualize distinctive problems that can be answered through empirical inquiry. Namely, what are the mechanisms at play within a racial structure working to (re)produce observable outcomes that solidify a malleable, but enduring racial hierarchy? It has been our aim throughout *State Looteries* to identify and explicate the lottery tax as one of these mechanisms, which, as Merton ([1949] 1967) argued, represent the conceptual building blocks of middle-range sociology. For the sake of clarity, let us define the meaning of "social mechanism." Simply put, a social mechanism refers to established sets of interactions between ideas and practices by which a set of outcomes takes place. These interactions are not mere abstract connections that link cause and effect (Hedström and Swedberg 1996, 1998; see also Hughey et al. 2015). Rather, they are contingent upon power relations (like racial conflict) that are located in particular socio-historical contexts (Hedström and Ylikosk 2010).

To offer more order on the functions of a social mechanism, we draw upon the work of Neil Gross (2009). He outlines unifying themes across the literature written on social mechanisms, which can at times be unclear and quite amorphous. According to Gross (2009), social mechanisms:

1) mediate between cause and effect,
2) unfold across time,
3) possess general properties, but can vary in degree,
4) and comprise elements at lower orders of aggregation than the phenomenon they help explain (p. 361–363).

Focus on the identification of these functions offers ways to distinguish coincidental association and causality, so the curtain can be raised on fundamental processes that account for observable outcomes. This approach goes beyond "black box" theoretical explanations in which the collective actions and practices that enact structure are inferred but not directly observed (Elster 1989; Hedström and Swedberg 1996, 1998).

In light of the above, we can think about state lotteries as tax arrangements that operate as a hidden mechanism within the racial structure. Focus on the lottery tax illuminates a new mode of "nonracial taxation" that enables and constrains certain capital flows mediated by a white-dominated state. These capital flows represent formalized relationships, which are enacted with the collection and reallocation of each lottery dollar, between the state and racial groups—ones that are justified by an ideology that justifies this mode of state finance. Our social mechanism approach permits the explication of systemic sets of established interactions ideas and practices that offer plausible accounts for how seemingly nonracial practices, though some explicit ones too, are linked to consequences of taxation. After all, *State Looteries* is a cautionary tale of the racial underpinning of how lotteries have reconfigured America's tax composition in ways that maintain or exacerbate existing racial hierarchy.

Saying It Plain: The Broader Racial Significance of Lotteries

Was Malcolm X correct when he said: "Racism is like a Cadillac, they bring out a new model every year" (qtd. in Lipsitz 1998: 182)? Today's models look very different in appearance compared to the models of yesterday; so do the tax structures of today compared to those of slavery and Jim Crow. Nonetheless, their essence remains the same. In Chapter 1, we discussed various forms of taxation that explicitly required different races to pay different taxes. Laws like these ended through legal reforms made possible by various social movements of Abolitionists and Black Freedom Struggles—if not in practice, then at least on paper. "Old Cadillacs never die," George Lipsitz's (1998) points out, "but they sometimes become too expensive to maintain" (p. 183). The racially disparate tax codes that predate the 1960s fell out of fashion due to changing social norms, but if Malcolm X were alive today, we "bet" he would caution against thinking these tax laws are dead—modes of state finance like the lottery tax included.

Racism survived the 1960s, despite claims to the contrary. Some celebratory figures have gone so far as to declare racism all but dead in America today. Following the presidential election of Barack Obama, numerous media pundits (e.g., Cohen 2008; Matthews 2010) and academics alike (e.g., Glaeser and Vigdor 2012; Heckman 2011) have declared that the United States has entered a "post-racism" era. In doing so, they dismiss, diminish, or deny the ways that racial discrimination continues to shape life circumstances, opportunities, and what resources people can attain. It is as though racial barriers are no more. To their point, racial dynamics can and do change. Malcolm X pointed out as much in his Cadillac analogy. While it is undeniable that some racial progress has occurred, it is another claim altogether to say that race no longer matters, or that past and present racial discrimination are no longer salient.

In a world that is supposedly beyond race, race remains a significant predictor in virtually every socioeconomic measure available to social scientists. What Dr. Martin Luther King (1967) observed long ago remains true even today: black people (and many Latinas/os too) have only half of what is good in life and double of what is bad. Moreover, minorities themselves are not responsible for their own subordinate position within the racial order. What is responsible are the systemic mechanisms like those we have outlined in the case of the lottery tax. Though tax laws like these give the appearance of a "new" racial order, they nonetheless share historical continuity with tax laws that preceded them. The lottery tax represents state finance that is by no means impartial and without racial consequence.

On the contrary, it entails hidden biases that have the capacity to reproduce racial inequalities over time. This tax blocks capital accumulation for people of color, hoards resources for many whites, and reallocates minority capital through unfair distributions of tax burdens. All the while, rationales for this mode of state finance places blame on minorities themselves for self-imposing these tax burdens. In doing so, lotteries represent a robust social mechanism of racial oppression that extends Jim Crow practices into the modern era. Yet the lottery tax is unlike Jim Crow of old because it lacks the explicit, in-your-face quality. Rather, it is a form of taxation that occurs behind the opaque curtain, away from direct view. This is what makes the lottery tax so potently dangerous, and perhaps all the more effective as a form of racial domination. It involves often-overlooked practices that most people partake in, but these practices are racial in every way but name. So let us never forget the words of Malcolm X, and let us call this new Cadillac what it is: Racism.

Notes

1 Quote taken from: Berger, Peter L. 1963. *Invitation to Sociology: A Humanist Perspective*. New York: Doubleday.
2 This view is hardly exclusive to representations common in everyday discourse and media representations, but even pervades "academic" viewpoints offered by conservatives like Shelby Steele (1990) and Stephen Thernstrom and Abigail Thernstrom (1997) or liberals like William Julius Wilson (1978, 1987).
3 This point owes heavily to the works of Barbara Cruikshank (1997), Kenneth J. Neubeck and Noel Cazenave (2001), and Patricia Hill Collins ([1990] 2010).
4 A number of others have also issued this critique (e.g., Carmichael and Hamilton 1967; Feagin and Eckberg 1980; Knowles and Prewitt 1969; Steinberg [1995] 2001; Wellman [1977] 1993).
5 This point extends Antonio Gramsci's ([1946] 1971) "war of position," in which he described the nature of cultural resistance to capitalism, to matters of race.
6 The reference alludes to Sam Cooke's 1964 song, "A Change is Gonna Come." It is one of the many songs commonly said to exemplify Black Freedom Struggles.
7 Racially explicit state-sponsored discrimination has been formally abolished on paper, but not in practice. Examples outside the realm of taxation include Arizona's SB1070 "Show Your Papers" law and Pennsylvania's "Voter ID" law. Arizona's SB1070 refers to the passage of among the broadest and strictest immigration measures of recent times. One of the most controversial provisions of the law was upheld by the U.S. Supreme Court decision (*Arizona et al. v United States* 567 U.S. 11–182 [2012]). It provides police officers the authority to check a person's immigration status should they have "reasonable suspicion," which remains broadly defined, that the person lacks citizenship. The Pennsylvania's "Voter ID" law, or Pennsylvania Election Code (25 P.S. § 2602(z.5)(2)), requires a government-approved form of identification to vote. Bell ([1973] 2008) compares these laws to historical poll taxes practiced in Jim Crow South because they negatively impact blacks and Latinas/os at disproportionate levels, and require many to drive great distances and pay extra money to merely participate in electoral politics.
8 Alternative sources to introduce readers to middle-range sociology are available. See also: Boudon (1991), Coleman (1990), Elster (1989), Granovetter (1978), Hedström and Swedberg (1996, 1998), and Lazarsfeld et al. (1944).
9 In Merton's ([1949] 1967) own words, he writes: "[I]t would seem reasonable to suppose that sociology will advance insofar as its major (but not exclusive) concern is with developing theories of the middle range, and it will be retarded if its primary attention is focused on developing total sociological systems" (p. 50). He goes on to say, "To concentrate entirely on a master conceptual scheme for deriving all subsidiary theories is to risk producing twentieth-century sociological equivalents of the large philosophical systems of the past, with all their varied suggestiveness, their architectonic splendor, and their scientific sterility" (p. 51).

Postscript
Going All In
Available Policy Alternatives

"We know everything about poor people: what they don't work at, what they don't eat, how much they don't weigh, how much they don't grow, what they don't think, how often they don't vote, and what they don't believe in.

The only thing left to learn is why poor people are poor.

Could it be because we are clothed by their nakedness and nourished by their hunger?"

~Eduardo Galeano[1]

The position we take on writing about existing social problems is one that understands politics as inseparable from academic life. When Howard Becker (1967) asked: "Whose side are you on?" his question was one that probed the longstanding divide in sociology between value-free and value-driven research. Those who push value-free research tend to place faith in the sociological dogma of objectivity, while supporters of value-driven research tend to be explicit about their advocacy position and the potential subjectivity this introduces (Furner 1975). Just because self-proclaimed impartial scientists claim neutral politics does not mean that their work goes without political consequence. Those that hide behind the veneer of objectivity or impartiality have already chosen a side. That side is "business as usual," and often an affirmation of the status quo.

We acknowledge that the political stance we outline throughout the postscript runs the risk of delegitimizing the perceived scientific integrity of the analysis we offer. To Stephen Steinberg's (2007) point, this is only because "value-free" sociology has been normalized as *the way* of doing science. Approaches that deviate from this stance, as scholars of marxist, feminist, and critical race traditions are well aware, are vulnerable to assertions that their positions fall outside the acceptable means of practicing research. These assertions are made by gatekeepers of sociology, who themselves are embedded within a power structure, and who then decide whether to open or close the door on what constitutes "truth," or at least how to arrive at it. Were we to stop short of offering solutions and taking actions to see them through, it would be us who are "clothed by the nakedness and nourished by the hunger" of those we write about. Our intent is not to reduce *State Looteries* to mere expressions of cynicism that propel our own career advancement (or lack thereof). Rather, we hope to confront and challenge the mechanized gears of racism, so that one day they might stop churning.

The problem with lotteries is not the lottery tax itself, but the fundamental conflicts surrounding a racialized fiscal crisis that remains unresolved. Lotteries are like placing a band-aid on a gaping wound in severe need of stitches. The racialized fiscal problems that lie ahead of us are systemic, and as such, they call for systemic solutions. Given that lotteries have ways of reproducing racial inequalities (and other social inequalities too), it would be quite convenient to call for an end to them altogether. In fact, some scholars have offered this suggestion (e.g., Borg, Mason, and Shapiro 1991). We sympathize with the underlying reasons for this solution, but we do not share this view. Many options are available, which we outline below, to make lotteries a social mechanism of progressive racial change. Of course, our suggestions might produce unintended consequences, but the outcome of not doing anything carries far more risk. It is for these reasons, among others, that we couple our critical view of the lottery tax with one that offers constructive alternatives and avenues of resistance. *Another world is possible.*

Acknowledge that Post-Racial America Is a Lie, a Dangerous One

We live in a world where race should not matter, but it does. The problem with post-racial views is not that they ignore racial inequality altogether. As Eduardo Bonilla-Silva (2001, [2003] 2014), Kimberlé Crenshaw (1997), and Charles Gallagher (2003) have pointed out, it is that they downplay, dismiss, or outright deny that past and present practices of racial oppression have anything to do with racial inequality. If people commit themselves to not seeing what reproduces racial inequality on an everyday basis, then they are not likely to understand how racial inequality works, let alone know how to squarely deal with it. The work of widely recognized analysts, like James Heckman (2011), for example, advances class-based solutions to problems confronting people of color. Their logic is that class-based prescriptions will do more to elevate minorities out of poverty, since they are overrepresented by this disparity, than will race-specific programs like affirmative action.

Others like William Julius Wilson (1987) have gone so far as to argue against affirmative action on the basis that it disproportionately benefits middle class people of color, all the while furthering class divisions within minority groups:

> Those with the greatest economic, educational, and social resources among the less advantaged individuals are the ones who are actually tapped for higher paying jobs and higher education through affirmative action
>
> (Wilson 1987: 115).

These views resonate with colorblind views across the political spectrum, but critics (e.g., Bonilla-Silva 2001; Collins 1997; Steinberg [1995] 2001) argue they are misguided at best and possibly wrong at worst. Steinberg ([1995] 2001) points out that Wilson's position has yet to be substantiated by evidence. They are opinion, not fact. Other studies, like those completed by Sharon Collins (1997), challenge Wilson's stance.

Collins (1997) reveals how even black corporate executives who have benefitted from affirmative action programs remain in fragile economic positions. This is because their climb up the occupational ladder was made possible not by market but political forces. The disruptive Black Freedom Struggles of the 1960s and 1970s forced a reorganization of the occupational structure. New positions that once did not exist were created for what would become the black middle class, tokenized positions like "diversity coordinators," "affirmative action compliance officers," and so on. Any withdrawal of the race-specific policies (e.g., the creation and enforcement of antibias public policies) that created these positions will threaten not only occupational stability but black stability. This is because the black middle class within the labor market remains without a stable foundation. In other words, successful government mandates must possess an explicit racial component if upward mobility of minority folks is to be expanded and stabilized. Only then will the persisting problems Collins (1997) identifies be addressed, as well as many other race-specific problems.

Despite claims otherwise, race-blind solutions will do little to address why "Emily and Greg" are more employable than "Lakisha and Jamal." In a study taking up this very question, Marianne Bertrand and Sendhil Mullainathan (2004) found that job applicants with "black-sounding" names were half as likely to be interviewed than those with "white-sounding" names, even when qualifications were held constant. Race-blind solutions will do little to address persisting problems in education. George Farkas (2003) identifies three of these. Minority students are more likely to: 1) be grouped as lower-ability students and placed in weak academic settings, 2) labeled as special education students (which corresponds with lower teacher expectations and student effort), and 3) attend lower-funded schools due to compounding factors of housing segregation (Farkas 2003). Race-blind solutions will do little to address why lasting consequences of a criminal record punish black men more than white men. Devah Pager (2003) points out that white convicted felons are preferred in entry-level jobs over black applicants with no criminal record at all. As these trends suggest, racial disparities on virtually every measure available to social scientists are not merely a corollary to something else like class, but they result from racially biased practices in institutional domains like employment, education, housing, and, most importantly to this study, taxation.

The tax revolts of the 1960s and 1970s contained a component that was irreducibly racial—so did the lottery advertisements, the structure and implementation of "numbers games," and so on. What we have shown throughout *State Looteries* is that the racial politics of yesterday, and the legacies they have spawned, remain very much alive and intact in contemporary tax ideas and practices. Today's racial structure persists in more pervasively insidious ways that are institutional, covert, and seemingly non-racial, but this makes it no less effective (Bonilla-Silva 2001, [2003] 2014; Bonilla-Silva and Lewis 1999). State lotteries may seem like a new political development in the world of racial inequality, but if we look just beneath the surface, it becomes clear that they have been shaped by the heavy hand of history—one that is filled with conflicts of taxation that are highly racialized. Therefore, the only solutions to race-specific problems involve those that are race-conscious solutions, and policy options that can bring them about should be unapologetically pursued.

Attain Tax Literacy, Label Lottery Purchases as Taxes

Reflecting on his time as Majority Leader of the New Jersey Legislature, Alan J. Karcher (1989) writes:

> Taxes of any description are not high on any legislator's list of favorite agenda items, and tax alternatives, such as a lottery, are easily viewed as some type of panacea. With their backs to the wall, legislators demonstrate a distinct preference for those measures least likely to incite heavy political reaction. Revenue-raising proposals that avoid easy identification as taxes—"surcharges for example—are much in style; and the more artfully hidden, the better, when it comes to taxes. Some levies are hidden so well that it is difficult to see on whom the burden actually falls, but it is even more common to see legislatures resort to expedient of adopting measures admitted to be regressive, and lotteries are what many consider to be the most regressive of all forms of taxation
>
> (p. 37).

When taxes are regressive, this generally means that they place higher tax burdens on those who can least afford to pay (Newman and O'Brien 2011). The state sales tax represents an example of a regressive tax. Policymakers and academics alike sometimes refer to taxation like this as "value added taxes" (or VAT for short). They can appear fair in form, since they are levied without discrimination and everyone is taxed the same flat rate, but they are not.

It is universal appeals to neutrality and impartiality like these that conceal how tax laws can serve partial interests (Brown and Fellows 1996; Infanti 2008). Practically speaking, regressive taxes cause the poor to pay higher portions of their income for the same products purchased by the wealthy. To illustrate our point, consider the Tennessee state sales tax (which is about a 10-percent rate on all consumption items) and two hypothetical families of four—one earns $5,000 per month, the other earns $2,000. Assuming both families budget $1,000 per month for groceries alone, each will pay about $100 to Tennessee in sales tax. Though both families pay the same absolute amount of taxes in these purchases, the family earning $5,000 per month pays about 2 percent of their total income toward sales taxes, whereas the other family pays 5 percent. This means that the lower-income family has to spend far more of their income just to survive.

Progressive taxes, on the other hand, possess qualities that run in opposition to regressive taxation. They are typically framed in terms of an individual's "ability to pay," since these taxes include rates that "progress" from low to high. The federal income tax of "the Code"[2] is a commonly cited example. It contains a tax rate, or a percentage of a person's total income, that is graduated in form. Higher-earning individuals and households (usually) fall into brackets that require them to pay higher percentages in taxes than their lower-income counterparts.[3] According to the 2010 Code (which includes the last year of "the Bush tax cuts"), the top statutory rate was 35 percent. The bottom rate was 10 percent.

The terminology of regressivity and progressivity does not represent an exhaustive account for how taxes are administered and revenues generated, but these labels are helpful in orienting people toward questions of how tax burdens are distributed. Still, these terms do not offer a language for answering questions of how different types of taxes comprise the overall tax structure. Those within the world of taxation, as Robin Einhorn (2006) points out, refer to these matters as tax incidence. The concept implies that those interested in tax matters, if they are to be understood holistically, must discern how taxes operate in a relational fashion alongside one another. The proliferation of lotteries during the late 20th century represents a broader trend in the overall tax structure of the United States. The country has moved from having a modestly (if at all) progressive tax structure to one that is increasingly regressive.

We say modestly progressive because, comparatively speaking, the United States has a far more progressive tax structure than many other countries— including European nations that have robust welfare states (Morgan and Prasad 2009). What has for the most part escaped taxation in America, however, are forms of wealth.[4] This is especially true for wealth that comes in the form of personal property that, unlike investments tied to real estate, is movable. The omission of taxation on wealth in the legal code should say something about the progressivity, or lack thereof, in American taxation and the political interests of "who rules America" (Domhoff [1967] 2013). Beginning with the legal codification of the United States as a nation-state, the people of "we the people" have always been defined by a few elite white men who owned wealth (Feagin 2006, 2012). And of course questions regarding wealth, like *what* constitutes it and *who* can legally possess it, have deeply rooted origins that are tied to slavery and white racial domination (Harris 1993).

Over the past half-century, the few progressive taxes that have been available in America have been steadily eroded. Federal statutory rates on income, for example, have been drastically reduced (Piven and Cloward 1982),[5] and branding efforts that stigmatize taxation on extreme accumulations of wealth, like labeling the estate tax "the death tax," have grown widely popular (Graetz and Shapiro 2005). Meanwhile, regressive forms of taxation are on the rise. This includes, for example, the growing implementation of sales taxes throughout the Southern and Western regions of the country (Newman and O'Brien 2011). It also includes other forms of taxation that often remain hidden in plain view, ones like the lottery tax. Because lottery participants are labeled as players rather than taxpayers, lotteries represent one form of taxing without taxation.

This sleight of hand is one way the relationship between individuals and the state becomes obscured—and tax burdens hidden. In the words of Karcher (1989):

> There is a certain romance in being referred to as a 'player'; a certain panache is associated with the word. It conjures up glamorous images of striped awnings over the clubhouse veranda at the race track or tuxedoed dealers passing the shoe at a baccarat table. There is nothing romantic or glamorous about being just another statistic—faceless and anonymous—a mere taxpayer
>
> (p. 38–39).

This kind of euphemism may sex up the lottery's appeal, but it does not change the fact that lottery revenues are tax revenues. Just like other taxes, taxplayer purchases of the lottery represent money-exchanges between two entities, with the state acting as an intermediary. The collection end of this exchange requires people to pay out of their own volition, but as other lottery scholars like Jens Beckert and Mark Lutter (2009), Charles Clotfelter and Philip Cook (1989), and David Nibert (2000) point out, these dollars carry the same value regardless of how they were collected.

Check Welfare Racism with Wealthfare AntiRacism

Throughout American history, as Joe Feagin (2006, 2012), George Lipsitz (1998), and others have shown, whites have been afforded exclusive wealthfare opportunities. One potent example to illustrate this includes New Deal-initiated housing practices of the 20th century. They represent a shift in public policy that transformed homeownership into the quintessential piece of the American Dream pie that it is today. No other asset is more central to a majority of Americans' wealth portfolio than homeownership (Wolff 1998). Homeownership is the most prized possession for those in the bottom 80 percent of America's wealth distribution. Less than one century ago, this was not the case. According to census records, only 47.8 percent of Americans owned their home in 1930 ("US Census Bureau" N.d.). This figure increased about 15 points to 62.9 percent by 1970. The federal government, as Kenneth Jackson (1985) argues, had forever altered how people came to own their homes.

Until the 1930s, most homeowners were required to pay nearly half their mortgage upfront and the rest soon thereafter. Lending initiatives of the newly created Federal Housing Authority (henceforth FHA), and later the Veteran's Administration, helped subsidize homeownership by creating mortgages that came with low down payments and interest rates, plus extended finance schedules that could be paid over many years. According to FHA (1959) records, it alone had financed three out of every four homes between the 1930s and 1959. Even a majority of mortgages obtained from private lending institutions followed the same conditions established by the federal government (Gotham 2002). Effectively, these new lending practices radically expanded homeownership opportunity. Not everyone received an invitation, though.

New Deal housing initiatives were, more or less, exclusive to white families (Gotham 2002; Kirp et al. 1995; Massey and Denton 1993; Ross and Yinger 2002).[6] Alongside new lending practices, New Deal policy established the Home Owners' Loan Corporation (henceforth HOLC) to create a nationwide property appraisal system. Its purpose was to assess property value by scores of neighborhood quality and creditworthiness (Jackson 1985). What the HOLC created, according to Douglas Massey and Nancy Denton (1993), was a valuation system that followed a racial continuum. The highest valued properties were those in virtually all white neighborhoods, while the lowest were those in neighborhoods mostly comprised of people of color, with racially diverse neighborhoods falling somewhere in between. By the count of David Kirp, Hohn Dwyer, and Larry Rosenthal (1995), this system caused less than one percent of all mortgages issued between 1930 and 1960 to go to black families. Effectively, New Deal housing initiatives assisted 28 million families in moving from urban to suburban spaces—27 million of which were white (Massey and Denton 1993). Meanwhile many minority families were left behind in concentrated areas of urban decay and economic divestment.

We bring up the example of New Deal-initiated housing practices because it contradicts and challenges commonplace racial stereotypes that some conservative scholars (e.g., Steele 1990; Thernstrom and Thernstrom 1997) use to say otherwise. These are the very stereotypical narratives that saturated tax revolts of the 1970s discussed in Chapter 3, which paint folks of color as free-riding moochers who would prefer nothing more than to live off of the government. Yet examples of white homeownership wealthfare reveal just how distorted this perspective is. People of color have long offered contributions that made possible the socioeconomic advancement of whites, only to be excluded from the very opportunities their material sacrifices made possible. If anyone has gotten a free ride throughout American history, whether we are talking about the eras of slavery, Jim Crow, or moderns times, it has not been people of color.

People of color have bailed out America time and time again. This is especially true in the area of taxation. We have already mentioned the various Jim Crow taxes that were imposed on black folks in the late 1800s and early 1900s (see Du Bois 1901, [1935] 1992; Stephenson [1910] 1969; Thornton 1982), but these examples are not the only ones. Minorities have been long subjected to pay many different types of taxes for services and resources from which they have been excluded. This was true, for example, with regard to the Social Security Act of 1935 whereby old-age and unemployment insurance was provided only to "qualified" beneficiaries. Despite paying payroll taxes, agricultural laborers and domestic servants (two occupations where black people were relegated and concentrated) were excluded from benefits by a Southern-controlled Congress (Quadagno 1988). Many of these restrictive provisions were slow to expand and did not incorporate agricultural laborers and domestic servants until 1976. Moving forward, this remains true with Social Security today. Many undocumented Latinas/os pay Social Security taxes for services they will never receive due to their noncitizen status. In 2005, for example, the Social Security Administration identified thousands of unauthorized workers who contributed US$7 billion that could not be credited properly to the appropriate beneficiaries (Porter 2005).

The lottery tax works in similar ways. It has shifted tax burdens away from property owners and corporate interests to those who play the lottery most (Borg and Mason 1988, 1990). In the process, people of color have steadily assumed larger shares of paying taxes that make possible public services we all enjoy. Those who deploy stereotypical narratives would have us believe that minorities are parasites on general society (e.g., Huntington 2004). They would have America believe that whites' tax dollars are being thrown away at the unsolvable "Negro problem" or "immigrant problem." As Richard Wright pointed out long ago, however, "there is only a white problem" (qtd. in Lipsitz 1998: 1). The evidence we offer throughout *State Lotteries* turns the misinformation on its head, and in the process, it represents our attempt at checking welfare racism with wealthfare antiracism. We need more truth-telling that aspires to this goal. After all, it is often the contributions of those "free-loading" people of color that are giving many of us a "free ride."

Equality Taxes by Design, Overhaul the Tax State

When state finance relies upon quick fix reforms, like the lottery tax, it is the people who are left in the wake to suffer. The property tax limitations of the 1970s, alongside the broader socioeconomic transformations of this time, have effectively left fewer resources, reduced quality, and dampened the performance of public services. This is especially true in the area of education

(Downes 1992; Downes and Figlio 1999; Downes et al. 1998; Figlio 1997). Lottery money has helped reduce these pains, but it does not resolve the problem of why this money was needed to begin with. A fundamental problem with fiscal policies in America is that they focus on the bare minimum (e.g., minimum wage, per pupil funding requirements, etc.)—nothing more, nothing less. Left unaddressed are levels of excess and waste. Yet sociologists like Charles Tilly (1998) remind us of the various ways that inequality, whether related to race, class, gender, or other factors, is a relational concept. It cannot be understood, let alone resolved, if only half the equation is considered (i.e., marginality). For these reasons, we suggest that one way to ease the problem of budgetary shortfalls for education (and government more generally) would be to raise revenues by eliminating unnecessary housing subsidies.

Homeowners qualify for a number of tax perks that are unavailable to those who do not own a home. The real property tax deduction (26 U.S.C. §164(a)(1)), for example, permits homeowners (really homebuyers) to subtract money paid toward local and state property taxes from their federally taxable income. Meanwhile the mortgage interest deduction (26 U.S.C. §163(h)(1), (h)(2)(D)) allows homeowners to reduce levels of federally taxable income by the amount of interest paid toward a mortgage.[7] These tax incentives are problematic on a number of counts. As Dorothy Brown (2010) points out, these types of homeownership subsidies surpassed more than $209 billion in foregone federal tax revenues in 2009 alone. One political scientist puts this figure into perspective by estimating that annual homeownership tax benefits routinely double what the federal government spends on low-income housing (Howard 1997). Another sociolegal scholar's approximation suggests this ratio is too conservative, as he argues that homeownership tax perks quadruple low-income housing expenditures in any given year (Salsich 1993). Despite these discrepancies, it is safe to conclude that both analysts agree, in relative terms, that homeownership is overly subsidized.

These homeownership subsidies are not evenly distributed by race either. A number of sociolegal scholars (e.g., Brown 2010; Moran and Whitford 1996; powell 1996) and sociologists (e.g., Oliver and Shapiro [1995] 2006; Shapiro 2004) point to the obvious housing wealth disparities and hypothesize that tax incentives are one reason for their perpetuation. john powell (1996) contends:

> [B]ecause home ownership is highly correlated with race, subsequent 'neutral' tax deductions benefitting homeowners have operated to the disproportionate benefit of whites, exacerbating [racial] disparity
> (p. 93).

Meanwhile, few tax incentives are available for the assets and liabilities (e.g., motor vehicles, credit card debt, or outstanding medical bills) most likely to be possessed by racial minorities (Brown 2010; Moran and Whitford 1996; powell 1996). These are among the reasons that these tax deductions should be abandoned. Still other options can help raise revenues too.

What if local governments were to raise property taxes? Hear us out before you dismiss the suggestion. As currently implemented, property taxes all too often subsidize the wealth of corporations that, technically speaking, own a good portion of the homes many Americans reside in. Banks and credit unions are not liable for property taxes on homes in the process of purchase, even though they retain the capacity to leverage this equity in their everyday business operations. Since these financial institutions continue to profit off of the homes they partially own, it makes good sense that they should be obligated to pay taxes on this vested capital too. An alternative mode of taxing property would prorate them accordingly. If Bank of America owns 90 percent of a family's home, for example, then they should pay 90 percent of the property tax bill. The structure of such a tax would ease the early costs that come with buying a home, and ultimately encourage homeownership, given the amortization structure of most home loans. Early payments of a standard installment schedule are high in interest but low in principle. This means that the liability of property taxes would gradually shift from financial institutions to homeowners.

We recognize that the solutions we have offered so far will do nothing to alleviate how property taxes are often passed down from landlords through rent (Fischer et al. 1996). To address this problem, a "Rental Tax Credit" (henceforth RTC) could be implemented. This policy could be modeled after the Earned Income Tax Credit (henceforth EITC), a federal law that was born out of the welfare debates of the 1960s and 1970s. It was President Richard Nixon and Democratic Congressman Russell Long who worked together to develop a plan that offers tax relief to low-income workers (Lui et al. 2006; Yin 1996). The EITC offsets the taxes of low- to moderate-income families, ones that earn too much for much welfare assistance but still struggle to make ends meet, by providing them with a refundable income tax credit. As a testament to its success, the law is often credited for having lifted millions of American families out of poverty (Oliver and Shapiro [1995] 2006).

A RTC could operate in a similar way so that people, especially those experiencing financial need or hardship, pay no more than a certain threshold of disposable income for housing—something that should constitute a basic human right. In some places like Illinois, Minnesota, and the District of Columbia, similar laws are already on the books. Those familiar with the world of residential taxation call them "homestead rebates" or "circuit breakers." Another version of a RTC would be what Thomas Shapiro (2004) labels Down Payment Accounts. "Similar to the home mortgage interest deduction," writes Shapiro (2004), "renters could deduct a portion of their rent on their tax form and have it put aside in a dedicated account to match their own savings for homeownership on a one-on-one basis" (p. 189). This program is ideal for working-class people of color who are first-time homebuyers, especially those who lack money for down payment and closing costs, and it could be funded in part by lottery money. In addition, we might consider supplementing this lottery money with pay-outs from class action settlements from banks, lending institutions, and insurance companies found guilty of discriminatory lending, racial steering, redlining, and other profiling practices.

Of course, eliminating homeownership subsidies, raising property taxes, and instituting a RTC, alone, will only go so far to remedy inequalities in school funding. The overreliance on local property taxes reinforces de facto disparities between communities, so that whiter, wealthier communities will always outspend poorer, minority concentrated communities (Kozol 1991; Walters 2001). Lasting patterns of segregation only worsen these trends, since enrollment in education remains organized by the proximity between residences and nearby schools (McKoy and Vincent 2006). These com-pounding factors inevitably lead to, as Pamela Barnhouse Walters (2001) argues, "inequalities in tax revenues among school districts [that] produce inequalities in educational resources, facilities, programs, and opportuni-ties" (p. 44). To remedy these disparities, it will be necessary to look beyond minimum per pupil funding requirements. These are discussed at length in Chapter 5 with regard to Illinois, but most states throughout the country have similar laws (Kozol 1991).

The problem with minimum per pupil standards is that they translate into what Claude Fischer and his colleagues (1996) label "inequality by design." Though these laws raise the standards of the social safety net, they do nothing to address excessive per pupil spending. This dilemma represents a similar dynamic present in ongoing battles over wage disparities and rais-ing the minimum wage. Most of us are likely familiar with these debates. Those who want to increase the minimum wage typically couch their argu-ment in terms of reducing levels of inequality so that those in poverty can earn enough money to eat, pay rent, and generally speaking, survive. What is missing in most of these debates is a notion of relativity. Since inequality is, by default, a relational notion between "haves" and "have nots," it only makes sense that we not let the "haves" off the hook. Our position supports a higher minimum wage,[8] but we remain skeptical of how effective it would be so long as a "maximum wage" and "pricing controls" remain unad-dressed (Barris 1992).

An alternative approach has been suggested by the late Congressman Martin Sabo in legislative bills he introduced throughout the 1990s and 2000s (see Stabile 2002). He recommended that corporate management executives, or general management members, could not earn 25 times the lowest paid worker.[9] To enforce these provisions and provide some regula-tory "teeth," should such a bill be enacted, government procurement could be linked to income disparities between executives and workers. Companies with persisting wage gaps, or those found guilty of racial discrimination, would become ineligible to receive federal contracts, forbidden from claiming tax deductions, and required to pay "a disparity tax." Per pupil funding requirements could draw inspiration from Sabo's policy recommendations. One possibility would be to establish a formula for maximum and minimum funding requirements throughout the nation, and set a threshold that prevents disparity levels beyond a certain point. School districts that violate this formula with excess spending would be levied a disparity tax, and this money could then be redistributed in Robin Hood fashion to school districts struggling to meet minimum standards—ones that are disproportionately located in poor and/or minority communities (Kozol 1991; McKoy and Vincent 2006; Walters 2001).

Towards a Racial Robin Hood Lottery Tax: Return Money to the People in Need

Collectively speaking, little relationship exists between who purchases lottery tickets and who benefits from the services they finance. This is true even though people are led to believe that lottery money cushions existing revenue streams. On the contrary, lotteries bring new money in the front door, while letting old money escape through the back. It is through budgetary reallocations and/or tax cuts that lottery money does not offer the additional money many promotional messages promised. Karcher (1989) suggests that one way of resolving this problem is to refund a portion of lottery proceeds to the very people who purchased them. By this, he does not mean returning the money directly to individuals but to the community at large. The Massachusetts Lottery represents one model of how this could be done. It has a decentralized, revenue-sharing style of distributing lottery funds to communities. "Net proceeds are distributed on a formula," Karcher (1989) points out, "that divides the population of each community into the total property tax base of the municipality. Using this method, towns with fewer resources receive more, and wealthier towns get less" (p. 97).

We agree with this recommendation, pending some qualification. We begin our proposal with demystifying the lottery tax with more transparency regarding the generation and expenditures of lottery revenues. No longer should it be acceptable to circulate this money in ways that are comparable to money laundering, as we describe with the Illinois Lottery in Chapter 5. Illinois is not the only state with these practices, though. Governments would be better poised to understand and measure matters of tax incidence if they possessed ledgers that show where lottery money originates with respect to where it is spent, all in relation to how other tax dollars are circulated, too. Our proposal of restructuring the lottery tax ends with reallocating how lottery proceeds are distributed.

It seems only fair that lottery money return to the communities where it originated, but what if those communities were racially exclusive communities of wealth and prosperity? This is quite possible if state lotteries took steps to reduce their racial regressivity, which is a socially responsible opportunity that is just within grasp. One strategy to reduce the racial regressivity of the lottery involves offering bigger, more frequent jackpots. Studies have shown (e.g., Olster 2004) that these types of games, typically of the lotto variety, bring in more taxplayers who otherwise do not buy lottery tickets. This broadens the tax-base so that lottery revenues no longer come disproportionately from those on the social margins. Another option is to increase the odds of winning.

When states increase the odds of winning, substantially more lottery tickets are purchased—by broader populations, too (Karcher 1989). The case of the Massachusetts Lottery, which is discussed in Chapter 4, serves as a prime example. It routinely has the highest grossing per capita sales in the country, largely because its payout rate is also the highest. More than three-fourths of every lottery dollar is returned to taxplayers through prize winnings. This structure permitted Massachusetts to generate the second highest sales of any lottery in the United States during 2011 ($4.2 billion), even with its comparatively smaller population base. These high payout rates do not necessarily translate into less money for state treasuries either. In fact, it is the high payout rates of the Massachusetts Lottery that permit it to transfer proceeds that compare in size to those of more populous states like Texas, Florida, and even California.

If these suggestions on easing the lottery's racial regressivity are taken to heart, then returning lottery money to the communities where these dollars originated could worsen existing racial inequality. An alternative solution to what Karcher (1989) proposes is a bit more complex but still straightforward. It would consider not only where lottery dollars originate, but which communities truly need the money. We suggest that lottery expenditures return to where they originated, but on the condition that these communities do not exceed a certain threshold of wealth and/or possess a certain racial makeup. Preferably, these communities would receive more lottery money than they contributed to begin with. An ideal, but still achievable, situation would return millions of lottery dollars to struggling schools to help lower class sizes, hire more teachers, or reduce projected budget pitfalls for the future. It could also mean returning much needed arts and physical education back to schools that had to eliminate them due to reduced budgets.

Lottery money does not have to be restricted to those already earmarked public services either. If the tax expansion recommendations we provided in the previous section were implemented, much of these revenues could be allocated to lottery-financed public services, and lottery proceeds could be allocated elsewhere. At least two options available involve redirecting lottery proceeds to finance savings-matching and community-based asset creation programs for people of color. The first of these refers to what Michael Sherradan (1991) calls "Individual Development Accounts" (henceforth IDAs). These are programs for individual wealth building, and they can be made possible through a special type of nontaxable, government-matched savings account that can be liquidated only to purchase a home, finance education, start a business, or retire. For IDAs to be effective, however, workers need an income stream that covers more than bare sustenance (i.e., a living wage).

The second option involves community-based asset creation programs. A number of these initiatives already exist throughout the country, and they are exemplified by the "regionalism" initiative spearheaded by powell (2000, 2002) and others. In his own words, powell (2002) describes the initiative as follows:

> We cannot solve unemployment disparities, the affordable housing crisis, and racially disparate school achievement levels, among other concerns, unless we act from a regional viewpoint. A single community, even a single municipality, faces enormous obstacles to linking low-income workers of color in the city with jobs emerging in the metropolitan periphery. A single community organization or advocacy group can be frustrated trying to improve schools in a high poverty, racially segregated district when 'racially neutral' policies privilege schools in affluent, majority White districts. The community's work is on target, but the dynamics of inequality are region-sized
>
> (p. 5).

Therefore, social problems cannot be solved solely with individual-based solutions. Rather, they require resources, services, and general infrastructure to be more equitably leveraged and distributed across races and spaces. In doing so, disparities in racial opportunity structures can be diminished. The fact that most these initiatives have been privately funded raises concerns about their longevity and sustainability, among other things. An injection of lottery money, however, could be just the revenue stream this initiative needs to remain effective. It would move us more toward retooling the lottery tax into a Robin Hood tax.

Play Responsibly, Advertise Responsibly

Though most lottery advertisements conform to "truth-in-advertising standards," the lottery ought to have higher standards. Those who operate lotteries, if they are to do it successfully, must have their eyes firmly planted on the bottom line. Many of them, especially the well-established ones, are required to expand sales without adding novelty. Yet there are only so many games that can be introduced and vendors established before states reach a certain point of saturation. This places quite the strain on lottery operators to boost sales by any means necessary. Out of necessity, many are induced to deliver predatory messages. Can we reasonably expect an institution, one that has the sheer purpose of generating revenue, to protect the public from messages aimed at boosting their bottom line?

That would be like a shepherd leaving her flock to be tended by a wolf. A preliminary solution to this problem would be to create an independent entity responsible for advertising, whether this entity would do the job itself or contract the work to private firms is an open question. Such a creation would establish a degree of independence and autonomy, so the aforementioned conflicts of interest could be minimized. It could also create an environment where advertising standards of accuracy and full disclosure, in addition to truth in advertising, could be upheld. The fact that state agencies pay for lottery promotional messages on television, billboards, and wherever else lends a degree of legitimacy and endorsement unavailable to other products sold by private industry. Lottery advertisements like those discussed in Chapters 2 and 5 say something about what is culturally tasteful or permissible, but more so they indicate social values.

Taken at face value, many lottery advertisements communicate implicit and explicit messages about racial minorities. Some of these messages are interlaced with the denigration of American values like hard work and self-sufficiency. This is exactly what can be communicated by Illinois Lottery ads placed in Chicago ghettos that read: "How to Get from Washington Boulevard to Easy Street" (see Brodt 1986; Congbalay 1986; Formanek 1986). It is as though the subtext of ads like these say the following:

"Why work and save up your money?
Those are chump activities.
What you need to do is buy this lottery ticket.
This will be your ticket to 'easy street.'"

Still other promotional messages of the lottery taunt the racialized poor with wealth they do not have. As Michael Heberling (2002) has pointed out, these messages include advertisement campaigns like "This could be your ticket out [the ghetto]" in Illinois or "[Dr. King's] vision lives on . . . honor the dream" in the District of Columbia. These messages need to stop not only because they prey upon the desperate and deprived, but because they communicate false hopes of unrealistic possibilities to the most vulnerable populations.

It is in poor taste enough that lotteries go without disclosing the odds of winning, but it is altogether something else that many advertisements go on to taunt them. As much is true in the Michigan Lottery advertisement discussed in Chapter 4. To refresh your memory, this ad shows a lottery cynic who complains about having better odds of being struck by lightning than winning the jackpot. Seconds later, lo and behold, a bolt strikes the man and he says, "One ticket, please" (Karcher 1989: 83). Such advertising tactics would be deemed a sheer absurdity in the context of other pressing social problems. Imagine the backlash that would occur, for example, if the state promoted a campaign that scoffed at statistics indicating how "texting while driving" leads to accidents, or worse, death. Though nothing horrendous happens to many drivers partaking in "texting while driving," statistics of tragic events that have occurred as a result nonetheless offer a compelling, if not sobering, message. Why not hold lottery-related messages to a similar standard?

In doing so, promotional messages about the lottery should also be prohibited from spreading misinformation. Lottery advertisements are quick to promote how they finance worthwhile causes like education, but they often do so in ways that simultaneously appeal to minority solidarity and paternalistic racism. In fact, they even communicate these messages in the democratic name of transparency and showing where government money is spent. Consider an example from the Missouri Lottery (see Figure P.1). The written text of the message communicates that the state's lottery has contributed more than $4 billion to public education. Not just any kids are getting "helped" by lottery revenues, though. The image of the advertisement says what words do not. By making a young black woman reading a book a focal point of attention, this lottery advertisement encourages black folks to buy lottery tickets so that they can promote "their own." This same ad also appeals to paternalistic "white guilt" by drawing upon white sympathies of how "bad" those young minority kids have it. For those of us who care about our children's

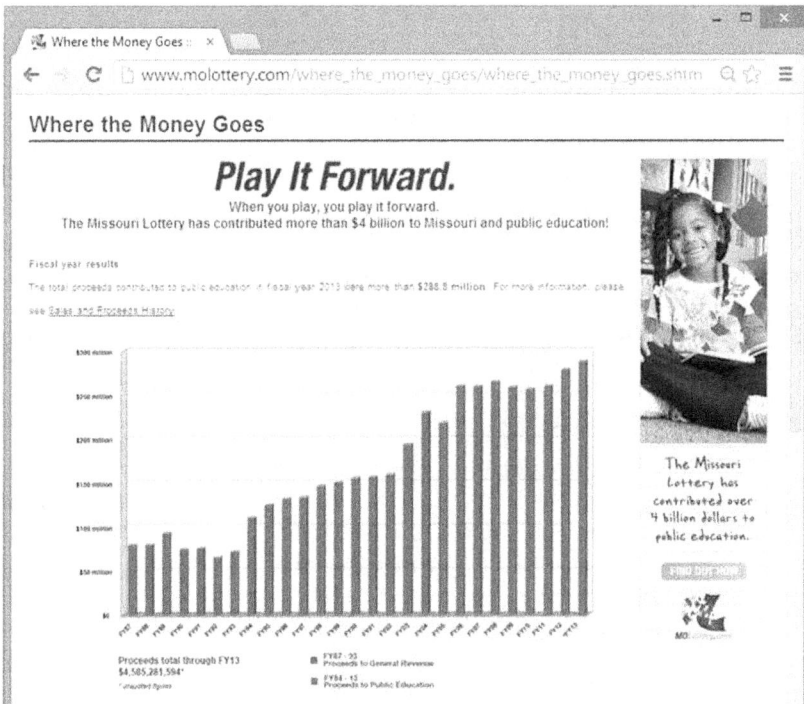

Figure P.1 Misleading Advertisements: The Missouri Lottery Example

future, why would we not help contribute to worthwhile lottery causes like equalizing education? And while we are doing so, we have a chance to strike it rich.

These scenarios are presented as a win/win situation for most of us. The irony in all this messaging is that the Missouri Lottery, like most other lotteries, is not really providing additional funds for this young woman's education. Many advertisements would have citizens believe otherwise. According to these messages, lotteries have been a boon to public finance. Though the evidence we and others (e.g., Borg and Shapiro 1988, 1990) have offered disproves this claim, these messages continue to fill television screens, radio waves, and the interwebs. Framing messages like this help to insulate lotteries from criticism, while obscuring the fact that the lottery tax paves an express route for extracting minority resources and distributing them elsewhere. So, please, could we have more honest advertising? Lotteries should follow their own advice of "play responsibly" in the world of advertising, and twisted messages of misinformation should be censored.

Any time recommendations of censorship arise, many rush to the absolute defense of the First Amendment. As much was true in the late 1970s, for example, when the American Civil Liberties Union defended a white nationalist group for organizing a march, one in which marchers would wear Nazi uniforms and display swastikas, in the predominantly Jewish community of Skokie, Illinois (i.e., *National Socialist Party of America v. Village of Skokie* 432 U.S. 43 [1977]). Yet just because speech ought to be free, that does not mean it should be worthless. Speech like this consists of power words, and Critical Race Theorists like Richard Delgado (1982) and Charles Lawrence III (1990) have linked it to verbal realism: This speech constitutes racism that ratifies marginality for people of color and preserves white dominance. Therefore, the regulation of lottery advertisements is less about matters of censorship and civil liberties than it is about transforming the connection between media messages, race, and power. If predatory messages or racial denigration are not consistent with state policy, then these messages should not be promoted by lotteries as if they are.

Louder, Louder: The People Speak

The whole notion of a colorblind tax code permits, as Karen Brown and Mary Louise Fellows (1996) argue, "participants in tax discourse to claim a position of innocence and avoid accountability for the role the tax law may play in perpetuating social injustices" (p. 6). With *State Looteries*, we hope to have disturbed any normative assumptions about the colorblind neutrality of tax laws or taken-for-granted views about taxation's hidden role in reproducing racial inequality. Central to all our suggestions outlined above is calling for an end to what we see as post-racial, colorblind nonsense. Audre Lorde ([1984] 2007) once wrote, "The master's tools will never dismantle the master's house" (p. 110), and her central point can be adapted here. It is quite difficult for people to acknowledge the consequences of race, which stem from past and ongoing racial discrimination, when they claim to not see it altogether. We must shift from a colorblind to color-conscious approach if a world where race no longer shapes life chances can be imagined. The lottery tax, for all intents and purposes, is a form of racialized fiscal policy that represents a host of social problems. We hope to see it change but recognize that without social change, a cold day in hell would be more likely.

The obstacles that lie ahead for those of us with a social justice agenda are daunting, but opportune moments for resistance are available. As Bonilla-Silva ([2003] 2006) puts it, "Thinking and theorizing about change is good, talking about change is better, but working toward change is the only way it will happen" (p. 236). *State Looteries* began as a project with this in mind. On August 20, 2008, a lawsuit spearheaded by the Chicago Urban League was filed against the State of Illinois and Illinois State Board of Education (Complaint # 08 CH 30490). Lawyers representing the Chicago Urban League (Jenner & Block) claim that the Illinois education finance system violates the education provision of the state's constitution and Illinois Civil Rights Act of 2003. Despite guarantees of high quality education for all, the funding schedule to school districts discriminates against communities of color not by intent but practice. Essentially these lawyers offer similar evidence discussed earlier: de facto disparities in property tax revenues between districts reinforces patterns of whiter, wealthier communities outspending poorer, minority concentrated communities (Kozol 1991; Walters 2001).

We agree with this argument, but it is one that has been offered on numerous other occasions—and results have not always ruled in the plaintiff's favor. This was the case of *San Antonio Independent School District v. Rodriguez* (411 U.S. 1 [1973]), a class action suit heard before the United States Supreme Court. In this case, the lawyers representing Rodriguez argued that the San Antonio Independent School District's financial system, which like Illinois is based on local property taxes, is in violation of the U.S. Constitution. In particular, the Fourteenth Amendment's "equal protection clause" was in question. The Majority Opinion determined that the Texas system did not disadvantage or discriminate against any definable class, and it claimed that the Court's position is not one to subject local education finance systems to strict judicial scrutiny. In light of rulings like these, we decided that the Chicago Urban League could use help in proving its case. As we write this very text, the lawsuit remains ongoing.

Though *State Looteries* has evolved into something much bigger, it began as our effort to not only theorize and talk about change, but work towards that change. Our project was designed from the onset to become an amicus brief for the lawsuit between the *Chicago Urban League v. State of Illinois and Illinois State Board of Education*. For those unfamiliar with what an "amicus brief" is and does, it literally translates from Latin as "friend of the court." Often, an independent person, group, or organization not represented in the lawsuit will petition the court to offer an informed statement on the conflict at hand. The goal of these briefs is to influence the court's decision one way or another. The evidence we have offered broadens the civil rights violation in question to include matters of the lottery tax, and we have advanced an argument that further substantiates claims for a more equitable and racially just means of education finance.

Long ago, Frederick Douglass ([1857] 1999) spoke these words:

> If there is no struggle, there is no progress. Those who profess to favor freedom, and yet depreciate agitation, are men who want crops without plowing up the ground. They want rain without thunder and lightning. They want the ocean without the awful roar of its many waters. This struggle may be a moral one, or it may be a physical one, or it may be both moral and physical, but it must be a struggle. Power concedes nothing without demand. It never did and it never will
>
> (p. 367).

State Looteries represents our struggle. It is our attempt at collective action through coalition politics that seeks to eliminate racial inequality. It is a small, targeted strategy that piggybacks upon the efforts of a local, but widely known organization in the Chicago Urban League. It is our hope in the near future to build upon the political effectiveness of this project, so that it can have broader reach and be tied to national and international resistance movements. This represents our frontal attack on an established racial structure that reproduces white racial domination. Nevertheless, we realize that our approach is certainly not the definitive answer. So long as ideology that blames minorities for their own subordinated position persists, we cannot foresee how tax law will fully redress the hidden mechanisms of racism.

Resisting racism and its many forms must not follow what Du Bois (1903) critiqued as a "singleness of vision," but involve a broadly based, pluralistic coalition of strategies. We are not alone in offering suggestions for antiracism. Scholars such as Floya Anthias and Cathie Lloyd (2002), Hamani Bannerji (1995), Andrew Barlow (2003), Bonilla-Silva ([2003] 2014), Melanie Bush (2004), Judith Katz (1978), and Amanda Lewis (2003) have already outlined innovative antiracist strategies (as well as advanced substantive critiques of antiracist movements). Where we depart from these scholars is merely a matter of focus. Our attention has been placed on public policy alternatives regarding taxation because it is an area that has been left largely under-addressed. If many of our suggestions offered throughout the postscript are taken seriously and implemented, they have much potential to expand the capacity of state finance and to do so in socially responsible ways that promote racial justice.

Notes

1 Quote taken from: Galeano, Eduardo. 2013. *Children of the Days: A Calendar of Human History*. New York: Nation Books.
2 Unless otherwise noted, all references to the U.S. Code (Title 26 —Internal Revenue Code) draw from the 2010 version to correspond with much of the data presented in this study. Most provisions of this version remain intact, including the ones central to this study, but some revisions have occurred (e.g., Taxpayer Relief Act of 2012, Public Law 112–240).
3 We say "usually" because numerous exemptions, deductions, and exclusions, which are buried within the tax code, can and often do offset the progressive structure of the federal income tax.
4 Not every form of wealth escapes taxation, but the taxation it is subjected to is often lower. Diversified assets such as stocks, bonds, and IRA accounts qualify for particular tax shelters that permit unrealized capital appreciation to go untouched, while capital gains qualify for reduced tax rates (Moran and Wildman 2007).
5 In 1980, the top statutory tax rate for personal income was 70 percent.
6 This is not to say New Deal policies were first to offer racially exclusive property acquisition. Besides the institution of slavery, the federal government encouraged westward expansion throughout the 19th century by transferring millions of acres to mostly white families (Fuchs 1990). These transfers were outright or sold at undervalued prices. Examples include President Andrew Jackson's Indian Removal Act of 1830, President John Tyler's Preemption Act of 1841, and President Abraham Lincoln's Homestead Act of 1862, among others.
7 This provision is capped at mortgages valued at $1 million or more.
8 To ensure that a high minimum wage does not penalize "small business," and to preemptively squash common conservative criticism, we suggest implementing a "Small Business Tax Credit" that could follow similar guidelines as the EITC or RTC.
9 The proposal incorporates a broadly defined notion of income that includes stock dividends, perquisites, and other forms of compensation (Barris 1992).

Appendix A
Supplementary Material

Table A.1 National Overview of Lottery States A–M: Total Revenues, Sales Per Capita, Prizes, Administrative Costs, and Available Proceeds to Public Services, Fiscal Year 2011*

	Total Lottery Revenues[a]	Sales Per Capita[b]	Total Prize Winnings[a] (% of Total Revenues)	Administrative Costs[a,c] (% of Total Revenues)	Proceeds Available to Public Services[a,d] (% of Total Revenues)
Arizona	$ 544,290	$122	$ 360,491 (66.2 %)	$ 39,023 (7.2 %)	$ 144,776 (26.6 %)
Arkansas	437,801	199	307,455 (70.2)	37,863 (8.6)	92,483 (21.1)
California	3,483,578	125	1,904,788 (54.7)	193,526 (5.6)	1,385,264 (39.8)
Colorado	479,337	126	326,624 (68.1)	40,904 (8.5)	111,809 (23.3)
Connecticut	959,650	348	620,134 (64.6)	41,218 (4.3)	298,298 (31.1)
Delaware	451,142	652	75,846 (16.8)	49,060 (10.9)	326,236 (72.3)
D.C.	231,749	463	125,860 (54.3)	11,767 (5.1)	94,122 (40.6)
Florida	3,781,550	256	2,460,219 (65.1)	134,339 (3.6)	1,186,992 (31.4)
Georgia	3,109,295	432	2,120,835 (68.2)	140,388 (4.5)	848,072 (27.3)
Idaho	135,379	119	90,230 (66.6)	8,669 (6.4)	36,480 (26.9)
Illinois	2,264,685	233	1,368,472 (60.4)	232,767 (10.3)	663,446 (29.3)
Indiana	735,206	151	494,516 (67.3)	48,202 (6.6)	192,488 (26.2)
Iowa	271,535	125	158,961 (64.3)	40,299 (14.8)	72,275 (26.6)
Kansas	218,590	103	132,332 (60.5)	20,175 (9.2)	66,083 (30.2)
Kentucky	672,069	203	422,410 (62.9)	35,154 (5.2)	214,505 (31.9)

Louisiana	362,222	113	202,902	(56.0)	24,351	(6.7)	134,969	(37.3)
Maine	202,314	192	135,587	(67.0)	15,710	(7.8)	51,017	(25.2)
Maryland	1,600,716	362	1,029,041	(64.3)	103,989	(6.5)	467,686	(29.2)
Massachusetts	4,167,142	813	3,199,444	(76.8)	88,634	(2.1)	879,064	(21.1)
Michigan	2,139,205	284	1,368,238	(64.0)	70,740	(3.3)	700,227	(32.7)
Minnesota	474,178	118	327,546	(69.1)	23,953	(5.1)	122,679	(25.9)
Missouri	981,542	215	639,011	(65.1)	42,234	(4.3)	300,297	(30.6)
Montana	43,322	57	24,778	(57.2)	7,616	(17.6)	10,928	(25.2)

Sources: "District of Columbia" 2011; "U.S. Census Bureau" 2011

*   All figures reported, aside from percentage values, are rounded to the nearest thousand.
a   Total Lottery Revenues is calculated as ticket sales minus commissions ("District of Columbia Lottery" 2011; "U.S. Census Bureau" 2011a).
b   Sales per capita is calculated as total lottery revenues divided by 2010 Census records of total state populations who are legally permitted, as determined by age, to purchase a lottery ticket. Lottery tickets can be purchased in a majority of states and in the District of Columbia by those 18 years of age and older, though some outliers deviate from this trend. The minimum age in Arizona and Iowa is 21 years.
c   Administrative costs reflect the costs associated with operating and maintaining lotteries ("District of Columbia" 2011; "U.S. Census Bureau" 2011a).
d   Proceeds available to public services reflect total lottery revenues less prize winnings and administration costs ("District of Columbia" 2011; "U.S. Census Bureau" 2011a).

Table A.2 National Overview of Lottery States N-W: Total Revenues, Sales Per Capita, Prizes, Administrative Costs, and Available Proceeds to Public Services, Fiscal Year 2011*

	Total Lottery Revenues[a]	Sales Per Capita[b]	Total Prize Winnings[a] (% of Total Revenues)	Administrative Costs[a c] (% of Total Revenues)	Proceeds Available to Public Services[a d] (% of Total Revenues)
Nebraska	$ 123,711	$ 90	$ 76,871 (62.1)	$ 16,546 (13.4)	$ 30,294 (24.5)
New Hampshire	216,229	210	139,262 (64.4)	14,552 (6.7)	62,415 (28.9)
New Jersey	2,489,474	370	1,505,220 (60.5)	53,118 (2.1)	931,136 (37.4)
New Mexico	129,756	84	76,699 (59.1)	11,636 (9.0)	41,421 (31.9)
New York	6,986,288	464	3,967,672 (56.8)	323,119 (4.6)	2,695,497 (38.6)
North Carolina	1,358,387	187	861,469 (63.4)	59,848 (4.4)	437,070 (32.2)
North Dakota	21,906	42	11,941 (54.5)	3,949 (18.0)	6,016 (27.5)
Ohio	2,439,667	277	1,603,054 (65.7)	89,232 (3.7)	747,381 (30.6)
Oklahoma	211,373	75	106,601 (50.4)	12,391 (5.9)	92,381 (43.7)
Oregon	838,595	283	208,673 (24.9)	75,156 (9.0)	554,766 (66.2)
Pennsylvania	2,905,632	293	1,958,432 (67.4)	69,238 (2.4)	877,962 (30.2)
Rhode Island	505,574	610	142,324 (28.2)	6,919 (1.4)	356,331 (70.5)
South Carolina	973,013	274	667,637 (68.6)	37,300 (3.8)	268,076 (27.6)
South Dakota	140,484	230	27,175 (19.3)	6,664 (4.7)	106,645 (75.9)
Tennessee	1,108,861	229	611,171 (55.1)	51,989 (4.7)	445,701 (40.2)
Texas	3,599,037	197	2,387,244 (66.3)	205,463 (5.7)	1,006,330 (28.0)
Vermont	89,935	181	50,613 (56.7)	7,943 (8.8)	31,379 (34.9)
Virginia	1,398,843	228	881,026 (63.0)	72,134 (5.2)	445,683 (31.9)

Washington	478,516	93	295,155	(61.7)	44,383	(9.3)	138,978	(29.0)
West Virginia	746,738	510	120,707	(16.2)	39,337	(5.3)	586,694	(78.6)
Wisconsin	502,654	116	290,459	(57.8)	33,765	(6.7)	178,430	(35.5)

Source: "U.S. Census Bureau" 2011a

*   All figures reported, aside from percentage values, are rounded to the nearest thousand.
a   Total Lottery Revenues is calculated as ticket sales minus commissions ("U.S. Census Bureau" 2011a).
b   Sales per capita is calculated as total lottery revenues divided by 2010 Census records of total state populations who are legally permitted, as determined by age, to purchase a lottery ticket. Lottery tickets can be purchased in a majority of states by those 18 years of age and older, though some outliers deviate from this trend. The minimum age in Louisiana and Nebraska is 21 years and 19 years, respectively.
c   Administrative costs reflect the costs associated with operating and maintaining lotteries ("U.S. Census Bureau" 2011a).
d   Proceeds available to public services reflect total lottery revenues less prize winnings and administration costs ("U.S. Census Bureau" 2011a).

Table A.3 National Overview of States A-M: Lottery-Funded Public Services, Fiscal Year 2011

Arizona	Economic and Business Development; Environment; Health and Public Welfare; K-12 and Higher Education
Arkansas	Higher Education Financial Aid
California	K-12 and Higher Education
Colorado	Conservation Education; Environmental Conservation; K-12 Education; Parks and Recreation; School Health and Safety
Connecticut	Chronic Gambler's Fund; Corrections; Conservation and Development; Debt Service; General Government; Grant Payments to Local Governments; Health and Hospitals; Human Services; Judicial, Regulation and Protection; K-12 and Higher Education; Legislative; Libraries and Education Services; Medicaid; Mental Health; Public Health; State Service
Delaware	Child, Youth, and Family Services; General Fund; Health and Social Services; Judicial and Corrections; K-12 and Higher Education; Natural Resources and Environmental Control; Public Safety
D.C.	Child Services; K-12 Education; Parks and Recreation; Public Housing; Public Safety; Senior Services
Florida	Higher Education Financial Aid; K-12 and Higher Education
Georgia	Higher Education Financial Aid; Pre-K Education
Idaho	K-12 and Higher Education; Public Building Construction and Preservation
Illinois	Breast Cancer Research and Education; HIV/AIDS Awareness and Support Initiatives; K-12 Education; Multiple Sclerosis Research; Veteran's Support Programs
Indiana	Offsetting Motor Vehicle Excise Taxes; Public Servant's Pension and Retirement
Iowa	Economic and Business Development; General Fund; K-12 Education; Public Building Construction and Preservation; Tourism; Veteran Support
Kansas	Economic Development; Gambling Treatment; General Fund; Juvenile Detention Facilities; Prison Construction and Maintenance
Kentucky	Early Childhood Reading; General Fund; Higher Education Financial Aid; Literacy
Louisiana	Gambling Treatment; K-12 Education
Maine	General Fund; Wildlife Preservation
Maryland	Environment; K-12 and Higher Education; General Fund; Public Health; Public Safety; Stadium Authority
Massachusetts	Arts and Culture; Gambling Treatment; Unearmarked Local Aid
Michigan	Gambling Treatment; General Fund; K-12 Education
Minnesota	Environmental Conservation; Gambling Treatment; General Fund; Parks and Recreation; Wildlife Preservation
Missouri	K-12 and Higher Education
Montana	General Fund; Health; K-12 Education; Public Safety

Source: Authors' Audited Material

Table A.4 National Overview of States N-W: Lottery-Funded Public Services, Fiscal
Year 2011

Nebraska	Environmental Conservation; Gambling Treatment; K-12 and Higher Education; State Fair; Wildlife Preservation
New Hampshire	K-12 Education
New Jersey	Human Services; K-12 and Higher Education; Military and Veteran's Affairs
New Mexico	Higher Education
New York	K-12 Education
North Carolina	Gambling Treatment; Pre-K-12 and Higher Education
North Dakota	Drug Task Force; Gambling Treatment; General Fund
Ohio	K-12 Education
Oklahoma	Gambling Treatment; K-12 and Higher Education
Oregon	Environmental Conservation; Gambling Treatment; Job Creation and Economic Development; K-12 and Higher Education; Parks and Recreation; Wildlife Preservation
Pennsylvania	Senior Services (rent/tax subsidies, free/reduced transit, prescription drug assistance, living services, senior community centers)
Rhode Island	General Fund; Human Services; K-12 Education; Public Safety; Natural Resources; Transportation
South Carolina	Gambling Treatment; K-12 and Higher Education; Libraries
South Dakota	Capital Construction (water and environment fund, ethanol fuel fund, state highway fund); Human Services; Property Tax Deduction
Tennessee	Business Creation and Economic Development (diversity and minority business participation); Pre-K-12 and Higher Education
Texas	General Fund; K-12 Education; Veteran's Support Programs
Vermont	K-12 Education
Washington	Economic Development; Gambling Treatment; General Fund; King County (Safeco Field); Pre-K-12 and Higher Education; Public Debt from Sports Forums and Exhibition Centers
West Virginia	General Fund; K-12 and Higher Education; Racetrack Reinvestment and Modernization; Senior Services; Tourism
Wisconsin	Gambling Treatment; General Fund; Law Enforcement; Property Tax Relief

Source: Authors' Audited Material

Table A.5 Descriptive Statistics and Coding Schemes for the Final Logit Models, N = 742*

Variables		Min.	Max.	Mean	(SE)
Played the Lottery in Past 7 Days?		0	1	.340	(.018)
Racial / Ethnic Status (Dummies, White Omitted)			1		
	Black	0	1	.078	(.010)
	Latina/o	0	1	.119	(.012)
Household Income[a]		1	4	2.300	(.034)
Highest Grade Attended[b]		1	5	2.890	(.042)
Current Employment Status		0	1	.780	(.015)
Received Unemployment, Disability, or SSI in Past Year		0	1	.060	(.009)
Received Social Security, Pension, or Annuity in Past Year		0	1	.160	(.014)
Current Marital Status		0	1	.760	(.016)
Sex Category (Female = 0, Male = 1)		0	1	.500	(.019)
Age of Interviewee[c]		1	5	2.940	(.045)
Currently Attending School		0	1	.070	(.009)
Importance of Faith[d]		1	5	4.480	(.033)
Lottery Purchase in Neighborhood		0	1	.780	(.015)

Source: GIBS

*   All variables coded with values ranging from "0" to "1" are dummy variables, unless otherwise noted, whereby "0" represents the absence and "1" represents the presence of some measurable outcome.

a   Household Include is coded as follows: "1" = Less than $24k; "2" = $24k-49k; "3" = $50-99k; and "4" = More than $100k.

b   Highest Grade Attended is coded as follows: "1" = Less than 12th Grade; "2" = 12th Grade; "3" Technical School or Some College; "4" = 4 Years of College; and "5" = Graduate or Professional School.

c   Age of Interviewee is coded as follows: "1"= 18–29 Years; "2" = 30–39 Years; "3" = 40–49 Years; "4" = 50–64 Years; and "5" = 65 Years and older.

d   Importance of Faith is coded as follows: "1" = Not At All Important; "2"= Not So Important; "3" = Don't Know or Refused; "4" = Important; and "5" = Very Important.

LOYOLA
UNIVERSITY CHICAGO

Illinois Lottery
100 W. Randolph, Suite 7-274
Chicago, IL 60601

January 28, 2011

Re: Illinois Freedom of Information Request

Kasey Henricks
Loyola University Chicago
Department of Sociology
1032 W. Sheridan Road
Coffey Hall 434
Chicago, IL 60660

Dear FOIA Officer,

This is a request for information under the Illinois Freedom of Information Act, 5 ILCS 140. I request that a copy of the following documents be provided to me: Annual Revenues Generated by Lottery Products per each Illinois Zip Code Tabulation Area (ZCTA) for fiscal year 2011. I would like to obtain these records in either electronic format or physical document form.

I understand that the Act permits a public body to charge a reasonable copying fee not to exceed the actual cost of reproduction and not including the costs of any search or review of the records, as stated in 5 ILCS 140(6). I request a waiver of all fees for this request. Disclosure of the requested information to me is in the public interest because it is likely to contribute to a public understanding of the operations regarding public education finance in the State of Illinois.

I am interested in measuring lottery sales as tax-generated revenues, and I want to learn of where across Chicago these revenues originate. Such a request does not concern commercial interest. Rather, the inquired information will be utilized in the fulfillment of a research project for the Department of Sociology at Loyola University Chicago.

I look forward to hearing from you in writing within seven working days, as required by the Act–5 ILCS 140(3).

Sincerely,

Kasey Henricks

Figure A.1 Sample Freedom of Information Request for Illinois Lottery Sales Information

Appendix B
Methods

The sources of data we rely upon to complete this study are scattered across a number of locations. These range broadly from nationally representative datasets to archival collections to public records. Essentially, the research questions we wrestle with cannot be answered by one master source. We synthesize and integrate a number datasets to, as the adage goes, "get the job done." Our analysis is highly descriptive, and at times historical, but when considered altogether, it sketches broad parameters of the lottery's role in state finance and its implications for racial inequality. Our strategy contextualizes the emergence of lotteries within historical transformations of government finance, specifies the role and scope of lotteries as a means for public finance, and details from whom this money comes. In what follows, we elaborate more on the datasets that empirically ground our study, how data were collected and analyzed, and why it is relevant to the analyses performed.

An Assortment of Archival Collections

Though the intent of *State Looteries* did not originate as a qualitative mode of inquiry, it proved quite difficult to complete our research objectives without the incorporation of historical archives. "Every social science—or better, every well considered social study—requires," argued C. Wright Mills (1959), "an historical scope of conception and a full use of historical materials" (p. 145). These materials help clarify what causal inferences we could generate, while linking them to broader theories of racial dynamics, regarding broader structural changes within America's tax code (Hunter 2013; Skocpol 1984; Vaughan 2004).

We utilize data from historical sources to anchor points made by other racial theorists, like Eduardo Bonilla-Silva (2001) and Charles Mills (1997), within the specific world of taxation. When Mills discusses modernity as a "racial contract," we extend his theoretical point to the legal codification of the "three-fifths clause" in Chapter 1 to empirically show how tax debate was racialized in the formation of the Constitution. We also rely upon archives to contextualize the proliferation of modern state lotteries in a specific socio-historical moment. The 1960s and 1970s represent a time of "great transformation" (Polanyi [1944] 1957) in terms of both race and taxation. With our preliminary analysis of discourse that saturated this time period, we attempt to connect two subjects that often go unconnected.

A focus on discourse is appropriate here because it illuminates the crystallizing medium that ultimately binds racial ideas and tax practices. It makes explicit the "common sense" ideology that people share, which represents views of how the world is, or ought to be, and where people are positioned within it (van Dijk 1998). The legitimating power of ideology—which "consists of the *broad mental and moral frameworks, or 'grids,' that social groups use to make sense of the world, to decide what is right and wrong, true or false, important or unimportant"*—lies in its ability to rationalize racial inequality in ways that are not only understandable but acceptable to the general public (Bonilla-Silva 2001: 62, emphasis original).

The archival texts we analyze are not conceptualized in an abstract manner where meaning and representation are uncoupled from social action, but as products and reflections of historically situated social relationships (Heritage 1984). Seen this way, archival materials represent portals into the racially contested terrain of past tax revolts in which racial hierarchy is justified and defended. These data permit analysts to study relations, and the people embedded within them, that are no longer available. Our data draws from a textual sum of original records, government documents, news articles, satirical prints, photographs, posters, speeches, correspondences, and personal accounts, among others.

Qualitative Orientation: Ethnographic Content Analysis

Tax revolts featured in our study have their own circumstances, conflicts, and histories, but each cannot be understood as an isolated event. The revolts in Alabama during Redemption and in California nearly 100 years later exemplify some of the most influential tax rebellions since the Civil War, so much so that they offer potent opportunities to probe culminating and systemic factors that produced the general waves of revolt in the first place. They are critical cases that illuminate political processes of who gets what, when, and how, and also what role racial ideology plays in shaping these events. To understand how racial conflict is discursively displaced onto the domain of taxation, we perform methods developed by David Altheide (1987) called ethnographic content analysis (ECA).

Simply defined, ECA is "an integrated method, procedure, and technique for locating, identifying, retrieving, and analyzing documents for their relevance, significance, and meaning," where "the emphasis is on discovery and description, including search for contexts, underlying meanings, patterns, and processes" (Altheide 2006: 93). As opposed to traditional orientations, ECA entails a research process that does not unravel in linear fashion. It "follows a recursive and reflexive movement between concept-development-sampling-data collection-data coding data analysis-interpretation" (Altheide and Schneider [1996] 2013: 26). The interactive nature of ECA is justified by its emphasis on discovery. ECA has been primarily used to study media discourses of topics like nationalism, fear, and terrorism (Altheide 2006; Del Russo 2011), but some notable exceptions have extended it to racial matters (e.g., Daniels 1997; Doane 2006; Hughey 2014).

Sampling Scheme: Deciding What to Study

Our data sources, which are listed at the section's end, are chosen for substantive reasons. They document bounded historical events of patterned, coherent, and sequenced activity. In fact, each case study possesses a degree of typicality (e.g., how actors collectively organized, formed coalitions, and ultimately, aimed for specific legal reforms), which as Diane Vaughn (1992) argues, serves as a launching point for learning something general from the specific. The selection of archives uses a hybrid approach of a progressive theoretical and snowball sampling strategy.

The process began by collecting data from archival sources documenting some of the most visible protests. These archives contain numerous texts of tax revolts that many credit as the spark that set fire to other revolts across the nation. More specifically, our sampling procedure is informed by Malcolm McMillan's (1955) work on Alabama and Clarence Lo's (1990) work on California. These authors rely upon the same archives and paper collections to a large extent. Yet it should be noted these archives are not exhaustive.

Archival data are often place-based by city or state, but the selected tax revolts possessed various degrees of regional and national reach. Therefore, we knew it was plausible that other data relevant to our study are scattered across sites outside those initially selected. To account for this possibility, we perform a preliminary analyses to learn of key actors, organizations, coalitions, and so on, and leave open the possibility of visiting additional archival sources that might otherwise remain "hidden" from plain view. Because of the overlap between the tax revolts and antibusing movements, for example, we also consult archival material in Massachusetts, Michigan, and Texas that focus on desegregation efforts.

Coding Strategy

Coding is performed by the primary author and two other secondary researchers. The reliability and validity of the themes presented in Chapters 1, 3, and 5 are scrutinized through triangulation processes (Denzin 1978). More specifically, two forms of triangulation are performed. One includes the cross-referencing of sources to confirm whether our observations meet a basic level of patterned activity. The other includes a reflective debriefing of coding decisions to verify whether the content of our observations is in agreement. These practices permit us to more holistically assess the ideological nature of the tax protests, how discourses can be seen from multiple perspectives, which outcomes they spawned, and above all, what role race played in these processes.

Annual Survey of State and Local Government Finance

Learning the size and contribution of lottery dollars is, by definition, a relational analysis. State lottery contributions are better understood in context, relating how they compare to other sources of state income such as property, excise, and corporate taxes, among others. The U.S. Census Bureau's *Annual Survey of State and Local Government Finance* (henceforth *SLGF*) is perhaps best suited for this analysis because it provides a comprehensive summary of all this information and more.[1] *SLGF* is a census collected from local and state governments every five years ending in "2" and "7." For our purposes, we select data from 1972 to 2007 because this timeline coincides with the expansion of taxpayer revolts and lottery adoptions.

The analysis we offer illuminates the changing makeup of state and local government revenue. It consists of simple univariate and bivariate statistical evaluations that measure how certain tax contributions have changed over time with respect to their total share of government revenue. In particular, we measure how property, sales, individual income, and miscellaneous taxes have risen and fallen over time as a proportional share of the state and local treasuries. A limitation of this dataset, however, is that it combines net lottery revenues with other sources of state income like interest earnings and assessments. Creating an umbrella category of miscellaneous state income dilutes the precision of measurement since lottery revenues cannot be disaggregated as their own separate entity. In light of this limitation, we complement our budgetary assessment with a timeline of state lottery adoptions. Since their emergence has been gradual, we can correlate lottery expansion with changes in miscellaneous revenue. These timeline lottery data are collected from various government documents, like budgets and annual reports, and can be readily accessed through formal audit.

Annual Survey of State Government Finances

Lottery expenditures are not consistent from year to year. This is because only some states earmark lottery proceeds to designated public services. States that do not earmark lottery revenues tend to place this money in a general fund for discretionary spending. Though lottery expenditures vary over time, Clotfelter and Cook (1989) document these variances to be subtle by most measures. If unearmarked lottery money is dispersed to public education one year, for example, odds are similar spending patterns will occur the following year. For this reason, as well as for reasons of timeliness, relevance, and brevity, we measure how lottery money is generated and spent by collecting data only from the most recent fiscal year available: 2011.

To complete this task, we rely upon the U.S. Census Bureau's *Annual Survey of State Government Finances* (henceforth *SGF*).[2] This is a recurring survey that collects finance data from all 50 state governments regarding their generated revenues by source, expended revenues by object and function, asset management by purpose, and indebtedness by term.[3] Not only does *SGF* statistically summarize state finances for the executive, legislative, and judicial branches of government, but it also offers detailed information about other state agencies like the lottery. Pertinent to this study, *SGF* records how much income each state lottery creates, what it costs to operate each state lottery, and the amount of money generated for public services.

Because lottery operations vary tremendously from state to state, we perform a series of univariate analyses to provide a national overview of the size, scope, and general role of lotteries. Utilizing the state as a unit of analysis, measures that are analyzed include lottery revenues (total sales and per capita), operating costs (prize winnings and administrative costs), and the proceeds made available for public services. Together these data answer questions about the general nature of lottery operations and how much money they contribute to state treasuries, but they do not specify which public services these funds finance. Alternative data are needed to address this question. To learn how lottery revenue is spent on public services, we turn to various government documents (e.g., budgets, annual reports) from lottery-operating states to highlight the variance between states and commonality across states. Our analysis offers an exhaustive state-by-state overview of every lottery-financed public service, and it summarizes these expenditures on a national scale. Most states disperse lottery money in identical ways, which standardizes the units of measure and makes a national summary readily possible.

Gambling Impact and Behavior Study, 1997–1999

Questions of who plays the lottery on a national level are measured with the *Gambling Impact and Behavior Study, 1997–1999* (henceforth *GIBS, 1997–1999*) dataset.[4] It yields the most comprehensive American dataset on gambling to date. Applying a stratified sampling design, the Random Digit Dial section of survey comprises a total of 2,417 individual respondents to correspond to a nationally representative sample of American households. Of this sample, 1,675 cases are omitted in the final analysis due to case-wise deletion of responses with missing values. This omission caused no significant differences in terms of demographics and representativeness, allowing a final sample size of 742. Participants were asked a host of questions regarding behavior and attitudes associated with the lottery, and gambling in general, but our focus is limited to describing who plays the lottery, how much money they spend, and what is their frequency of participation.

To sketch a general picture of the differences in lottery play between social groups, we rely upon bivariate and multivariate analyses. First performing the bivariate analysis, we crosstabulate several socio-demographic variables to determine whether some groups lose more money on the lottery and play the lottery more frequently than do others. This analysis is then supplemented with a more sophisticated one: binary logistic regression. We perform this technique to build a profile of who frequently plays the lottery.[5] It enables us to measure the simultaneous and independent effects of multiple variables at once. Throughout these analyses, we consider a host of socio-demographic variables that have preoccupied the academic literature, but my primary attention is given to measuring the differences of lottery play between whites, blacks, and Latinas/os.

The Illinois Case Study, A Synthetic Integration of Multiple Data

The analytic logic for much of the analysis offer in Chapter 5 draws one of the golden principles of investigative journalism: "follow the money." In other words, we incorporate and integrate some of the timeliest data available from multiple sources to document where lottery revenues originate and how they are distributed. These sources of data include: 1) 2011 financial records from the Illinois Department of Revenue (henceforth *IDOR, 2011*) financial records, 2) socio-demographic from the *2010 Census*, and 3) documentation of how Illinois funds public education via the IL Public Act 90–548. The financial records from *IDOR, 2011* were collected by following the guidelines laid forth by the state's Freedom of Information Act (§5–140). (The instrument we relied upon to probe this information is available in Figure A.1 of Appendix A.) Because a portion of lottery revenues pays for a service provided by the state, financial documents that detail them constitute public records of interest and are available to the public upon request. These records contain information on annual lottery sales per zip code tabulation area, as defined by the United States Postal Service.

The U.S. Census Bureau utilizes these same spatial units to aggregate decennial census information. *Census 2010* represent among the most comprehensive datasets available.[6] Collected every 10 years, this study counts every resident in the United States and collects various socio-demographic information. Since these data are collected at the household level, they can be aggregated to a broader unit of measure like the zip code. This consistency in measurement between *Census 2010* and *IDOR, 2011* permits us to readily integrate the two datasets. It is further worth noting that, despite the fact that census data are gathered decennially and IDOR records annually, the cross-sections of data we rely upon were collected at relatively similar points in time. This lends more precision to our measurement of lottery revenues and from which communities this money originates. To better evaluate social factors associated with lottery-generated revenues, we replicate bivariate and multivariate analyses similar to the analysis offered in the preceding chapter. Like our logistic regression analysis in Chapter 4, an ordinary least squares regression analysis permits a more nuanced under-standing of how multiple variables simultaneously and independently affect lottery sales. The primary difference is that this mode of analysis permits us to predict numerical outcomes.

Meanwhile, to measure how lottery revenues are distributed, we rely upon documentation that outlines how Illinois finances public education. Most lottery proceeds are earmarked, after all, toward the state's primary and secondary schools. To learn how lottery money is distributed across the state, we turn to information contained in Public Act 90–548. This law outlines the General State Aid (henceforth GSA) formula, which determines how the Illinois State Board of Education delegate state funds to local school districts. It includes criteria that can be evaluated to discern how lottery rev-enues are expended, or to "follow the money."

Notes

1 *SLGF* is a public-use dataset available at http://www.census.gov/govs/estimate/. Here, one can also find an in-depth summary of the research design, description of the sampling frame, data collection (i.e., collection periods and methods) and processing (i.e., editing and imputation), and data quality (i.e., response rates and sampling error).

2 Data for the 2011 fiscal year ends on June 30 with the exception of four states: Alabama and Michigan (September 30), New York (March 31) and Texas (August 31).

3 *SGF* is a public-use dataset available at http://www.census.gov/govs/state/. Here, one can also find an in-depth summary of the research design, description of the sampling frame, data collection (i.e., collection periods and methods) and pro-cessing (i.e., editing and imputation), and data quality (i.e., response rates and sampling error).

4 *GIBS, 1997–1999* is a public-use dataset made available by the Inter-university Consortium for Political and Social Research at http://www.icpsr.umich.edu/icp srweb/SAMHDA/studies/2778. Here, one can also find an in-depth summary of the study and its design.

5 We do not perform a logistic regression analysis on the outcome variable of the net amount of money lost to the lottery. This omission is purposeful because of the variable's frequency distribution and coding scheme. Responses were aggre-gated in a way that reports the vast majority (78.7 percent) of money lost to be $100 or less. Because the function of logistic regression is to predict probabilities that improve upon the modal output, such an analysis loses substantive meaning for a mode that is already correct 78.7 percent of the time.

6 While census data represents the most comprehensive dataset of demographic data, it has problems of internal and external validity. The census defines race as a fixed characteristic. On the contrary, it is a social process of everyday behavior (Lewis 2003, 2004). "[Race] is something learned and achieved in interactions and institutions. It is something we live and perform" (Lewis 2004: 629). Another problem regards selection bias. Model (2008) clarifies, "The greatest source of inaccuracy in censuses is that individuals absent from the data differ in some sys-tematic way from individuals present. The converse also occurs: censuses include persons who should be excluded, but that problem is less severe" (p. 166). Some are overrepresented among the data, and others are underrepresented.

Data Sources

Public Datasets

"National Gambling Impact Study Commission." [2002] 2007. *Gambling Impact and Behavioral Study, 1997–1999.*
"U.S. Census Bureau." 2011a. *Income and Apportionment of State-Administered Lottery Funds: 2011.*
———. 2011b. *State Government Finances: 2011 Annual Survey of State Government Finances.*
———. 2011c. *2010 Census.*
———. 2010. *American Community Survey, 2005–2009.*

Archival Collections

California State University, Northridge, Oviatt Library, Special Collections and Archives, *Daily News* Morgue Files of the Bustop Campaign Collection, 1928–1988.
The Library of Congress, American Memory, A Century of Lawmaking for a New Nation: U.S. Congressional Documents and Debates.
State of Alabama, Alabama Department of Archives and History, Alabama History Initiative.
State of California, California State Library, Howard Jarvis Collection, 1970–1986.
State of California, California State Library, Paul Gann Archive, 1978–1986.
State of Massachusetts, Boston Public Library, Spencer Grant Collection.
State of Texas, Dallas History and Archives Division, Dallas Public Library.
University of Illinois at Urbana-Champaign, Historical Papers Online Collection, *The Chicago Tribune 1849–1989.*
University of Michigan, Bentley Historical Library, Carmen A. Roberts Papers.
Legal Documents and Records
"Alabama Secretary of State." 1875. *Alabama Constitution of 1875.*
"Arizona State Lottery." 2011. *Arizona Lottery: A Component Unit of the State of Arizona, Financial Statements Year Ended June 30, 2011.*
"Arkansas Lottery Commission." 2011. *Comprehensive Annual Financial Report for the Fiscal Year Ended June 30, 2011.*
"California Lottery." 2011. *Report to the Public for the Fiscal Year Ended June 30, 2011.*
"Colorado Lottery." 2011. *2011 Annual Report.*
"Commonwealth of Massachusetts." 2011. *Statutory Basis Financial Report: For the Fiscal Year Ended June 30, 2011.*
———. 2011. *Comprehensive Annual Financial Report: For the Fiscal Year Ended June 30, 2011.*
"Commonwealth of Pennsylvania, Department of Revenue, Pennsylvania Lottery Bureau." 2011. *Comparative State of Income and Expenditures.*
"Connecticut Lottery Corporation." 2011. *2011 Annual Report Year Ended June 30, 2010.*
"Delaware Lottery." 2011. *2011 Annual Report for the Fiscal Year Ending June 30, 2010.*
"District of Columbia." 2011a. *Basic Financial Statements.*

———. 2011b. *Fiscal Year 2011 Annual Report.*

"Florida Lottery." 2011. *2010–2011 Annual Report.*

"Georgia Lottery Corporation." 2011. *Management's Discussion and Analysis for the Years Ended June 20, 2011 and 2010, Financial Statements as of and for the Years Ended June 30, 2011 and 2010, and Independent Auditor's Report.*

"Hoosier Lottery." 2011. *Annual Report 2011: It's Amazing!*

"Idaho Lottery." 2011. *Annual Report FY2011 Luck Happens: Benefiting Idaho Public Schools and the Idaho Permanent Building Fund.*

"Illinois Department of Revenue." 2011. *Sales Report SLS989–01, IDOR FY2011 Lottery Sales by Zip Code.*

"Illinois House of Representatives, Policy Numbers Game Committee." 1975. *Report and Recommendations to the Legislature.*

"Illinois Lottery." 2010. *State of Illinois Department of Revenue Illinois Lottery 2010 Annual Report: A Win, Win. . .Celebration!*

———. 2009. *Dream by Numbers: Illinois Lottery Annual Report 2008.*

———. 2005. *Winning Big: Illinois Lottery Annual Report 2005.*

"Illinois State Board of Education." 2011. *General State Aid—FY 2011 Overview.*

———. 2004. *Illinois Public School Enrollment Projections: 2004–05–2012–13.*

"Illinois State Comptroller." N.d. "The General State Aid Formula." *Fiscal Focus Magazine, A Publication of the Illinois State Comptroller.*

"Iowa Lottery." 2011. *Games that Help the Cause: Iowa Lottery Annual Report Fiscal Year 2011.*

———. N.d. *Lottery Fact Book.*

"Kansas Legislative Research Department." N.d. *FY13 Appropriations Report.*

"Kansas Lottery." 2012. "Where the Money Goes." *www.kslottery.com.*

"Kentucky Lottery Corporation." 2011. *Fiscal Year 2011 Annual Report.*

"Michigan Lottery, Bureau of State Lottery, An Enterprise Fund of the State of Michigan." 2011. *Comprehensive Annual Financial Report, For Fiscal Years Ended September 30, 2011 and 2010.*

"Minnesota State Lottery." 2011. *FY2011 Annual Report.*

"Missouri State Lottery Commission, An Enterprise Fund of the State of Missouri." 2011. *Comprehensive Annual Financial Report, For Fiscal Year Ended June 30, 2011.*

"Montana Lottery." 2011. *Annual Report 2011: Winners Happen!*

"Nebraska Lottery." 2011. *2011 Annual Report and Resource Guide.*

"New Jersey Lottery." 2010. *Give Your Dreams a Chance: 2011 Annual Report.*

"New Mexico Lottery." 2011. *Happy 15th Birthday!: Annual Report Fiscal Year 2011.*

"New York Lottery, An Enterprise of the State of New York." 2012. *Comprehensive Annual Financial Report: For the Fiscal Year Ended March 31, 2012.*

"North Carolina Education Lottery." 2011. *North Carolina Education Lottery: Annual Report FY 2011.*

"North Dakota Lottery." 2011. *North Dakota Lottery: Audit Report for the Tears Ended June 30, 2011 and 2010.*

"The Ohio Lottery Commission, An Enterprise Fund of the State of Ohio." 2011. *Comprehensive Annual Financial Report: For the Fiscal Years Ended June 30, 2011 and 2010.*

"Oklahoma Lottery Commission." 2011. *Comprehensive Annual Report of the Oklahoma Lottery Commission for the Fiscal Year Ended June 30, 2011.*

"Oregon State Lottery, An Enterprise Fund of the State of Oregon." 2011. *Comprehensive Annual Financial Report: For the Fiscal Year Ended June 30, 2011.*

"Rhode Island Lottery, An Enterprise Fund of the State of Rhode Island and Providence Plantations." 2011. *Comprehensive Annual Financial Report: For the Fiscal Year Ended June 30, 2011.*

"South Carolina Education Lottery Commission." 2011. *Report on Financial Statements: For the Years Ended June 30, 2011 and 2010.*

"South Dakota Lottery." 2011. *Fiscal Year 2011 Annual Report.*

"State of Florida, General Auditor." 2012. *Department of the Lottery: Financial Audit for the Fiscal Year Ended June 30, 2011.*

"State of Illinois, Department of Revenue Illinois Lottery." 2011. *Financial Statements Individual Nonshared Funds June 30, 2011.*

"State of Louisiana, Louisiana Lottery Corporation." 2012. *Comprehensive Annual Financial Report for the Fiscal Years Ended June 30, 2012 and 2011.*

"State of Maine." 2011. *Compendium of State Fiscal Information: Through Fiscal Year Ending June 30, 2011.*

"State of Maryland, Maryland State Lottery Agency." 2011. *Comprehensive Annual Financial Report for the Years Ended June 30, 2011 and 2010.*

"State of New Hampshire, New Hampshire Lottery Commission." 2011. *Comprehensive Annual Financial Report for the Fiscal Year Ended June 30, 2011.*

"Tennessee Education Lottery Corporation." 2011. *$2,000,000,000 for Education: Tennessee Education Lottery Corporation Annual Report 2011.*

"Texas Lottery Commission." 2011. *Annual Financial Report for the Year Ended August 31, 2011 and Independent Auditors' Report.*

"Vermont Lottery." 2011. *Good. Clean. Fun.: Annual Report, Fiscal Year 2011.*

"Virginia Lottery." 2011. *We're Game: 2012 Virginia Lottery Annual Financial for Year Ended June 30, 2012.*

"Washington's Lottery, An Agency of the State of Washington." 2011. *Whose World Could You Change?: Comprehensive Annual Financial Report, For the Fiscal Year Ended June 30, 2011.*

"West Virginia Lottery, A Component Unit of the State of West Virginia." 2011. *25 Years: 1986–2011, Comprehensive Annual Financial Report for the Fiscal Year Ended June 30, 2011.*

"Wisconsin Lottery." 2012. An Audit: Wisconsin Lottery, Department of Revenue Report.

References

Abreu, Alice G. 2001. "Tax Counts: Bringing Money-Law to LatCrit." *Denver University Law Review* 78(4): 575–594.

Adams, Douglas J. 2001. "My Ticket, My 'Self': Lottery Ticket Number Selection and the Commodification and Extension of the Self." *Sociological Spectrum* 21(4): 455–477.

Alexander, Michelle. 2010. *The New Jim Crow: Mass Incarceration in the Age of Colorblindness*. New York, New York: Free Press.

Allport, Gordon. 1954. *The Nature of Prejudice*. Reading, Massachusetts: Addison-Wesley.

Alm, James, Michael McKee, and Mark Skidmore. 1993. "Fiscal Pressure, Tax Competition, and the Introduction of State Lotteries." *National Tax Journal* 46(4): 463–476.

Altheide, David L. 2006. *Terrorism and the Politics of Fear*. Lanham, Maryland: AltaMira Press.

———. 1987. "Ethnographic Content Analysis." *Qualitative Sociology* 10(1): 65–77.

Altheide, David L. and Christopher J. Schneider. [1996] 2013. *Qualitative Media Analysis*. Thousand Oaks, California: Sage.

Anderson, James D. 1988. *The Education of Blacks in the South, 1860–1935*. Chapel Hill, North Carolina: University of North Carolina Press.

Anthias, Floya and Cathie Lloyd. eds. 2002. *Rethinking Anti-Racisms: From Theory to Practice*. New York: Routledge.

Balzac, Honoré de. [1842] 1897. *La Rabouilleuse*. Philadelphia: George Barrie & Son.

Bannerji, Hamani. 1995. *Thinking Through: Essays on Feminism, Marxism, and Anti-Racism*. Toronto: Women's Press.

Barlett, Donald L. and James B Steele. 1994. *America: Who Really Pays the Taxes?* New York: Simon & Schuster.

Barlow, Andrew L. 2003. *Between Fear and Hope: Globalization and Race in the United States*. Lanham, Maryland: Rowman and Littlefield.

Barris, Linda J. 1992. "The Overcompensation Problem: A Collective Approach to Controlling Executive Pay?" *Indiana Law Journal* 68(1): 59–100.

Becker, Howard S. 1967. "Whose Side Are We On?" *Social Problems* 14(3): 239–247.

Beckert, Jens and Mark Lutter. 2013. "Why the Poor Play the Lottery: Sociological Approaches to Explaining Class-Based Lottery Play." *Sociology* 47(6): 1152–1170.

———. 2009. "The Inequality of Fair Play: Lottery Gambling and Social Stratification in Germany." *European Sociological Review* 25(4): 475–488.

Bell, Derrick A. [1973] 2008. *Race, Racism, and American Law*. New York: Aspen Publishers.

———. 1980. "Brown v. Board of Education and the Interest-Convergence Dilemma." *Harvard Law Review* 93(3): 518–533.

Bell, Joyce M. and Douglas Hartmann. 2007. "Diversity in Everyday Discourse: The Cultural Ambiguities and Consequences of 'Happy Talk'." *American Sociological Review* 72(6): 895–914.

Bennett, William J. 1993. *The Book of Virtues: A Treasury of Great Moral Stories*. New York: Simon and Schuster.

Berger, Peter L. 1963. *Invitation to Sociology: A Humanist Perspective*. New York: Doubleday.

Berry, Brent and Eduardo Bonilla-Silva. 2008. " 'They Should Hire the One with the Best Score': White Sensitivity to Qualification Differences in Affirmative Action Hiring Decisions." *Ethnic and Racial Studies* 31(2): 215–242.

Berry, Frances Stokes and William D. Berry. 1990. "State Lottery Adoptions as Policy Innovations: An Event History Analysis." *American Political Science Review* 84(2): 395–416.

Bertrand, Marianne and Sendhil Mullainathan. 2004. "Are Emily and Greg More Employable than Lakisha and Jamal? A Field Experiment on Labor Market Discrimination." *The American Economic Review* 94(4): 991–1013.

Black, Earl and Merle Black. 1987. *Politics and Society in the South*. Cambridge, Massachusetts: Harvard University Press.

Blackmon, Douglas A. 2008. *Slavery by Another Name: The Re-Enslavement of Black Americans from the Civil War to World War II*. New York: Anchor Books.

Blakey, G. Robert. 1979. "State Conducted Lotteries: History, Problems, and Promises." *Journal of Social Issues* 35(3): 62–86.

Blalock, Garrick, David R. Just, and Daniel H. Simon. 2007. "Hitting the Jackpot or Hitting the Skids: Entertainment, Poverty, and the Demand for State Lotteries." *American Journal of Economics and Sociology* 66(3): 545–570.

Bloch, Herbert A. 1951. "The Sociology of Gambling." *American Journal of Sociology* 57(3): 215–221.

Blumer, Harold. [1939] 2000. "The Nature of Race Prejudice." Pp. 183–195 in *Selected Works of Herbert Blumer: A Public Philosophy for Mass Society*, edited by Stanford M. Lyman and Arthur J. Vidich. Chicago: University of Illinois Press.

———. 1971. "Social Problems as Collective Behavior." *Social Problems* 18(3): 298–306.

———. 1958. "Race Prejudice as a Sense of Group Position." *The Pacific Sociological Review* 1(1): 3–7.

Bobo, Lawrence D. 1988. "Attitudes toward the Black Political Movement: Trends, Meaning, and Effects on Racial Policy Preferences." *Social Psychology Quarterly* 51(4): 287–302.

———. 1983. "Whites' Opposition to Busing: Symbolic Racism or Realistic Group Conflict?" *Journal of Personality and Social Psychology* 45(6): 1196–1210.

Bobo, Lawrence D., Camille Z. Charles, Maria Krysan, and Alicia D. Simmons. 2012. "The Real Record on Racial Attitudes." Pp. 38–83 in *Social Trends in American Life: Findings from the General Social Survey*, edited by Peter V. Marsden. Princeton, New Jersey: Princeton University Press.

Bonastia, Christopher. 2012. *Southern Stalemate: Five Years without Public Education in Prince Edward County, Virginia*. Chicago: University of Chicago Press.

———. 2009. "White Justifications for School Closings in Prince Edward County, Virginia, 1959–1964." *The Du Bois Review* 6(2): 309–333.

Bonilla-Silva, Eduardo. 2015. "More than Prejudice: Restatement, Reflections, and New Directions in Critical Race Theory." *Sociology of Race & Ethnicity* 1(1): 73–87.

———. [2003] 2014. *Racism without Racists: Color-Blind Racism and the Persistence of Racial Inequality in America.* Lanham, Maryland: Rowman and Littlefield.

———. [2003] 2006. *Racism without Racists: Color-Blind Racism and the Persistence of Racial Inequality in America.* Lanham, Maryland: Rowman and Littlefield.

———. 2004. "From Bi-Racial to Tri-Racial: Towards a New System of Racial Stratification in the USA." *Ethnic and Racial Studies* 27(6): 931–950.

———. 2001. *White Supremacy and Racism in the Post-Civil Rights Era.* Boulder, Colorado: Lynne Rienner.

———. 1999. "The Essential Social Fact of Race." *American Sociological Review* 64(6): 899–906.

———. 1997. "Rethinking Racism: Toward a Structural Interpretation." *American Sociological Review* 62(3): 465–480.

Bonilla-Silva, Eduardo and Amanda E. Lewis. 1999. "The 'New Racism': Toward an Analysis of U.S. Racial Structure, 1960–1990s." Pp. 100–150 in *Race, Nation, and Citizenship*, edited by Paul Wong. Boulder, Colorado: Westview Press.

Bonilla-Silva, Eduardo, Amanda E. Lewis, and David G. Embrick. 2004. "'I Did Not Get that Job Because of a Black Man . . .': The Story Lines and Testimonies of Color-Blind Racism." *Sociological Forum* 19(4): 555–581.

Bonilla-Silva, Eduardo, Carla Goar, and David G. Embrick. 2006. "When Whites Flock Together: White Habitus and the Social Psychology of Whites' Social and Residential Segregation from Blacks." *Critical Sociology* 32(2–3): 229–254.

Bonilla-Silva, Eduardo, Tyrone A. Forman, Amanda E. Lewis, and David G. Embrick. 2003. "'It Wasn't Me!': How will Race and Racism Work in 21st Century America." *Political Sociology for the 21st Century* 12: 111–134.

Borg, Mary O. and Paul M. Mason. 1990. "Earmarked Lottery Revenues: Positive Windfalls or Concealed Redistribution Mechanisms." *Journal of Education Finance* 15(3): 289–301.

———. 1988. "The Budgetary Incidence of a Lottery to Support Education." *The National Tax Journal* 41(1): 75–86.

Borg, Mary O., Paul M. Mason, and Stephen L. Shapiro. 1991. *The Economic Consequences of State Lotteries.* New York: Praeger.

Boudon, Raymond. 1991. "What Middle-Range Theories Are." *Contemporary Sociology* 20(4): 519–522.

Bracey II, Glenn E. 2015. "Toward a Critical Race Theory of State." *Critical Sociology* 41(3): 553–572.

Brennen, David A. 2004. "Race and Equality Across the Law School Curriculum: The Law of Tax Exemption." *Journal of Legal Education* 54(3): 336–350.

Brown, Daniel J., Dennis O. Kaldenberg, and Beverly A. Browne. 1992. "Socioeconomic Status and Playing the Lotteries." *Sociology and Social Research* 76: 161–167.

Brown, Dorothy A. 2012. "Tax Law: Implicit Bias and the Earned Income Tax Credit." Pp. 164–178 in *Implicit Racial Bias Across the Law*, edited by Justin D. Levinson and Robert J. Smith. New York: Cambridge University Press.

———. 2010. "Shades of the American Dream." *Washington University Law Review* 87(2): 329–378.

———. 2007. "Race and Class Matters in Tax Policy." *Columbia Law Review* 107(3): 790–831.

———. 1999. "Racial Equality in the Twenty-First Century: What's Tax Policy Got to Do with It?" *University of Arkansas Little Rock Law Review* 21(4): 759–768.

Brown, Karen B. and Mary Louise Fellows (Eds.). 1996. *Taxing America*. New York: New York University Press.

Brown, Michael K. 1999. *Race, Money, and the American Welfare State*. Ithaca, New York: Cornell University Press.

Brunori, David. [2001] 2005. *State Tax Policy: A Political Perspective (2nd Edition)*. Washington, DC: The Urban Institute.

Bryce, James D. 1998. "A Critical Evaluation of the Tax Crits." *North Carolina Law Review* 76(5): 1687–1728.

Bush, Melanie E. L. 2004. *Breaking the Code of Good Intentions: Everyday Forms of Whiteness*. Lanham, Maryland: Rowman and Littlefield.

Calcagno, Peter T., Douglas M. Walker, and John D. Jackson. 2010. "Determinants of the Probability and Timing of Commercial Casino Legalization in the United States." *Public Choice* 142(1–2): 69–90.

Campbell, Andrea L. 2009. "What Americans Think of Taxes." Pp. 48–67 in *The New Fiscal Sociology: Taxation in Comparative and Historical Perspective*, edited by Isaac William Martin, Ajay K. Mehrotra, and Monica Prasad. New York: Cambridge University Press.

Carmichael, Stokely and Charles V. Hamilton. 1967. *Black Power: The Politics of Liberation*. New York: Vintage.

Caudill, Steven B., Jon M. Ford, Franklin G. Mixon Jr., and Ter Chao Peng. 1995. "A Discrete-Time Hazard Model of Lottery Adoption." *Applied Economics* 27(6): 555–561.

Clark, Kenneth and James Baldwin. 1963. " 'There Is No Compromise': Total Freedom or Total Oppression." Pp. 25–31 in *Negro Digest*, edited by John H. Johnson. Chicago, Illinois: Johnson Publishing Company.

Clotfelter, Charles T. and Philip J. Cook. 1989. *Selling Hope: State Lotteries in America*. Cambridge, Massachusetts: Harvard University Press.

Clotfelter, Charles T., Philip J. Cook, Julie A. Edell, and Marian Moore. 1999. *State Lotteries at the Turn of the Century: Report to the National Gambling Impact Study Commission*. Durham, North Carolina: Duke University.

Coleman, James S. 1990. *Foundations of Social Theory*. Cambridge, Massachusetts: Harvard University Press.

Collins, Patricia Hill. [1990] 2010. *Black Feminist Thought: Knowledge, Consciousness, and the Politics of Empowerment*. New York: Routledge.

Collins, Sharon M. 1997. *Black Corporate Executives: The Making and Breaking of a Black Middle Class*. Philadelphia: Temple University Press.

Conlisk, John. 1993. "The Utility of Gambling." *Journal of Risk and Uncertainty* 6(3): 255–275.

Coughlin, Cletus C., Thomas A. Garret, and Rubén Hernández-Murillo 2006. "The Geography, Economics, and Politics of Lottery Adoption." *Federal Reserve Bank of St. Louis Review* 88(3): 165–180.

Crenshaw, Kimberlé Williams. 1997. "Color-blind Dreams and Racial Nightmares: Reconfiguring Racism in the Post-Civil Rights Era." Pp. 97–168 in *Birth of a Nation'hood*, edited by Toni Morrison and Claudia Brodsky Lacour. New York: Pantheon.

Cruikshank, Barbara. 1997. *The Will to Empower: Democratic Citizens and Other Subjects.* Ithaca, New York: Cornell University Press.

Daniels, Jessie. 1997. *White Lies: Race, Class, Gender, and Sexuality in White Supremacist Discourse.* New York: Routledge.

Darity, Jr., William A. 2008. "Forty Acres and a Mule in the 21st Century." *Social Science Quarterly* 89(3): 656–664.

———. 2002. "Intergroup Disparity: Why Culture is Irrelevant." *The Review of Black Political Economy* 29(4): 77–90.

Davis, J. Ronnie, John E. Filer, and Donald L. Moak. 1992. "The Lottery as an Alternative Source of State Revenue." *Atlantic Economic Journal* 20(2): 1–10.

de Genova, Nicholas. 2005. *Working the Boundaries: Race, Space, and 'Illegality' in Mexican Chicago.* Durham, North Carolina: Duke University Press.

Delgado, Richard. 1982. "Words that Wound: A Tort Action for Racial Insults, Epithets, and Name-Calling." *Harvard Civil Rights–Civil Liberties Review* 17: 133–181.

Denzin, Norman K. 1978. *Sociological Methods: A Sourcebook.* New York: McGraw-Hill.

Devereux, Edward Clifton. [1949] 1980. *Gambling and the Social Structure: A Sociological Study of Lotteries and Horse Racing in Contemporary America.* New York: Arno Press.

Doane, Ashley "Woody." 2006. "What is Racism? Racial Discourse and Racial Politics." *Critical Sociology* 32(2–3): 255–274.

———. 1997. "Dominant Group Ethnic Identity in the United States: The Role of 'Hidden' Ethnicity in Intergroup Relations." *The Sociological Quarterly* 38(3): 375–397.

Domhoff, G. William. [1967] 2013. *Who Rules America? The Triumph of the Corporate Rich.* New York: McGraw-Hill.

Douglass, Frederick. [1857] 1999. "West India Emancipation, speech delivered before American Anti-Slavery Society, New York, May 14, 1857." Pp. 358–368 in *Frederick Douglass: Selected Speeches and Writings*, edited by Philip S. Foner. New York: International Publishers.

Downes, Thomas A. 1992. "Evaluating School Impact of School Finance Reform on the Provision of Public Education." *National Tax Journal* 45(4): 405–419.

Downes, Thomas A. and David N. Figlio. 1999. "Do Tax and Expenditure Limits Provide a Free Ride? Evidence on the Link between the Limits and Public Sector Quality." *National Tax Journal* 52(1): 113–128.

Downes, Thomas A., Richard F. Dye, and Therese McGuire. 1998. "Do Limitations Matter? Evidence on the Effects of Tax Limitations on School Performance." *Journal of Urban Economics* 43(3): 401–417.

Downs, Anthony. 1970. *Racism in America and How to Combat It.* Washington, DC: U.S. Commission on Civil Rights.

Drake, St. Clair and Horace R. Cayton. [1945] 1993. *Black Metropolis: A Study of Negro Life in a Northern City.* Chicago: University of Chicago Press.

———. 1967. "Policy: Poor Man's Roulette." Pp. 3–10 in *Gambling*, edited by Robert D. Herman. New York: Harper & Row.

Du Bois, W.E.B. [1935] 1992. *Black Reconstruction in America.* New York: Atheneum.

———. 1910. "Reconstruction and Its Benefits." *American Historical Review* 15(4): 781–799.

———. 1903. *The Souls of Black Folk*. Chicago: McClurg & Co.

———. (Ed.). 1901. *The Negro Common School*. Atlanta, Georgia: Atlanta University Press.

Eckblad, Gudrun Fleischer and Anna Louise von der Lippe. 1994. "Norwegian Lottery Winners: Cautious Realists." *Journal of Gambling Studies* 10(4): 305–322.

Edgar, David. 1981. "Reagan's Hidden Agenda: Racism and the New Right." *Race & Class* 22(3): 221–238.

Edsall, Thomas Byrne and Mary D. Edsall. 1991. *Chain Reaction: The Impact of Race, Rights, and Taxes on American Politics*. New York: W.W. Norton.

Einhorn, Robin L. 2006. *American Taxation, American Slavery*. Chicago: University of Chicago Press.

———. 2001. "Species of Property: The American Property-Tax Uniformity Clauses Reconsidered." *The Journal of Economic History* 61(4): 974–1008.

Elster, Jon. 1989. *Nuts and Bolts for the Social Sciences*. New York: Cambridge University Press.

Embrick, David G. 2015. "Two Nations, Revisited: The Lynching of Black and Brown Bodies, Police Brutality, and Racial Control in 'Post-Racial' Amerikkka." *Critical Sociology* 41(6): 1–10.

Embrick, David G. and Kasey Henricks. 2013 "Discursive Colorlines at Work: How Epithets and Stereotypes are Racially Unequal." *Symbolic Interaction* 36(2): 197–215.

Erekson, O. Homer, Glenn Platt, Christopher Whistler, and Andrea L. Ziegert. 1999. "Factors Influencing the Adoption of State Lotteries." *Applied Economics* 31(7): 875–884.

Essed, Philomena. 1991. *Understanding Everyday Racism: An Interdisciplinary Theory*. New York: Sage.

Farkas, George. 2003. "Racial Disparities and Discrimination in Educaiton: What Do We Know, How Do We Know It, and What Do We Need to Know?" *Teachers College Record* 105(6): 1119–1146.

Farmer, Stephanie and Chris D. Poulos. 2015. "Tax Increment Financing in Chicago: Building Neoliberal Exclusion One School at a Time." *Critical Sociology* 41(1): 153–171.

Feagin, Joe R. 2012. *White Party, White Government: Race, Class, and U.S. Politics*. New York: Routledge.

———. 2006. *Systemic Racism: A Theory of Oppression*. New York: Routledge.

———. 2000. *Racist America: Roots, Current Realities, and Future Reparations*. New York: Routledge.

Feagin, Joe R. and Douglas Lee Eckberg. 1980. "Discrimination: Motivation, Action, Effects, and Context." *Annual Review of Sociology* 6(1): 1–20.

Feagin, Joe R. and Sean Elias. 2013. "Rethinking Racial Formation: A Systemic Racism Critique." *Ethnic and Racial Studies* 36(6): 931–960.

Figlio, David N. 1997. "Did the 'Tax Revolt' Reduce?" *Journal of Public Economics* 65(3): 245–269.

Filer, John E., Donald L. Mozak, and Barry Uze. 1988. "Why Some States Adopt Lotteries and Others Don't." *Public Finance Quarterly* 16(3): 259–283.

Fischel, William A. 1989. "Did *Serrano* Cause Proposition 13?" *National Tax Journal* 42(4): 465–473.

Fischer, Claude S. and Michael Hout. 2006. *Century of Difference: How America Changed in the Last One Hundred Years*. New York: Russell Sage.

Fischer, Claude S., Michael Hout, Martín Sánchez Jankowski, Samuel R. Lucas, Ann Swindler, and Kim Voss. 1996. *Inequality by Design: Cracking the Bell Curve Myth*. Princeton, New Jersey: Princeton University Press.

Fisher, Glenn W. 1969. *Taxes and Politics: A Study of Illinois Public Finance*. Urbana: University of Illinois Press.

Foner, Eric. 1988. *Reconstruction: America's Unfinished Revolution*. New York: HarperCollins.

Forrest, David, Robert Simmons, and Neil Chesters. 2002. "Buying a Dream: Alternative Models of Demand for Lotto." *Economic Inquiry* 40(3): 485–496.

Franklin, John Hope. [1961] 1994. *Reconstruction after the Civil War*. Chicago, Illinois: University of Chicago Press.

Franklin, John Hope and Alfred A. Moss. 1947. *From Slavery to Freedom: A History of African Americans*. New York: A.A. Knopf.

Fuchs, Lawrence H. 1990. *The American Kaleidoscope: Race, Ethnicity, and the Civic Culture*. Hanover, New Hampshire: Wesleyan University Press.

Furner, Mary. 1975. *Advocacy and Objectivity: A Crisis in the Professionalization of American Social Science, 1865–1905*. Lexington, Kentucky: University of Kentucky Press.

Galeano, Eduardo. 2013. *Children of the Days: A Calendar of Human History*. New York: Nation Books.

Gallagher, Charles A. 2003. "Color-Blind Privilege: The Social and Political Functions of Erasing the Color Line in Post Race America." *Race, Gender & Class* 10(4): 1–17.

Galvin, Charles O. 1998. "Taking Critical Tax Theory Seriously—A Comment." *North Carolina Law Review* 76(5): 1749–1752.

Garrett, Thomas A. and Thomas L. Marsh. 2002. "The Revenue Impacts of Cross-Border Lottery Shopping in the Presence of Spatial Autocorrelation." *Regional Science and Urban Economics* 32(4): 501–519.

Garvía, Roberto. 2007. "Syndication, Institutionalization, and Lottery Play." *American Journal of Sociology* 113(3): 603–652.

Ghent, Linda S. and Alan P. Grant. 2007. "Are Voting and Buying Behavior Consistent? Evidence from the South Carolina Education Lottery." *Public Finance Review* 35(6): 669–688.

Gilens, Martin. 1999. *Why Americans Hate Welfare: Race, Media, and the Politics of Antipoverty Policy*. Chicago: University of Chicago Press.

Glaeser, Edward and Jacob Vigdor. 2012. *The End of the Segregated Century: Racial Separation in America's Neighborhoods, 1890–2010*. New York: Center for State and Local Leadership at the Manhattan Institute.

Glickman, Mark M. and Gary D. Painter. 2004. "Do Tax and Expenditure Limits Lead to State Lotteries? Evidence from the United States: 1970–1992." *Public Finance Review* 32(1): 36–64.

Goodman, Jack. 2006. "Houses, Apartments, and the Incidence of Property Taxes." *Housing Policy Debate* 17(1):1–26.

Goodman, Robert. 1995. *The Luck Business: The Devastating Consequences and Broken Promises of America's Gambling Explosion*. New York: Free Press.

Gotham, Kevin. 2000. "Racialization and the State: The Housing Act of 1934 and the Origins of the Federal Housing Administration (FHA)." *Sociological Perspectives* 43(2): 291–316.

Gotham, Kevin Fox. 2002. *Race, Real Estate, and Uneven Development: The Kansas City Experience, 1900–2000*. Albany, New York: State University of New York Press.

Graetz, Michael J. and Ian Shapiro. 2005. *Death by a Thousand Cuts: The Fight Over Taxing Inherited Wealth*. Princeton, New Jersey: Princeton University Press.

Gramsci, Antonio. [1949] 1974. *Note sull Machiavelli sulla Politica e sullo Stato Moderno*. Turin, Italy: Giulio Einaudi.

———. [1946] 1971. *Selections from the Prison Notebooks*. New York: International Publishers.

Granovetter, Mark. 1978. "Threshold Models of Collective Behavior." *American Journal of Sociology* 83(6): 1420–1443.

Gribbin, Donald W. and Jonathan J. Bean. 2005. "Adoption of State Lotteries in the United States, with a Closer Look at Illinois." *Independent Review* X(3): 351–364.

Gross, Neil. 2009. "A Pragmatist Theory of Social Mechanisms." *American Sociological Review* 74(3): 358–379.

Guillén, Mauro F., Roberto Garvía, and Andrés Santana. 2012. "Embedded Play: Economic and Social Motivations for Sharing Lottery Tickets." *European Sociological Review* 28(3): 344–354.

Guryan, Jonathan and Melissa S. Kearney. 2008. "Gambling at Lucky Stores: Empirical Evidence from State Lottery Sales." *American Economic Review* 98(1): 458–473.

Hall, Stuart (Ed.). 1997. *Representation: Cultural Representations and Signifying Practices*. London: Sage Publications.

———. 1984. "The Narrative Construction of Reality: An Interview with Stuart Hall." *Southern Review* 17(1): 3–17.

Haller, Mark H. 1979. "The Changing Structure of American Gambling in the Twentieth Century." *Journal of Social Issues* 35(3): 87–114.

Hamilton, Darrick, William A. Darity, Jr., Anne E. Price, Vishnu Sridharan, and Rebecca Tippett. 2015. *Umbrellas Don't Make It Rain: Why Studying or Working Hard Isn't Enough for Black Americans*. Oakland, California: Insight Center for Community Economic Development.

Haney-López, Ian F. 2000. "Judicial Conduct and a New Theory of Racial Discrimination." *The Yale Law Journal* 109(8): 1717–1884.

———. 1996. *White By Law: The Legal Construction of Race*. New York: New York University Press.

Hansen, Ann. 1995. "The Tax Incidence of the Colorado State Instant Lottery Game." *Public Finance Quarterly* 23(3): 385–398.

Hansen, Ann, Anthony D. Miyazaki, and David E. Sprott. 2005. "The Tax Incidence of Lotteries: Evidence from Five States." *The Journal of Consumer Affairs* 34(2): 2000.

Harris, Cheryl I. 1993. "Whiteness as Property." *Harvard Law Review* 106(8): 1707–1791.

Harris, Jerome and William D. McCullough. [1973] 1998. "Quantitative Methods and Black Community Studies." Pp. 331–343 in *The Death of White Sociology: Essays on Race and Culture*, edited by Joyce A. Ladner. Baltimore, Maryland: Black Classic.

Hartley, Roger and Lisa Farrell. 2002. "Can Expected Utility Theory Explain Gambling?" *American Economic Review* 92(3): 613–624.

Heberling, Michael. 2002. "State Lotteries: Advocating a Social Ill for the Social Good." *The Independent Review* 6(4): 597–606.

Heckman, James J. 2011. "The American Family in Black and White: A Post-Racial Strategy for Improving Skills to Promote Equality." *Daedalus* 140(2): 70–89.

Hedström, Peter and Petri Ylikoski. 2010. "Causal Mechanisms in the Social Sciences." *Annual Review of Sociology* 36: 49–67.

Hedström, Peter and Richard Swedberg. 1998. *Social Mechanisms: An Analytical Approach to Social Theory.* New York: Cambridge University Press.

———. 1996. "Social Mechanisms." *Acta Sociologica* 39(3): 281–308.

Henricks, Kasey. 2014. "Who Plays? Who Pays?: Education Finance Policy that Supplant Tax Burdens along Lines of Race and Class." *Race Ethnicity and Education* doi: 10.1080/13613324.2013.868343.

Henricks, Kasey, Bill Byrnes, and Victoria Brockett. 2014. "Celebrating a Return to Jim Crow?: A Reflexive Analysis and Methodological Query on Measuring Segregation." *Critical Sociology* 40(1): 89–101.

Henricks, Kasey and Daina Cheyenne Harvey. 2015. "Black Dollars, White Pockets: Looting by Another Name." *Humanity & Society* 39(1): 3–8.

Heritage, John. 1984. *Garfinkel and Ethnomethodology.* New York: Polity.

Howard, Christopher. 1997. *The Hidden Welfare State: Tax Expenditures and Social Policy in the United States.* Princeton, New Jersey: Princeton University Press.

Hughey, Matthew W. 2015. "We've Been Framed! A Focus on Identity and Interaction for a Better Vision of Racialized Social Movements." *Sociology of Race and Ethnicity* 1(1): 137–152.

———. 2014. *The White Savior Film: Content, Critics, and Consumption.* Philadelphia: Temple University Press.

———. 2012. *White Bound: Nationalists, Antiracists, and the Shared Meanings of Race.* Stanford, California: Stanford University Press.

Hughey, Matthew W., David G. Embrick, and Ashley "Woody" Doane. 2015 "Paving the Way for Future Race Research: Exploring the Racial Mechanisms within a Color-Blind, Racialized Social System." *American Behavioral Scientist* 59(11): 1347–1357.

Hunter, Marcus Anthony. 2013. *Black Citymakers: How the Philadelphia Negro Changed Urban America.* New York: Oxford University Press.

Huntington, Samuel P. 2004. *Who Are We? The Challenges to America's National Identity.* New York: Simon and Schuster.

Infanti, Anthony C. 2008. "Tax ~~Equity~~." *Buffalo Law Review* 55(4): 1191–1260.

Jackman, Mary R. 1994. *The Velvet Glove: Paternalism and Conflict in Gender, Class, and Race Relations.* Berkeley, California: University of California Press.

Jackson, Kenneth T. 1985. *Crabgrass Frontier: The Suburbanization of the United States.* New York: Oxford University Press.

Jameson, Fredric. 1988. "Cognitive mapping." Pp. 347–360 in *Marxism and the Interpretation of Culture,* edited by Cary Nelson and Lawrence Grossberg. Urbana, Illinois: University of Illinois Press.

Jarvis, Howard. 1979. *I'm Mad as Hell: The Exclusive Story of the Tax Revolt and Its Leader.* New York: Times Books.

Johnston, David Cay. 2003. *Perfectly Legal: The Covert Campaign to Rig our Tax System to Benefit the Super Rich.* New York: Portfolio.

Johnson, Donald R. 1999. *Public School Finance Programs of the United States and Canada 1998–1999.* Washington, DC: US Department of Education, National Center for Education Statistics.

Johnson, Walter. 2015. "Ferguson's Fortune 500 Company." *The Atlantic* 4(26). Retrieved May 1, 2015 (http://www.theatlantic.com/politics/archive/2015/04/fergusons-fortune-500-company/390492/).

Jones Jeffery, M. 2008. "One in Six Americans Gamble on Sports: State Lotteries Are Most Common Form of Gambling." Gallup, Inc., February 1, Social Issues Section.

Jung, Moon-Kie. 2015. *Beneath the Surface of White Supremacy: Denaturalizing U.S. Racisms Past and Present.* Stanford, California: Stanford University Press.

Jung, Moon-Kie, João H. Costa Vargas, and Eduardo Bonilla-Silva. 2011. *The State of White Supremacy: Racism, Governance, and the United States.* Stanford, California: Stanford University Press.

Kaplan, H. Roy. 1987. "Lottery Winners: The Myth and Reality." *Journal of Gambling Behavior* 3(3): 168–178.

Karcher, Alan J. 1992. "State Lotteries." *Society* 29(4): 51–56.

———. 1989. *Lotteries.* New Brunswick, New Jersey: Transaction Publishers.

Katz, Judith H. 1978. *White Awareness: Handbook for Anti-Racism Training.* Norman, Oklahoma: University of Oklahoma Press.

Katznelson, Ira. 2005. *When Affirmative Action was White: An Untold History of Racial Inequality in Twentieth-Century America.* New York: W.W. Norton.

Kefelas, Maria. 2003. *Working Class Heroes: Protecting Home, Community, and Nation in a Chicago Community.* Berkeley: University of California Press.

Kidder, Jeffrey L. and Isaac William Martin. 2012. "What We Talk About When We Talk About Taxes." *Symbolic Interaction* 35(2): 123–145.

King, Jr., Martin Luther. 1967. *Where Do We Go from Here? Chaos or Community?* Boston, Massachusetts: Beacon Press.

Kirp, David L., John P. Dwyer, and Larry Rosenthal. 1995. *Our Town: Race, Housing, and the Soul of Suburbia.* New Brunswick, New Jersey: Rutgers University Press.

Knowles, Louis L. and Kenneth Prewitt. 1969. *Institutional Racism in America.* Englewood Cliffs, New Jersey: Prentice-Hall, Inc.

Kousser, J. Morgan. 1980. "Progressivism—for Middle-Class Whites Only: North Carolina Education, 1880–1910." *Journal of Southern Economic Hisotry* 46(2): 169–195.

Kozol, Jonathan. 1991. *Savage Inequalities: Children in America's Schools.* New York: HarperCollins.

Kruse, Kevin Michael. 2005. *White Flight: Atlanta and the Making of Modern Conservatism.* Princeton, New Jersey: Princeton University Press.

Lakoff, George. 2004. *Don't Think of an Elephant: Know Your Values and Frame the Debate.* White River Junction: Chelsea Green Publishing.

Larsson, Bengt. 2011. "Becoming a Winner but Staying the Same: Identities and Consumption of Lottery Winners." *American Journal of Economics and Sociology* 70(1): 187–209.

Lawrence, Charles R., III. 1990. "If He Hollers Let Him Go: Regulating Racist Speech on Campus." *Duke Law Journal* 3: 431–483.

Lazarsfeld, Paul F., Bernard Berelson, and Hazel Gaudet. 1948. *The People's Choice, How the Voter Makes Up His Mind in a Presidential Campaign.* New York: Columbia University Press.

Lesieur, Henry R. 1998. "Costs and Treatment of Pathological Gambling." *Annals of the American Academy of Political and Social Science* 556(March): 153–171.

Lesieur, Henry R. and Shelia B. Blume. 1987. "The South Oaks Gambling Screen (SOGS): A New Instrument for the Identification of Pathological Gamblers." *American Journal of Psychiatry* 144(9): 1184–1188.

Lewis, Amanda. 2004. "What group? Studying Whites and Whiteness in the Era of 'Color-blindness.'" *Sociological Theory* 22(4): 623–646.

———. 2003. *Race in the Schoolyard: Negotiating the Color Line in Classrooms and Communities.* New Brunswick, New Jersey: Rutgers University Press.

Lewis-Beck, Michael S. 1980. *Applied Regression: An Introduction.* Beverly Hills, California: SAGE Publications.

Lieberman, Robert C. 1998. *Shifting the Color Line: Race and the American Welfare State.* Cambridge, Massachusetts: Harvard University Press.

Lipman, Francine J. 2011. "The 'ILLEGAL' Tax." *Connecticut Public Interest Law Journal* 11(1): 93–131.

Lipsitz, George. 2011. *How Racism Takes Place.* Philadelphia: Temple University Press.

———. 1998. *The Possessive Investment in Whiteness: How White People Profit from Identity Politics.* Philadelphia: Temple University Press.

Lo, Clarence Y. H. 1990. *Small Property Versus Big Government: Social Origins of the Property Tax Revolt.* Berkeley: University of California Press.

Loewen, James. 2005. *Sundown Towns: A Hidden Dimension of American Racism.* New York, New York: The New Press.

Lombardo, Robert M. 2002. "The Black Mafia: African-American Organized Crime in Chicago 1890–1960." *Crime, Law & Social Change* 38(1): 33–65.

Lorde, Audre. [1984] 2007. *Sister Outsider.* Berkeley, California: Crossing Press.

Ludwig, Jack. 1999. "Charge That Gambling Industry Preys on the Poor Not Borne out in Gallup Survey: High-Income and High-Education Americans Play Heavily." Gallup, Inc., July 8, Business Section.

Lui, Meizhu, Bárbara Robles, Betsy Leondar-Wright, Rose Brewer, and Rebecca Adamson, with United for a Fair Economy. 2006. *The Color of Wealth: The Story Behind the U.S. Racial Wealth Divide.* New York: New Press.

Lustig, Richard. 2010. *Learn How to Increase Your Chances of Winning the Lottery.* Bloomington, Indiana: AuthorHouse.

Luttmer, Erzo F.P. 2001. "Group Loyalty and the Taste for Redistribution." *Journal of Political Economy* 109(3): 500–528.

Marable, Manning. [1983] 2000. *How Capitalism Underdeveloped Black America: Problems in Race, Political Economy and Society.* Boston: South End Press.

Martin, Isaac William. 2008. *The Permanent Tax Revolt: How the Property Tax Transformed American Politics.* Stanford, California: Stanford University Press.

Martin, Isaac William, Ajay K. Mehrotra, and Monica Prasad (Eds.). 2009. *The New Fiscal Sociology: Taxation in Comparative and Historical Perspective.* Cambridge, England: Cambridge University Press.

Martin, Isaac William and Kevin Beck. Forthcoming. *Property Tax Limitation and Racial Inequality in Effective Tax Rates. Critical Sociology.*

Martin, Isaac William and Monica Prasad. 2014. "Taxes and Fiscal Sociology." *Annual Review of Sociology* 40: 331–345.

Marx, Karl. [1844] 1972. "Contribution to the Critique of Hegel's *Philosophy of Right*: Introduction." Pp. 11–23 in *The Marx-Engels Reader*, edited by Robert C. Tucker. New York: W.W. Norton & Company.

———. [1852] 1963. *The Eighteenth Brumaire of Louis Bonaparte.* New York: International Publishers.

Marx, Karl and Friedrich Engels. [1848] 2002. *The Communist Manifesto.* London: Penguin.

Massey, Douglas S. and Nancy A. Denton. 1993. *American Apartheid: Segregation and the Making of the Underclass.* Cambridge, Massachusetts: Harvard University Press.

Mayorga-Gallo, Sarah. 2014. *Behind the White Picket Fence: Power and Privilege in a Multiethnic Neighborhood.* Chapel Hill, North Carolina: University of North Carolina Press.

McCrary, Joseph L. and Thomas J. Palvak. 2002. *Who plays the Georgia Lottery?: Results of a Statewide Survey.* Athens, Georgia: University of Georgia, Carl Vinson Institute of Government.

McKoy, Deborah L. and Jeffrey M. Vincent. 2006. "Housing and Education: The Inextricable Link." Pp. 125–150 in Segregation: The Rising Costs for America, edited by James H. Carr and Nandinee K. Kutty. New York: Routledge.

McMillan, Malcolm Cook. [1955] 1978. *Constitutional Development in Alabama, 1798–1901: A Study in Politics, the Negro, and Sectionalism.* Chapel Hill, North Carolina: University of North Carolina Press.

Merton, Robert K. [1949] 1967. *On Theoretical Sociology: Five Essays, Old and New.* New York: Free Press.

Mikesell, John L. 1989. "A Note on the Changing Incidence of State Lottery Finance." *Social Science Quarterly* 70(2): 513–521.

Mikesell, John L. and C. Kurt Zorn. 1988. "State Lotteries for Public Revenue." *Public Budgeting and Finance* 8(1): 38–47.

———. 1986. "State Lotteries as Fiscal Savior or Fiscal Fraud: A Look at the Evidence." *Public Administration Review* 46(4): 311–320.

Mills, C. Wright. [1959] 2000. *The Sociological Imagination.* New York: Oxford University Press.

Mills, Charles W. 1997. *The Racial Contract.* Ithaca, New York: Cornell University Press.

Miyazaki, Anthony D., Ann Hansen, and David E. Sprott. 1998. "A Longitudinal Analysis of Income-Based Tax Regressivity of State-Sponsored Lotteries." *Journal of Public Policy & Marketing* 17(2): 161–172.

Model, Suzanne. 2008. *West Indian Immigrants: A Black Success Story?* New York: Russell Sage Foundation.

Moore, Wendy Leo. 2014. "The *Stare Decisis* of Racial Inequality: Supreme Court Race Jurisprudence and the Legacy of Legal Apartheid in the United States." *Critical Sociology* 40(1): 67–88.

Moore, Wendy Leo and Joyce M. Bell. 2010. "Embodying the White Racial Frame: The (In)Significance of Barack Obama." *Journal of Race & Policy* 6(1): 123–138.

Moore, Wendy Leo and Joyce Bell. 2011. "Maneuvers of Whiteness: 'Diversity' as a Mechanism of Retrenchment in the Affirmative Action Discourse." *Critical Sociology* 37(5): 597–613.

Moran, Beverly I. 2010. "Wealth Redistribution and the Income Tax." *Howard Law Journal* 53(2): 319–336.

Moran, Beverly I. and Stephanie M. Wildman. 2007. "Race and Wealth Disparity: The Role of Law and the Legal System." *Fordham Urban Law Journal* XXXIV: 1219–1238.

Moran, Beverly I. and William Whitford. 1996. "A Black Critique of the Internal Revenue Code." *Wisconsin Law Review* 71(4): 751–820.

Morgan, Kimberly J. and Monica Prasad. 2009. "The Origins of Tax Systems: A French-American Comparison." *American Journal of Sociology* 114(5): 1350–1394.

Murguia, Edward and Rogelio Sáenz. 2002. "An Analysis of the Latin Americanization of Race in the United States A Reconnaissance of Color Stratification among Mexicans." *Race and Society* 5(1): 85–101.

Myers, Dowell. 2009. *The Demographics of Proposition 13.* Los Angeles, California: University of Southern California Population Dynamics Research Group.

"National Opinion Research Center." 1999. *Gambling Impact and Behavior Study: Report to the National Gambling Impact Study Commission.* Chicago: University of Chicago.

Neubeck, Kenneth J. and Noel A. Cazenave. 2001. *Welfare Racism: Playing the Race Card Against America's Poor.* New York: Routledge.

Newman, Katherine S. and Rourke O'Brien. 2011. *Taxing the Poor: Doing Damage to the Truly Disadvantaged.* Berkeley: University of California Press.

Nibert, David. 2000. *Hitting the Lottery Jackpot: Government and the Taxing of Dreams*. New York: Monthly Review.

Norušis, Marija J. 2008. *SPSS Statistics 17.0 Guide to Data Analysis*. Upper Saddle River, New Jersey: Prentice Hall.

O'Connor, James. [1973] 2002. *The Fiscal Crisis of the State*. New Brunswick, New Jersey: Transaction Publishers.

Oliver, Melvin L. and Thomas M. Shapiro. [1995] 2006. *Black Wealth/White Wealth: A New Perspective on Racial Inequality*. New York: Routledge.

Omi, Michael and Howard Winant. [1986] 1994. *Racial Formation in the United States: From the 1960s to the 1990s (2nd Edition)*. New York: Routledge.

Orfield, Gary, and Chungmei Lee. 2005. *Why Education Matters: Poverty and Educational Inequality*. Cambridge, Massachusetts: Harvard University Press.

Orwell, George. [1949] 1961. *1984, With an Afterword by Erich Fromm*. New York: The New American Library, Inc.

Oster, Emily. 2004. "Are All Lotteries Regressive? Evidence from the Powerball." *National Tax Journal* 57(2): 179–187.

Pager, Devah. 2003. "The Mark of a Criminal Record." *American Journal of Sociology* 108(5): 937–975.

Pareto, Vilfredo. [1920] 1980. *Compendium of General Sociology*. Minneapolis: University of Minnesota Press.

———. [1906] 1971. *Manual of Political Economy*. New York: Augustus M. Kelley.

Peppard, Jr., Donald M. 1987. "Government as Bookie: Explaining the Rise of Lotteries for Revenue." *Review of Radical Political Economics* 19(3): 56–68.

Peterson, George E. 1982. "The State and Local Sectors." Pp. 157–217 in *The Reagan Experiment*, edited by John L. Palmer and Isabel V. Sawhill. Washington, DC: The Urban Institute.

Phillips, Kevin. 1990. *The Politics of Rich and Poor: Wealth and the American Electorate in the Reagan Aftermath*. New York: Random House.

Pincus, Fred L. 2003. *Reverse Discrimination: Dismantling the Myth*. Boulder, Colorado: Lynnne Rienner.

Pinkney, Alphonso. 1984. *The Myth of Black Progress*. New York: Oxford University Press.

Pirog-Good, Maureen and John L. Mikesell. 1995. "Longitudinal Evidence of the Changing Socio-Economic Profile of a State Lottery Market." *Policy Studies Journal* 23(3): 451–465.

Piven, Frances Fox and Richard A. Cloward. 1982. *The New Class War*. New York: Pantheon Books.

Polanyi, Karl. [1944] 1957. *The Great Transformation*. Boston, Massachusetts: Beacon Press.

Porter, Eduardo. 2005. "Illegal Immigrants are Bolstering Social Security with Billions." *The New York Times* April 5: A1, C6.

powell, john A. 2002. *Racism and Metropolitan Dynamics: The Civil Rights Challenge of the 21st Century*. Minneapolis, Minnesota: Institute on Race & Poverty.

———. 2000. "Addressing Regional Dilemmas for Minority Communities." Pp. 218–246 in *Reflections on Regionalism*, edited by Bruce Katz. Washington, DC: Brookings Institute Press.

———. 1996. "How Government Tax and Housing Policies have Racially Segregated America. Pp. 80–115 in *Taxing America*, edited by Karen B. Brown and Mary Louise Fellows. New York: New York University Press.

Prasad, Monica. 2012. "The Popular Origins of Neoliberalism in the Reagan Tax Cut of 1981." *The Journal of Policy History* 24(3): 351–383.

Price, Donald I. and E. Shawn Novak. 1999. "The Tax Incidence of the Three Texas Lottery Games: Regressivity, Race, and Education." *National Tax Journal* 52(4): 741–751.

Quadagno, Jill. 1994. *The Color of Welfare: How Racism Undermined the War on Poverty.* New York: Oxford University Press.

———. 1988. *The Transformation of Old Age Security: Class and Politics in the American Welfare State.* Chicago: University of Chicago Press.

Quiroz, Pamela Anne. 2007. *Adoption in a Color-Blind Society.* Lanham, Maryland: Rowman and Littlefield.

Quiroz, Pamela Anne and Vernon Lindsay. 2015. "Selective Enrollment, Race, and Shifting the Geography of Educational Opportunity: Where 'Diversity' and Opportunity Compete with Tax Increment Financing." *Humanity & Society* doi: 10.1177/0160597615603749.

Reed, Douglas S. 1998. "Twenty-Five Years after *Rodriguez*: School Finance Litigation and the Impact of the New Judicial Federalism." *Law & Society Review* 32(1): 175–209.

Reith, Gerda. 1999. *The Age of Chance: Gambling in Western Culture.* New York: Routledge.

Rogers, William Warren. 1970. *The One-Gallused Rebellion: Agrarianism in Alabama, 1865–1896.* Baton Rouge, Louisiana: Louisiana State University.

Ross, Stephen L. and John Yinger. 2002. *The Color of Credit: Mortgage Discrimination, Research Methodology, and Fair-Lending Enforcement.* Cambridge, Massachusetts: M.I.T. Press

Rubin, Lillian B. 1972. *Busing and Backlash: White Against White in an Urban School District.* Berkeley: University of California Press.

Ryan, William. 1971. *Blaming the Victim.* New York: Pantheon Books.

Sáenz, Rogelio and Aurelia Lorena Murga. 2011. *Latino Issues: A Reference Handbook.* San Diego, California: ABC-CLIO.

Sáenz, Rogelio, Janie Filoteo, and Aurelia Lorena Murga. 2007. "Are Mexicans in the United States a Threat to the American Way of Life? A Response to Huntington." *Du Bois Review* 4(2): 375–393.

Saito, Leland T. 2009. *The Politics of Exclusion: The Failure of Race-Neutral Policies in Urban America.* Palo Alto, California: Stanford University Press.

Salsich, Jr., Peter W. 1993. "A Decent Home for Every American: Can the 1949 Goal Be Met?" *North Carolina Law Review* 71(5): 1619–1646.

Saxton, Alexander. 1990. *The Rise and Fall of the White Republic: Class Politics and Mass Culture in Nineteenth-Century America.* New York: Verso.

Schuman, Howard, Charlotte Steeh, Lawrence D. Bobo, and Maria Krysan. [1985] 1997. *Racial Attitudes in America: Trends and Interpretation.* Cambridge, Massachusetts: Harvard University Press.

Schumpeter, Joseph. [1918] 1991. "The Crisis of the Tax State." Pp. 99–140 in *The Economics and Sociology of Capitalism*, edited by Richard Swedberg. Princeton, New Jersey: Princeton University Press.

Seamster, Louise. 2015. "Emergency Management and Urban Redevelopment in a New Company Town." Durham, North Carolina: Duke University.

Seamster, Louise and Kasey Henricks. 2015. "A Second Redemption? Racism, Backlash Politics, and Public Education." *Humanity & Society* doi: 10.1177/0160597615604926.

Sears, David O. and Donald R. Kinder. 1971. "Racial Tensions and Voting in Los Angeles." Pp. 51–88 in *Los Angeles: Viability and Prospects for Metropolitan Leadership*, edited by Werner Z. Hirsch. New York: Praeger.

Sears, David O. and Jack Citrin. 1982. *Tax Revolt: Something for Nothing in California*. Cambridge, Massachusetts: Harvard University Press.

Seligman, Edwin R. A. 1895. *Essays in Taxation*. New York: MacMillan and Co.

Shapiro, Thomas M. 2004. *The Hidden Cost of Being African American: How Wealth Perpetuates Inequality*. New York: Oxford University Press.

Shaw, Dennis. 2000. "Lottery Security." Pp. 261–272 in *Protection, Security, and Safeguards: Practical Approaches and Perspectives*, edited by Dale L. June. Boca Raton, Florida: CRC Press.

Sherradan, Michael. 1991. *Assets and the Poor: A New American Welfare Policy*. Armonk, New York: M.E. Sharp, Inc.

Simmel, Georg. [1907] 2004. *The Philosophy of Money*. New York: Routledge.

Skocpol, Theda. Ed. 1984. *Vision and Method in Historical Sociology*. New York: Cambridge University Press.

Smith, Adam. [1776] 2010. *The Wealth of Nations*. West Sussex, United Kingdom: Capstone Publishing.

Smith, Daniel A. 1999. *Tax Crusaders and the Politics of Direct Democracy*. New York: Routledge.

Stabile, Susan J. 2002. "Enron, Global Crossing, and Beyond: Implications for Workers." *St. John's Law Review* 76(4): 815–834.

Stranahan, Harriet A. and Mary O. Borg. 2004. "Some Futures are Brighter than Others: The Net Benefits Received by Florida Bright Futures Scholarship Recipients." *Public Finance Review* 32(1): 105–126.

———. 1998. "Separating the Decisions of Lottery Expenditures and Participation: A Truncated Tobit Approach." *Public Finance Review* 26(2): 99–117.

Steinberg, Stephen. 2007. *Race Relations: A Critique*. Stanford, California: Stanford University Press.

———. [1995] 2001. *Turning Back: The Retreat from Racial Justice in American Thought and Policy*. Boston: Beacon Press.

———. 1981. *The Ethnic Myth: Race, Ethnicity, and Class in America*. Boston, Massachusetts: Beacon Press.

Stephenson, Gilbert Thomas. [1910] 1969. *Race Distinctions in American Law*. New York: AMS Press.

Takaki, Ronald. 1993. *A Different Mirror: A History of Multicultural America*. Boston: Little, Brown, and Company.

Tedin, Kent L. 1994. "Self-Interest, Symbolic Politics and the Financial Equalization of the Public Schools." *Journal of Political Studies* 56(3): 628–649.

Thomas, W.I. and Dorothy S. Thomas. 1928. *The Child in America: Behavior Problems and Programs*. New York: Knopf.

Thornton III, J. Mills. 1982. "Fiscal Policy and the Failure of Radical Reconstruction in the Lower South." Pp. 349–394 in *Region, Race, and Reconstruction*, edited by J. Morgan Kousser and James M. McPherson. New York: Oxford University Press.

Tilly, Charles. 2009. "Foreword." Pp. xi-xiii in *The New Fiscal Sociology: Taxation in Comparative and Historical Perspective*, edited by Isaac William Martin, Ajay K. Mehrotra, and Monica Prasad. New York: Cambridge University Press.

———. 2007. *Democracy*. New York: Cambridge University Press.

———. 1998. *Durable Inequality.* Berkeley: University of California Press.

United States Department of Justice, Civil Rights Division. 2015. *Investigation of the Ferguson Police Department.* Washington, DC: United States Department of Justice.

van den Berghe, Pierre L. 1967. *Race and Racism: A Comparative Perspective.* New York: Wiley.

van Dijk, Teun A. 1998. *Ideology: A Multidisciplinary Approach.* London: Sage.

Vargas, Nicholas. 2015. "Latina/o Whitening? Which Latina/os Self-Classify as White and Report Being Perceived as White by Other Americans?" *Du Bois Review* 12(1): 119–136.

Vaughan, Diane. 2004. "Theorizing Disaster: Analogy, Historical Ethnography, and the Challenger Accident." *Ethnography* 5(3): 315–347.

———. 1992. "Theory Elaboration: The Heuristics of Case Analysis." Pp. 173–202 in *What is a Case? Exploring the Foundations of Social Inquiry,* edited by Charles C. Ragin and Howard S. Becker. New York: Cambridge University Press.

Vyse, Stuart A. [1997] 2014. *Believing in Magic: The Psychology of Superstition.* New York: Oxford University Press.

Walker, Ian. 1998. "The Economic Analysis of Lotteries." *Economic Policy* 13: 359–401.

Walsh, Camille. Forthcoming. "White Backlash, the 'Taxpaying' Public, and Educational Citizenship." *Critical Sociology.*

Walters, Pamela Barnhouse. 2001. "Education Access and the State: Historical Continuities and Discontinuities in Racial Inequality in American Education." *Sociology of Education* 74(1): 35–49.

Warren, Donald I. 1976. *The Radical Center: Middle Americans and the Politics of Alienation.* South Bend, Indiana: University of Notre Dame Press.

Weber, Max. [1919] 1946. "Science as a Vocation." Pp. 129–156 in *From Max Weber: Essay in Sociology,* edited by H.H. Gerth and C. Wright Mills. New York: Oxford University Press.

Wells, Ida B. 1892. *Southern Horrors: Lynch Law in All Its Phases.* New York: The New York Age.

Wellman, David T. [1977] 1993. *Portraits of White Racism.* New York: Cambridge University Press.

Wetzel, Christopher. 2012. "Moral Markets and the Problematic Proprietor: How Neoliberal Values Shape Lottery Debates in Nevada." *University of Nevada, Las Vegas, Center for Gaming Research—Occasional Paper Series* 20: 1–12

Wills, Garry. 2003. *Negro President: Jefferson and the Slave Power.* New York: Mariner.

Wilson, Carter A. 1996. *Racism: From Slavery to Advanced Capitalism.* New York: Sage.

Wilson, George. 1997. "Pathways to Power: Racial Differences in the Determinants of Job Authority." *Social Problems* 44(1): 38–54.

Wilson, William Julius. 1987. *The Truly Disadvantaged: The Inner City, the Underclass, and Public Policy.* Chicago: University of Chicago Press.

———. 1978. *The Declining Significance of Race: Blacks and Changing American Institutions.* Chicago: University of Chicago Press.

Wilson, William Julius and Richard P. Taub. 2006. *There Goes the Neighborhood: Racial, Ethnic, and Class Tensions in Four Chicago Neighborhoods and their Meaning for America.* New York: Vintage Books.

Wise, Tim J. [2003] 2008. "Overclass Blues: Class, Race, and the Ironies of Privilege." Pp. 318–324 in *Speaking Treason Fluently: Anti-Racist Reflections from an Angry White Male*, edited by Tim J. Wise. Berkeley, California: Soft Skull.

Wohl, Michael J.A. and Michael E. Enzle. 2002. "The Deployment of Personal Luck: Sympathetic Magic and Illusory Control in Games of Pure Chance." *Personality and Social Psychology Bulletin* 28(10):1388–1397.

Wolff, Edward N. 1998. "Recent Trends in the Size Distribution of Household Wealth." *Journal of Economic Perspectives* 12(3): 131–150.

Woodward, C. Vann. 1971. *Origins of the New South, 1877–1913*. Baton Rouge, Louisiana: Louisiana State University.

Yin, George K. 1996. "The Uncertain Fate of the Earned Income Tax Program." Pp. 297–321 in *Taxing America*, edited by Karen B. Brown and Mary Louise Fellows. New York: New York University Press.

Index

For Product Safety Concerns and Information please contact our EU
representative GPSR@taylorandfrancis.com
Taylor & Francis Verlag GmbH, Kaufingerstraße 24, 80331 München, Germany